Lecture Notes in Computer Science 5842

Commenced Publication in 1973
Founding and Former Series Editors
Gerhard Goos, Juris Hartmanis, and

T0216752

Tom Pfeifer
Paolo Bellavista (Eds.)

Wired-Wireless Multimedia Networks and Services Management

12th IFIP/IEEE International Conference on Management
of Multimedia and Mobile Networks and Services, MMNS 2009
Venice, Italy, October 26-27, 2009
Proceedings

 Springer

Volume Editors

Tom Pfeifer
Waterford Institute of Technology
Telecommunications Software and Systems Group
Cork Road, Waterford, Ireland
E-mail: t.pfeifer@computer.org

Paolo Bellavista
Università di Bologna
Dipartimento di Elettronica, Informatica e Sistemistica (DEIS)
Viale Risorgimento 2, 40136 Bologna, Italy
E-mail: paolo.bellavista@unibo.it

Library of Congress Control Number: 2009936722

CR Subject Classification (1998): C.2, H.4, H.5, H.2.4, H.4.3

LNCS Sublibrary: SL 5 – Computer Communication Networks and
Telecommunications

ISSN   0302-9743
ISBN-10   3-642-04993-1 Springer Berlin Heidelberg New York
ISBN-13   978-3-642-04993-4 Springer Berlin Heidelberg New York

springer.com

© IFIP International Federation of Information Processing, Hofstrasse 3, A-2361 Laxenburg, Austria 2009
Printed in Germany

Typesetting: Camera-ready by author, data conversion by Scientific Publishing Services, Chennai, India
Printed on acid-free paper   SPIN: 12775910   06/3180   5 4 3 2 1 0

Preface

This volume presents the proceedings of the 12th IFIP/IEEE International Conference on Management of Multimedia and Mobile Networks and Services (MMNS 2009), which was held in Venice, Italy, during October 26–27 as part of the 5th International Week on Management of Networks and Services (Manweek 2009). As in the previous four years, the Manweek umbrella allowed an international audience of researchers and scientists from industry and academia – who are researching and developing management systems – to share views and ideas and present their state-of-the-art results.

The other events forming Manweek 2009 were the 20th IFIP/IEEE International Workshop on Distributed Systems: Operations and Management (DSOM 2009), the 9th IEEE Workshop on IP Operations and Management (IPOM 2009), the 4th IEEE International Workshop on Modeling Autonomic Communications Environments (MACE 2009), and the 6th International Workshop on Next Generation Networking Middleware (NGNM 2009).

Under this umbrella, MMNS proved itself again as a major conference for research and innovation in the management of multimedia technology and networked services.

The scope of MMNS has been expanded in recent years to include management of emerging mobile and wireless networks and their integration with more traditional network infrastructures. The objective of the conference is to bring together researchers and scientists, from both academia and industry, interested in state-of-the-art management of converged multimedia networks and services across heterogeneous networking infrastructures, while creating a public venue for result dissemination and intellectual collaboration.

The convergence of existing and emerging technologies such as broadband, mobile, and broadcast networks is considered as a promising opportunity for existing providers to increase their service subscriber base, so that the 4G vision and beyond becomes a reality. An important research effort is undertaken by main actors to face the multidimensional heterogeneity (in terms of transport technology, session signaling, and QoS provisioning) of next-generation networks (NGNs). Efficient management of these services is a key ingredient in the effort to provide cost-effective innovative services and mass market solutions that are likely to become a major source of income for different stakeholders.

The need to evolve management tools, solutions, platforms and methodologies to keep pace with emerging networks is at a critical juncture with the proliferation of mobile and wireless systems, intelligent and broadband networks, quadruple play convergence, and the integration of embedded systems in different domains, from smart homes/cities to next-generation automotive systems. The academic and industry research communities should join forces to address the challenges of developing and operating converged multimedia networks and services. Inevitably, integrated management is a key element in addressing this challenge.

MMNS 2009 continued the success of the outstanding agendas of the past, with special emphasis on novel research in the management of wired-wireless multimedia networks and services.

The research community contributed a total of 37 paper submissions from 21 different countries. A comprehensive review process was carried out by the Technical Program Committee and additional subject area experts, with all papers receiving three to four reviews, in controversial cases up to six. Subsequently, all submissions were ranked based on review scores as well as the Technical Program Committee's view of their contribution and relevance to the conference scope.

After a thorough discussion, it was decided to accept 13 full papers for MMNS, resulting in an acceptance rate of 35% which is in line with previous events and contributes to a high-quality technical program. In addition, five papers were accepted for the poster session presenting work in progress, with short-paper abstracts also printed in this volume. Two papers of good quality could be referred to other events in Manweek where they fitted better in the scope, demonstrating the synergy of the umbrella event.

The diverse topics in this year's program included Multimedia Networks and Systems Management, Multimedia Quality, VoIP and Vocal Applications, and Peer-to-Peer Multimedia Networks – all contributing to the management of Wired-Wireless Multimedia Networks and Services, as expressed in this year's motto.

The high-quality MMNS 2009 program is owed, first of all, to the original and novel contributions of all the authors who submitted their work to the conference, purified by the hard work of the MMNS 2009 Technical Program Committee members and the rigorous review process accomplished by this set of worldwide experts, supported by the 2009 Manweek Organizing Committee, and enabled with the generous contribution of IFIP, IEEE, and the sponsor companies, all of whom are gratefully thanked by the Conference and Program Committee chairs. In addition, we thank the Publication Chairs and the Springer LNCS team for their support in the preparation of these proceedings, which we hope can pleasantly introduce the readers to the challenging arena of the management of multimedia and mobile networks/services and can help in giving a fresh sketch of currently hot topics and state-of-the-art solutions in the field.

Enjoy your reading.

October 2009   Tom Pfeifer
                                                        Paolo Bellavista

MMNS 2009 Organization

Conference and Program Co-chairs

Tom Pfeifer   Waterford Institute of Technology, Ireland
Paolo Bellavista   University of Bologna, Italy

Publication Advisory Chair

Tom Pfeifer   Waterford Institute of Technology, Ireland

Publication Chair

Alberto Gonzalez Prieto   Royal Institute of Technology (KTH), Sweden

Finance Chair

Raouf Boutaba   University of Waterloo, Canada

Infrastructure Chair

Sven van der Meer   Waterford Institute of Technology, Ireland

Local Arrangements Chair

Massimo Foscato   Telecom Italia Labs, Italy

Registration Chair

Idilio Drago   University of Twente, The Netherlands

Publicity Co-chair

Carlos Becker Westphall   Federal University of Santa Catarina (UFSC), Brazil

Manweek 2009 General Co-chairs

Aiko Pras   University of Twente, The Netherlands
Roberto Saracco   Telecom Italia Labs, Italy

Manweek 2009 Advisors

Raouf Boutaba	University of Waterloo, Canada
James Hong	POSTECH, Korea
Aiko Pras	University of Twente, The Netherlands

MMNS 2009 Technical Program Committee

Aiko Pras	University of Twente, The Netherlands
Alan Marshall	The Queen's University of Belfast, UK
Alexander Clemm	Cisco Systems, USA
Bert-Jan van Beijnum	University of Twente, The Netherlands
Brendan Jennings	TSSG, Waterford Institute of Technology, Ireland
Burkhard Stiller	University of Zurich and ETH Zurich, Switzerland
Christian Timmerer	Klagenfurt University, Austria
Danny Raz	Technion University, Israel
Dilip Krishnaswamy	Qualcomm Inc., USA
Dorgham Sisalem	Tekelec, Germany
Francine Krief	LaBRI Laboratory, Bordeaux University, France
Gabriel-Miro Muntean	Dublin City University, Ireland
Gang Ding	Olympus Communication Technology of America, USA
George Pavlou	University College London, UK
Gerard Parr	University of Ulster, UK
Go Hasegawa	Osaka University, Japan
Guy Pujolle	Université de Paris 6 Pierre et Marie Curie, France
Hanan Lutfiyya	University of Western Ontario, Canada
John Vicente	Intel Corporation, USA
Karim Seada	Nokia Research Center, Finland
Liam Murphy	University College Dublin, Ireland
Lukas Kencl	Czech Technical University in Prague, Czech Republic
Maja Matijasevic	University of Zagreb, Croatia
Mohammad Ghanbari	University of Essex, UK
Nazim Agoulmine	University of Evry, France
Nicola Cranley	ACRA Control, USA
Paolo Bellavista	University of Bologna, Italy
Ralf Steinmetz	Technical University of Darmstadt, Germany
Roger Zimmermann	National University of Singapore, Singapore
Sasitharan Balasubramaniam	Waterford Institute of Technology, Ireland
Sven van der Meer	Waterford Institute of Technology, Ireland

Tasos Dagiuklas	TEI of Mesolonghi, Greece
Theodore Willke	Intel Corporation, USA
Thomas Magedanz	Fraunhofer FOKUS, Germany
Tom Pfeifer	Waterford Institute of Technology, Ireland
Toufik Ahmed	University of Bordeaux, France
Yacine Ghamri-Doudane	LRSM – ENSIIE, France
Yangcheng Huang	Ericsson, USA

Additional Reviewers

Alan Walsh	Waterford Institute of Technology, Ireland
Alberto Diez	Technical University of Berlin, Germany
Andrei Vancea	University of Zurich, Switzerland
Carlo Giannelli	University of Bologna, Italy
Cedric Lamoriniere	University College Dublin, Ireland
Chamil Kulatunga	Waterford Institute of Technology, Ireland
Dalibor Peric	University of Zurich, Switzerland
Enda Fallon	Athlone Institute of Technology, Ireland
Fabricio Gouveia	Fraunhofer FOKUS, Germany
Giovane Moura	University of Twente, The Netherlands
Ismail Djama	CNRS-LaBRI, University of Bordeaux I, France
Jan Rudinsky	Czech Technical University in Prague, Czech Republic
Jiri Danihelka	Czech Technical University in Prague, Czech Republic
John Floroiu	Tekelec, Germany
Jordi Jaen Pallares	Fraunhofer FOKUS, Germany
Jose Simoes	Fraunhofer FOKUS, Germany
Konstantinos Birkos	University of Patras, Greece
Luca Foschini	University of Bologna, Italy
Martijn van Eenennaam	University of Twente, The Netherlands
Mehdi Nafaa	Université Evry Val d'Essonne, France
Micheal Crotty	Waterford Institute of Technology, Ireland
Mohamed Aymen Chalouf	University of Bordeaux, France
Mubashar Mushtaq	University of Bordeaux, France
Ramin Sadre	University of Twente, The Netherlands
Ray Carroll	Waterford Institute of Technology, Ireland
Seung-Bum Lee	Dublin City University, Ireland
Thomas Bocek	University of Zurich, Switzerland
Tiago Fioreze	University of Twente, The Netherlands
Victor Pascual Ávila	iptelorg-Tekelec, Germany
Wouter Klein Wolterink	University of Twente, The Netherlands
Yuansong Qiao	Athlone Institute of Technology, Ireland

Table of Contents

Multimedia Networks and Systems Management

Multimedia Quality

VoIP and Vocal Applications

Peer-to-Peer Multimedia Networks

Short Papers

Design of an Online Charging System to Support IMS-Based Inter-domain Composite Services

M. van Le[1], G.B. Huitema[2], F.J. Rumph[3], L.J.M. Nieuwenhuis[1],
and B.J.F. van Beijnum[4]

[1] Faculty of Information Systems and Change Management, University of Twente,
The Netherlands
[2] Faculty of Economics and Business, University of Groningen, The Netherlands
[3] TNO, The Netherlands
[4] Faculty of Electrical Engineering, Mathematics and Computer Science,
University of Twente, The Netherlands
van-minh.le@atosorigin.com, g.b.huitema@rug.nl,
frens_jan.rumph@tno.nl, l.j.m.nieuwenhuis@utwente.nl,
beijnum@ewi.utwente.nl

Abstract. For service providers online charging of composite services is necessary in order to manage financial risks of service delivery in multi-domain environments. At service level, inter-domain composite services consist of one or more service components, e.g. access service, IMS communication service or content service, delivered by different service providers. The 3rd Generation Partnership Project (3GPP) has developed a framework for off-line and online charging of IMS-based services. However, the current Online Charging System (OCS) specified by 3GPPP does not support an online charging function for composite services. The contribution of this work lies in the design of an online charging system that addresses the required charging functionalities based on the IMS online charging architecture. The design consists of a service composition information model guided by the NGOSS and SID concepts of the Tele-Management Forum, a set of functional charging system components and their interactions at their interfaces.

Keywords: Online charging, IP Multimedia Subsystem (IMS), inter-domain composite services.

1 Introduction

Today, customers consume a broad variety of multimedia services. The growth of data-centric mobile devices and mobile broadband network capacity is pushing multimedia services into the mainstream. Most of these multimedia services are *composite services*. A composite service is composed of many service components provided by third party providers to the service provider.

In general there are *off-line* and *online* charging mechanisms. Here off-line charging means that the charging for service usage occurs after a service event or service session has occurred (i.e. postpaid). On the other hand online charging means that the

T. Pfeifer and P. Bellavista (Eds.): MMNS 2009, LNCS 5842, pp. 1–14, 2009.

charging occurs during a service session usage or right after a service event has occurred. We note that the notion of online charging may refer to prepaid as well as
postpaid. In the latter case online charging will allow consumers to set charge limits
when desired (e.g. roaming in foreign countries).

Now, the delivery of composite services imposes a huge complexity on online
charging mechanisms, especially when dealing with dynamic online charging
schemes. That is, when the charge of an individual service component depends on the
existence of other components during a service session. For example, see Figure 1, a
TVoD (TV-on-demand) session may be combined with an advertising service component. During the service session, the customer, here Jane, may decide to remove the
advertising component, which results in an immediate increase of the TVoD service
charge.

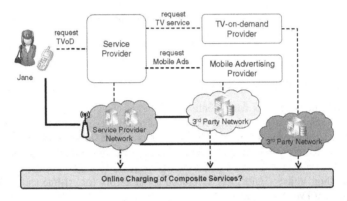

Fig. 1. Inter-domain service scenario depicting functional relationships (dash lines) and the
physical paths of the delivered data (solid lines). The arrows and the blue box denote the problem domain of online charging across multiple administrative domains.

In order to deal with online charging of composite services based on dynamic pricing, new online charging architectures are needed. With the uptake of more valuable,
complex services most customers of composite multimedia services want to obtain
(near) real-time charging and billing information to manage their expenses during
usage. Furthermore, also service providers need (near) real-time management information in order to manage their financial risks. However, today's charging systems
are not capable of dealing with requirements related to composite services. In particular, the 3rd Generation Partnership Project (3GPP) has developed the IP Multimedia
Sub-system (IMS) [1] to support multimedia services but their framework for current
Online Charging Systems (OCS) do not support online charging functions for inter-
domain composite services.

The contribution of this work lies in the design of an online charging system to
support IMS-based inter-domain composite services. The design uses the IMS online
charging architecture as a basis to develop a refined online charging system that addresses the required charging functionalities. The design is also based on the New
Generation Operations Systems and Software (NGOSS), in particular the Information
Framework (SID), concepts of the TeleManagement Forum [9].

The remainder of this paper is organized as follow: Section 2 provides a brief overview of related work. Section 3 presents the problem domain of online charging of composite services. Section 4, 5 and 6 proposes a design of an online charging system solving the stated problem, by respectively defining a service composition information model, defining the functional charging system components and by defining the interactions at their interfaces. Finally, Section 7 presents the conclusion together with some future research directions.

2 Related Work

In this section related work with respect to online charging of composite services is described. The 3GPP has proposed two reference charging models for service scenarios [2], namely: an off-line and an online charging model. The latter charging model covers near real-time charging issues such as charging authorization, credit control during service sessions. However, it lacks a service composition model to deal with charging of composite services. For instance, a video conference can fall back from video plus voice to only voice due to some network problem. This introduces a change in charging of the voice component for the rest of the conversation. In this kind of situation, it is necessary for a charging system to keep track of the service composition information to adapt charging accordingly.

The Akogrimo project [3] has proposed a charging architecture called A4C (Authentication, Authorization, Accounting, Auditing, and Charging). A4C consists of a number of basic system components based on the IETF's AAA architecture [4]. This architecture offers charging solutions for mobile grid services in a multi-provider service environment and is designed to support charging of inter-domain composite services. However, the architecture lacks a specification of composite services, and real-time service charging and billing have not received detailed attention.

Koutsopoulou [5] has proposed an architecture to support billing processes which also accounts for inter-domain billing. In this architecture, the authentication, authorization and event-based billing in roaming service scenarios is well addressed. However, the charging of composite services has not been considered in detail.

Xu and Jennings [13] have proposed a framework for automated generation of charging schemes for composite IMS services. This framework provides a comprehensive approach to ease the modification of charging schemes. Nonetheless, it does not address the issues of online charging for composite IMS services.

Our approach contributes to the above related work in a number of ways. We propose a service composition information model and a charging system that deals with online charging of inter-domain composite services. To this extent, we propose a concrete refinement of the Online Charging System (OCS) that has been specified by the 3GPP thus far.

3 Problem Domain of Online Charging of Composite Services

This section deals with the focus of our research: the setup of an online charging system for inter-domain composite services. Depending on the implementation strategy online charging may involve different distributed Online Charging Systems (OCS).

However, we abstract from a concrete distribution and focus on one single OCS. We assume that the composite services will be delivered across several administrative domains and across several delivery platforms. Hence, a combination of web services and IMS services based on SOA (Service Oriented Architecture) [6] is considered.

In order to master the complexity of such a service delivery, the concept of service broker as advocated in [6, 7] is used. There are different possible configurations of service brokers in an actual deployment. Here we consider two types of service broker: 1. An IMS Service Broker within the IMS domain and 2. An Inter-domain Service Broker within the Web-Services domain. Here, the Inter-domain Service Broker is leading and is responsible for the end-to-end service composition for the user.

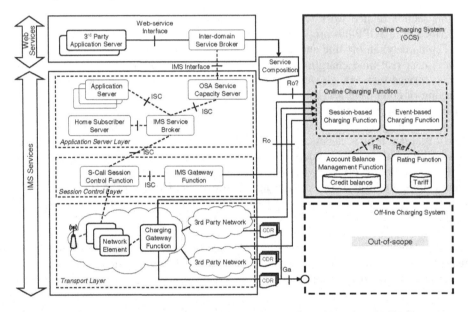

Fig. 2. Provisioning and Charging of Composite Services in an Inter-domain Environment

Figure 2 above illustrates a possible model for provisioning and charging of composite services in a multi-domain environment. A composite service is delivered across different administrative domains: the service provider domain, which is supported by IMS core infrastructure, and the third party domains, which are not necessarily supported by an IMS but some different network infrastructures. The service composition and orchestration occurs at the web-service level through the Inter-domain Service Broker. This implies that the Inter-domain Service Broker has the knowledge of the service composition and needs to communicate this information with the OCS for online charging purposes. Note that here off-line charging is out-of-scope.

The 3GPP framework describes online charging for both events and sessions. However, there exists no standard model yet for service composition within 3GPP specifications. Although an IMS service may consist of different service components (e.g. VoIP over IP-access), current online charging systems do not correlate charges between service components. As a result, when a service component is added or removed from an incurred composite service session, adjustment of online charging due to possible tariff changes (e.g. zero rate bearer usage when a VoIP session is active) cannot be handled. Since the composition of a composite service may change at run time, online charging needs to adapt to this dynamic behavior as well. This implies that the OCS needs to have knowledge about how the ongoing service composition is built up and the corresponding tariff of an individual service component. Furthermore, charging policies need to be enforced appropriately according to some pre-defined service level agreement between the customer and the service provider.

Hence we come up to the following research questions regarding online charging of inter-domain composite services:

1. What is the service composition information model used by the OCS?
2. What are the functional components embodied within the OCS?
3. How do these functional components interact at their interfaces?

The above questions will be addressed respectively in the sections 4, 5 and 6 below.

4 A Service Composition Model

This section presents a service composition information model for online charging of inter-domain composite services.

According to the Service Delivery Framework of the TeleManagement Forum (TMForum) [8], there are three steps to arrive at the eventual service delivery, namely: product design, service creation and service execution. During the product design phase, a service designer from the service provider domain can look up available service components in a catalog and chooses the necessary service components to form a composite service. During the creation phase, the designed composite service is tested throughout. When a composite is accepted, a meta information model of the composite service is created and stored in a composite service catalog. In the last phase, whenever a user requests a composite service, an instance to the corresponding meta information model is generated. Figure 3 depicts when a meta service composition model comes into existence.

In order to compose a composite service, the service provider mostly needs external services from third party providers. A service composition model therefore must express the relationship between the constituent service components. The TMForum

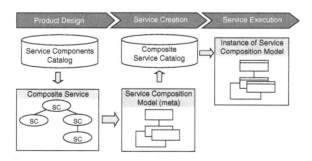

Fig. 3. Service Composition Information in the context of Service Delivery Framework of TMForum

also has been working on the SID (Information Framework) model [9], which provides guidelines for the modeling of information/data for the purpose of product design, service construct and service provisioning. Currently, the SID model is widely accepted as standard in the industry. Among many aspects, the SID model addresses the basic entities: product, service, end-user-facing service and provider-facing service and their relationships.

The service composition information model contains necessary detail information to ensure the correlation of service components and their corresponding charge. Based on SID the following pieces of information are crucial:

- `serviceID` – a unique identifier of a provided composite service or a service component.
- `interOperatorID` – a unique identifier of a service provider or a third party provider.
- `chargingKey` – an identifier used by the OCS to determine the tariff of a composite service or a service component.

The combination of an `interOperatorID`, the corresponding `serviceID` and the `chargingKey` allows for an appropriate credit authorization request at the OCS. For more details on the service composition information model see our previous work in [10, 11].

5   The Proposed Online Charging System

This section describes the functional components embodied within the proposed Online Charging System (OCS). It presents a description of OCS and their interactions at the interfaces.

5.1   Intertwinement of Service Life Cycle and Charging Life Cycle

The rationale of the processes for the online charging of services is to intertwine the service life cycle and the charging life cycle as we have proposed in [12]. The intertwining of these two different life cycles is described by the process given in Figure 4.

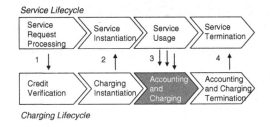

Fig. 4. Intertwinement of Service Life Cycle and Charging Life Cycle

In short, the use of a service comprises the following phases:

1. *Service Request Processing* - In this phase, a request initiated by the end-user is processed.
2. *Service Instantiation* - In this phase, the requested service is orchestrated (i.e. composed) and set-up for use.
3. *Service Usage* - In this phase the service is actually provided for use by the service provider to the end-user.
4. *Service Termination* - In this phase the service use is terminated, this is either initiated by the end-user or by the service provider.

For the online charging of this service usage, the following phases are defined:

1. *Credit Verification* - This process validates if the Subscriber's credit conforms to the requirements allowing the service request to be granted.
2. *Charging Instantiation* - This process prepares the charging of the orchestrated service.
3. *Accounting and Charging* - During this phase usage events (i.e. usage records) are received by the OCS and processed as to determine in (near) real-time the charge of the service.
4. *Accounting and Charging Termination* - In this phase, the accounting and charging is terminated (gracefully).

For more details on the credit control mechanisms and the interactions with the Inter-domain Service Broker see [11].

5.2 Functional Components of the Online Charging System

In this sub-section the refinement of the OCS is discussed. The OCS consists of the following functional components:

- *Mediation* – The *Mediation* acts as a gateway with the capability to receive and to route incoming messages from provisioning systems to the *Charge Aggregator*. As the *Charge Aggregator* is a computation-intensive system component, the *Mediator* can take care of the load balancing by distributing the charging process over multiple *Charging Aggregator* instances. The *Mediation* component has a port that connects to "outward" interfaces to provisioning systems.
- *Charge Aggregator* – The *Charge Aggregator* is mainly responsible for credit verification. It has knowledge of service composition information to conduct the accumulation of charge reservations (or claims) that belong to a particular service session. Unlike conventional post-paid billing where charge records are produced by rating engines, here charge records are produced by the *Charge Aggregator*. The rationale behind this design choice is related to the assigned intelligence of the *Charge Aggregator* to keep track of all states of all charging sessions and to aggregate the charges of the involved components. Hence, this information is used to generate the charge records.
- *Balance Manager* – The *Balance Manager* manages and updates the credit balances of subscribers. When a subscriber credit balance reaches a certain pre-defined threshold, the *Balance Manager* informs the *Charge Aggregator* about

the balance status so that appropriate action can be taken by the provisioning system. For instance, the provisioning system may decide to proceed with the service provisioning based on the good history of the subscriber in question or the provisioning system may decide to immediately terminate the ongoing service provisioning.

- *Rating Engine* – The *Rating Engine* conducts the calculations for charge reservation for the individual service components based on the incoming charge requests. The *Rating Engine* retrieves the tariff and discount information (i.e. user specific charging profile) from the *Tariff & Discount Database* for a specific End-user and calculates the costs for different service components involved. The *Rating Engine* retains the tariff and discount information for the entire Charging Life Cycle.

- *Balance Database* – The *Balance Database* stores the credit balance information of subscribers. When a charging session starts, the *Balance Manager* retrieves the current credit balance status of a specific End-user and his associated Subscriber from the *Balance Database*. The state of the credit balance changes during a charging session and the *Balance Manager* maintains this state. When the charging session terminates, the *Balance Database* is updated with the actual total cost of the service session. The credit information can be made accessible to Subscribers/End-users so as to provide them with (near) real-time information about their credit balance.

- *Charge Record Database* – The *Charge Record Database* stores charge records for invoicing and auditing purposes. A charge record is sent by the *Charge Aggregator* after the termination of a charging session.

- *Tariff & Discount Database* - The *Tariff & Discount Database* stores the information related to the service portfolio offered by the Service Provider. A tariff and discount plan can be tailored down to a Subscriber or End-user specific profile according to the SLA signed between the Subscriber and the Service Provider.

Figure 5 below gives an overview of the functional components comprised by the OCS and the interfaces between these functional components.

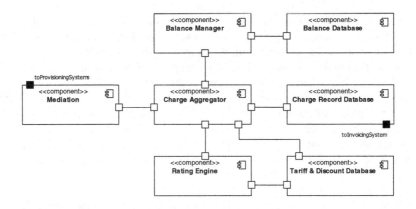

Fig. 5. Functional Components and Interfaces of the Online Charging System; the shaded ports indicates the external ports outward the OCS

6   Interaction between the System Components

This section details the phases of the Online Charging System (OCS), the involved system components and their interactions at the interfaces.

6.1   Credit Verification

The purpose of Credit Verification is to find out whether the Subscriber's credit balance is sufficient to allow the provisioning of a requested service. When a credit verification operation arrives at the Mediation, it is forwarded to the Charge Aggregator. The Charge Aggregator looks at this request message and then tries to retrieve the estimated charge of the requested composite service session from the Tariff & Discount Database. The reason to estimate the charge is because the duration of the requested service session is not known beforehand (e.g. the user might terminate a service session anytime). From a business perspective, it is desirable to ensure that the Subscriber has a minimum credit to be able to request a certain type of composite service. Charge estimation for different types of (composite) services can be predefined and stored in the Tariff & Discount Database. Based on the estimated charge, the Charge Aggregator requests the Balance Manager to verify the Subscriber's credit balance. If the credit balance is sufficient, the Balance Manager returns a "positive" response. In turn, the Charge Aggregator returns a "positive" credit verification response to the Mediation, which then forwards this response to the provisioning system. If the credit balance is not sufficient, the Balance Manager returns a "negative" response. As a result, the Charge Aggregator returns a "negative" credit verification response the Mediation, which then forwards this response to the provisioning system. One of the novel aspects of the proposed design is the exchange of the service composition information in the Credit Verification case. This allows the OCS to prepare for the charging process and to estimate the charge before service provisioning. Figure 6 shows the sequential interactions between the involved functional components in the Credit Verification phase.

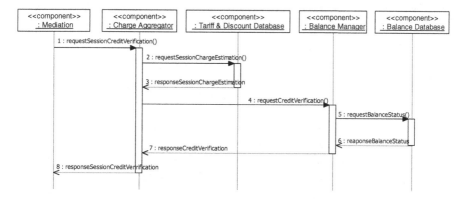

Fig. 6. Interactions between functional components involved in the Credit Verification phase

6.2 Accounting and Charging Instantiation

The purpose of the Accounting and Charging Instantiation phase is to set up a charging session for individual service components of a composite service.

When a credit authorization request arrives at the Mediation, it is forwarded to the Charge Aggregator. A credit authorization request allows a (sub) provisioning system (i.e. a network element) requesting authorization to provision a service component. This operation provides the provisioning system with a possibility to submit authorization, which depends on the service unit. A service unit may be some data volume (e.g. megabyte), certain time units (e.g. second) or a number of internet pages, etc. The Service Provider may enforce provisioning sub-systems to apply a specific frequency of charge.

In order to proceed with the credit authorization request, the Charging Aggregator needs to know the cost of the service component. Therefore, it requests the Rating Engine to calculate this cost. The service component cost depends on the component tariff, the assigned discount and the service unit. Furthermore, the tariff and discount plan for a specific Subscriber and the relevant End-user may depend on a number of other parameters such as time of day, quality of service, current location of the End-user, etc. These parameters are defined in a so-called "tariff & discount profile" according to the SLA between the Service Provider and the Subscriber. Upon receiving the component rating request, the Rating Engine retrieves the End-user's profile from the Tariff & Discount Database to calculate the cost.

Thereafter, the Rating Engine returns a component rating response to the Charging Aggregator, which includes the calculated cost. Note that the End-user's tariff & discount profile is retained within the Rating Engine during the entire Charging Life Cycle. Now the cost of the service component is known, the Charge Aggregator can ask the Balance Manager to create a credit reservation by indicating the required amount. Based on the current credit balance status of the End-user, the Balance Manager creates a credit reservation and provides a response to the Charging Aggregator

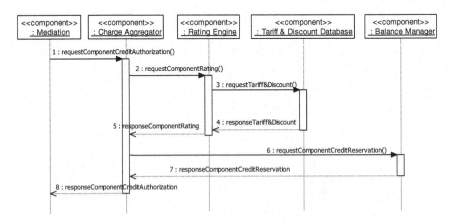

Fig. 7. Interactions between functional components involved in the Accounting and Charging Instantiation phase

indicating that the credit reservation has been accepted. Figure 7 shows the sequential interactions between the involved functional components in the Accounting and Charging Instantiation phase.

6.3 Accounting and Charging

In the previous phase, service provisioning has been authorized for a certain number of service units. The purpose of the Accounting and Charging phase is to re-authorize the individual provisioning sub-systems to continue with their service provisioning. Hence, during this phase, subsequent credit re-authorization requests will be sent from the provisioning system and third party provisioning systems to the OCS.

The handing of credit-reauthorization requests arriving at the Mediation in this phase is similar to the previous phase. When a credit re-authorization request operation arrives at the Mediation, the request message is forwarded to the Charge Aggregator via the Charge Request interface. The Charge Aggregator replies to this message with a credit re-authorization response, which can be either "positive" or "negative" depending on the remaining credit balance status.

As the Charge Aggregator retains and keeps track of the costs of all continuing composite services, it can easily associate a credit re-authorization request of a specific service component with the cost, which has been calculated previously by the Rating Engine. Based on this (pre-calculated) cost, the Charge Aggregator requests the Balance Manager to create an interim credit reservation. This approach contributes to the efficiency of the Charging Aggregator and at the same time releases the load of the Rating Engine because no re-rating is necessary. Here, it is assumed that service units contained in credit re-authorization requests originating from a provisioning sub-system, remain the same. There are special occasions where the Charge Aggregator needs to ask the Rating Engine to conduct a new rating. For instance, when a credit re-authorization request arrive at the boundary of two time zones where different tariff and discounting are applied.

When the Balance Manager receives the credit re-authorization request, this request is held against the latest credit balance status so that a new credit reservation can be deducted. The Balance Manager returns a response to the Charging Aggregator, which can be either "positive" (i.e. sufficient credit balance) or "negative" (i.e. insufficient credit balance). In turn, the Charging Aggregator provides a response to

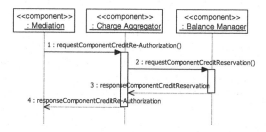

Fig. 8. Interactions between functional components involved in the Accounting and Charging phase

the Mediation. In order to create credit reservations, the Balance Manager does not need to distinguish the difference between credit authorization and credit reauthorization. This helps to simplify its functionality and at the same time to increase its efficiency. Figure 8 shows the sequential interactions between the involved functional components in the Accounting and Charging phase.

6.4 Accounting and Charging Termination

In a dynamic service provisioning environment, participating service components in a composite service session might be terminated in an arbitrary order. The termination order depends on the service orchestration and service delivery logics of the provisioning system [8]. The OCS is not in control of the termination of service provisioning. Instead, it receives final usage records at the Mediation and is expected to stop the charging process for the associated service components or service session in the most logical and secure way. Hence, in this phase, it is assumed that whenever a provisioning sub-systems terminates its service provisioning, it will generate a final usage record. The final usage record contains (amongst other details) the information about the service usage of the total session, which can be either incremental or cumulative service usage.

Two termination scenarios are possible:

- The OCS first receives a service session charging termination request, and then the corresponding component charging termination requests.
- The OCS first receives different component charging termination requests, and then the corresponding service session termination request. This occurs, for example, when a service component is removed from a composite service session.

Regardless of which of the above scenarios is used, the Charging Aggregator will process every component charging termination requests that arrives. In parallel, it keeps track of all terminated service components. Once the charging processes of all service components have been terminated, the charging process of the corresponding service component can also be terminated.

When a final usage record arrives at the Mediation, the Mediation requests the Charging Aggregator to terminate the charging process of this particular service component. As the final usage may be less than the (re)-authorized service usage in the Accounting and Charging phase, the Charge Aggregator requests the Rating Engine to re-calculate the cost of the final usage. Upon this request, the Rating Engine returns a response, which contains the calculated cost of the final usage. Next, the Charging Aggregator requests the Balance Manager to release the current credit reservation of the service component in question. The Balance Manager compares the actual cost of the final usage and then it adjusts the credit reservation with this final cost. This mechanism allows the Balance Manager to manage the Subscriber's credit balance appropriately in accordance with the actual service usage. Once the credit reservation of a service component has been released, the Balance Manager returns a confirmation to the Charge Aggregator and updates the Balance Manager with the actual total cost of the service component usage.

The above termination process has a recurrent character because it repeats itself for individual service components involved in a composite service session. Once the charging termination of the last service component in a composite service session has been processed, the Charge Aggregator sends a notification via the Mediation to the provisioning system to report that the service session charge is (properly) terminated. Finally, the Charge Aggregator generates a charge record for the entire composite service session and stores it in the Charge Record Database. Figure 9 below shows the sequential interactions between the involved functional components in the Accounting and Charging Termination phase.

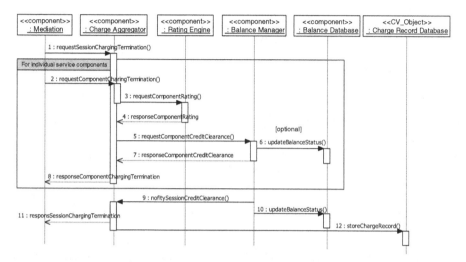

Fig. 9. Interactions between functional components involved in the Accounting and Charging Termination phase

7   Conclusion and Future Research

In this paper we address the problem of online charging for inter-domain composite services which are delivered across IMS-based and web-based infrastructures. A main issue here is the lacking of an adequate service composition information model that relates the constituent service components and the corresponding charging keys. In this paper we overcome this problem by giving a design of a refined IMS based Online Charging System (OCS) together with a composition model based on the SID framework of the TM Forum. Since the design applies the principle of separation of concerns one may expect that it simplifies an implementation and support a large variety of business models between service partners in different domains.

Future investigation on performance aspects of the system components embodies by the proposed OCS will provide insights about their performance indicators. In particular, attention will be paid to the charge aggregation system component since this component is expected to be computing intensive. To achieve high performance, efficient engineering techniques will be explored in combination with state-of-the-art technology such as in-memory databases.

References

1. Cuevas, A., Moreno, J.I., Vidales, P., Einsiedler, H.: The IMS service platform: a solution for next-generation network operators to be more than bit pipes. IEEE Communication Magazine 44(8) (August 2006)
2. 3GPP, Charging Architecture and Principles, TS 32.240, version 8.4.0 (September 2008)
3. Jahnert, J., Wesner, S.: Overall Architecture Definition and Layer Integration, Akogrimo, deliverable 3.1.1 (July 2005)
4. de Laat, C., Gross, G., Gommans, L., Vollbrecht, J., Spence, D.: Generic AAA Architecture, IETF RFC 2903 (August 2000)
5. Koutsopoulou, M., et al.: Charging, Billing & Accounting in a multi-Operator and multi-Service Provider Environment. In: ANWIRE, Workshop on Reconfigurability, Mykonos Greece (September 2003)
6. Huslak, N.S., McQuaide, A.C.: Service Brokering: Opportunities and Challenges. In: International Conference on Intelligent Network (ICIN), Bordeaux France (October 20-23, 2008)
7. 3GPP, Study on Architecture Impacts of Service Brokering, TR 23.810, release 8.0 (September 2008)
8. TMForum, Service Delivery Framework Overview, release 2.0 (September 2008)
9. TMForum, Shared Information/Data (SID) Model – Business View Concepts, Principles and Domains, release 6 (November 2005)
10. van Le, M., Beijnum, B.J.F., Nieuwenhuis, L.J.M., Huitema, G.B.: An Enterprise Model for Real-time Inter-domain Billing of Services. In: Workshop on ODP Enterprise Computing (WODPEC), Muchen, Germany (September 2008)
11. van Le, M., Rumph, F.J., Huitema, G.B., Beijnum, B.J.F., Nieuwenhuis, L.J.M.: Online Charging for IMS-based Inter-Domain Composite Services. In: 6th International Workshop on Internet Charging and QoS Technologies, Aachen (May 2009)
12. van Le, M., van Beijnum, B.J.F., de Goede, B.L.: Real-time Service Accounting. In: IEEE Workshop on IP Operations and Management (IPOM2002), Dallas, TX, USA, October 29-31 (2002)
13. Xu, L., Jennings, B.: Automating the Generation, Deployment and Application of Charging Schemes for Composed IMS Services. In: IFIP/IEEE International Symposium on Integrated Network Management (IM 2007), Munich, Germany, May 21-25 (2007)

Telecom Network and Service Management: An Operator Survey

Stefan Wallin and Viktor Leijon

Luleå University of Technology LTU
SE-931 87 Skelleftea Sweden
stefan.wallin@ltu.se, leijon@csee.ltu.se

Abstract. It is hard to know which research problems in network management we should focus our attention on. To remedy this situation we have surveyed fifteen different telecom operators on four continents to gather some feedback on what they desire and expect from the network management research community. Their input forms a foundation for future directions in network management research, and provides us with valuable insight into what the most urgent problems are in industry.

1 Introduction

Network management research covers a wide range of different topics, and it is hard for the individual researchers to prioritize between them. One factor to take into account is the requirements emanating from the telecom industry.

In order to get an objective view of what the industry considers important we have surveyed fifteen different companies, to gather their opinions on the current state of network management systems, as well as their expectations on the future of Operational Support Systems (OSS).

As far as we can tell, there have been no previous surveys of this type for telecommunications network management. The process control and power industry areas seems to have a higher degree of industry feedback to the research [1,2,3], probably because of the human safety risks involved.

The results of this survey has strategic value both for researchers and solution vendors. It identifies areas where there is a strong need for further research and point to what changes are needed in order to stay competitive.

The contributions of this paper are:

- We present survey results from fifteen different companies, with a total of over 100 million customers, covering the current state (Section 3) and most important change drivers (Section 4).
- The respondents were then asked about their view on the future of OSS systems (Section 5) and what they expected from the OSS research community (Section 7.1).
- We conclude with a discussion of the focus areas identified in the survey: service topology and alarm quality in Section 7.2.

T. Pfeifer and P. Bellavista (Eds.): MMNS 2009, LNCS 5842, pp. 15–26, 2009.

2   Method

We distributed the survey questions by e-mail to 20 operators of different sizes
and on different continents. The individuals were selected based on their roles as
network management architects or managers. 15 out of 20 operators answered.
The respondents are a mix of fixed, broadband and mobile operators with a total
customer base of over 100 million subscribers, see Table 1. The operators were
classified by number subscribers into the categories [< 10 M, < 20 M, < 100 M]
to avoid giving out identifying information.

Some clarifying questions were sent over e-mail and a draft version of this
paper was sent to all operators that provided answers. All questions except one
were essay questions to avoid limiting the answers by our pre-conceived ideas.
We have aggregated similar answers into groups, often using eTOM [4] processes
as targets. The eTOM (enhanced Telecom Operations Map), published by the
TM Forum, is the most widely used and accepted standard for business processes
in the telecommunications industry. The operators were allowed to select several
alternatives for every question.

Table 1. Summary of responding operators

Services	Customers	Region
Mobile and Broadband	< 10 million	North America
Mobile	< 20 million	Europe
Mobile	< 10 million	Europe
Mobile	< 20 million	South America
Mobile	< 20 million	North Africa
Managed OSS, Mobile, transmission	< 20 million	Europe
Mobile, broadband, transmission	<100 million	Europe
Mobile, broadband	< 10 million	Europe
Mobile, broadband, transmission	<100 million	Asia Pacific
Outsourced OSS, Mobile internet, broadband, 3G	< 10 million	Europe
Broadcast, virtual network, capacity	< 10 million	Europe
Mobile, broadband	< 10 million	Europe
Mobile, broadband, managed services	< 10 million	Asia Pacific
Full service carrier, wireline, wireless	< 10 million	Asia Pacific
Mobile and broadband	< 10 million	Asia Pacific

3   Current Status of Network Management

The network and service management solution for a telecom operator is referred
to as the OSS, the Operation Support System. We divide the OSS solutions into
two types depending on maturity, either *Classic* or *Advanced.*

Classic OSS solutions covers service assurance and trouble ticketing. Element
Managers are used to perform configuration management activities and performance management is only partially implemented.

Advanced OSS solutions have expanded the solution to include service management tools such as active and passive probes; and service models. General configuration management tools are used to some degree, spanning several different vendors.

Common to both types is that security is not generally covered by the OSS solution. IT and Telecom is typically still split into different organizations and the IT department manages the customer care and billing processes.

All of the operators said that they focused on making the OSS a proactive solution, but admitted that in reality most of the OSS work is reactive, responding to alarms and problems reported to customer care. The proactive activities were typically based on probes and statistics, where the data was used to predict problems such as capacity limitations, but these were not really integrated into the overall OSS solution.

An interesting comment from one of the operators was about "OSS culture", they had problems transitioning their network administrators from using the element managers to using the full OSS solution. This resulted in underutilization of the OSS and decreased the motivation to develop it.

4   OSS Motivation and Drivers

We asked the operators to identify the most important external drivers that motivates changes in their OSS. The answers are shown in Figure 1.

Increased focus on *services and service quality* was identified as the most important factor behind changes in the OSS. In order to understand this subject better we asked the operators to elaborate on how they viewed service management, one of the operators summarized it in the following way:

> *Services are not currently managed well in any suite of applications and requires a tremendous amount of work to maintain.*

Fig. 1. Change Drivers for OSS

The competitive market is pushing operators to offer more and more innovative services, including SLAs, which require the OSS solution to measure the service quality.

One operator described the experience with the two major alternatives to service monitoring, either using probes or mapping existing events and alarms to a service model. The latter approach failed since there was no good way to describe which alarms were really critical. They made the decision to use only probing for future services, stressing that future services will have service probing from the service deployment phase.

Some of the operators stressed the importance of standards for service models. The problem with models is that services are rapidly changing, therefore requiring a large amount of customization work. One operator expressed reservations about how detailed services can be:

> *Time and money will not be available to [develop] sophisticated approaches over a long period. Customers will have to accept limited quality assurance and quality documentation. Service levels will always be high level, if [they exist] at all.*

Another operator commented on how the use of service models is evolving:

> *Service models are becoming more and more important: currently [they are] not implemented in core processes but used as means to semi-document and analyze when evaluating impact of faults, new services, etc.*

As indicated by Figure 1 *cost reduction* is clearly another key factor. We asked the operators to further break down the cost drivers and the results are shown in Figure 2.

The first two items can be considered two sides of the same coin: Integration costs are high in OSS due to the introduction of new technologies and services. When a new type of network element is deployed it needs to be integrated into the OSS solution and while most solutions are based on well established products,

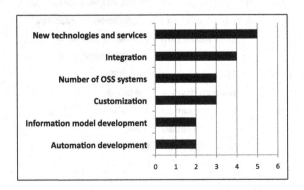

Fig. 2. Cost drivers for OSS

there is still a high degree of customization needed to adopt the tools to user needs and processes.

In order to get a unified view of the solution, the resource oriented interfaces needs to be mapped into an overall service model. Operators are struggling with this challenge, the "information model development" in Figure 2. Finally the OSS itself is expensive due to the number of components that are needed. Even in the case where an OSS is built using only one vendor, it is still made up of a portfolio of modules which add up to a relatively costly software solution.

Returning to the change drivers (Figure 1) the next items are *network growth* and increased focus on *customer satisfaction*. While network growth is inherent in network management, customer satisfaction has not historically been a primary goal for OSS solutions.

To put the true business role of the OSS solution in focus, we asked if it was seen as a competitive tool or not. The answers were divided into two general streams:

- *Yes.* Motivations are the desire to decrease time-to-repair, decrease OPEX, and improve customer satisfaction by quicker response to new requirements and customer complaints. Two thirds of the responses fall into this category.
- *No.* These operators felt that it will be outsourced. The out-sourcing scenario was partly motivated by internal failures and a desire to give the problem to someone else.

5   The Future of OSS

5.1   Organizational Changes

The answers regarding future OSS changes are summarized in Figure 3, it is no surprise that Service management is seen as one of the most important upcoming changes. One of the larger operators predicted a "focus on service management - bringing this up to 40% from [the] current level of 5-10%".

Further, we see the strategic need for a service inventory to enable service quality, service provisioning and a service life-cycle view. Most of the operators are providing broadband services and this makes automatic service provisioning a must.

Service management was summarized in the following way by one of the operators:

> *Managing services must be the focus of the future development, while pushing network management into a supporting role, [...] service models [should be] constructed from auto-discovered infrastructure components that have auto-discovery deeply integrated. [...] [The] service models should be abstracted from physical and logical inventory to ensure there is a life cycle. [...] If the service models were to be constructed from scratch, with no base layer that is managed separately (auto-discovered or abstraction over inventory), that will most probably undermine the layered service level management solution.*

Fig. 3. OSS organizational changes

Common to all respondents is an increased focus on customer care, customer service, self-management, and self-provisioning. An interesting point made by one of the operators is the shift from eTOM verticals to a more supply chain based production model. Classical OSS systems have had separate solutions for fulfillment, assurance, and billing. The supply chain model will focus on the whole life-cycle from service definition to billing and retirement. This will remove the obstacles between eTOM verticals and help relieve the hand-over problem from "eTOM Strategy" to "eTOM Operations" areas.

Another trend is a radical transformation of the OSS from being a network-oriented function to becoming a customer-oriented organization. The surveyed operators mentioned features such as "more focus on customer service, customer experience, and self-management".

5.2   Focus Processes

The eTOM process framework defines the processes in several abstraction layers. We asked the operators to identify the three most important processes (Figure 4).

The prefixes of the legend in Figure 4 refers to the eTOM vertical (**F**ulfillment, **A**ssurance, **B**illing) and horizontal (**C**ustomer, **S**ervice, **R**esource, **S**upplier) end-to-end processes. For instance F-S refers to Fulfillment-Service. Again, we see the focus on the service life-cycle through order handling, provisioning, service quality, problem management and billing.

6   Standards and Research Efforts

6.1   Standards

The attitude towards standards was not very enthusiastic: "They are too complicated and are actually adding to the cost of ownership", in this case the 3GPP

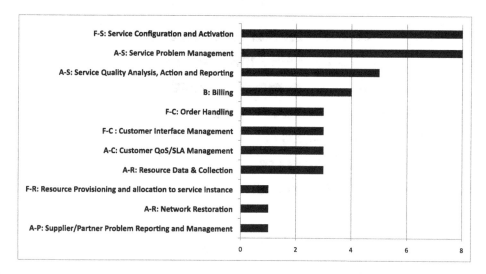

Fig. 4. The most important eTOM processes

Alarm Interface was the main source for concern. Another operator had similar distrust for standards: "[In] alarm integration to the OSS, most of the vendors do not follow any one. We are pushing [our] internal standard to have useful alarm information for the end users". Some operators mentioned SNMP as a working protocol that is easy to integrate, however the lack of standard OSS interface MIBs is a problem, and the vendor MIBs vary in quality.

As important areas for future standardization efforts they mentioned "interfaces, data and semantic models, standardization of procedures" and "well defined top level common framework and common languages". We see from these comments that the current practice of using different protocols for different interfaces and having weak formal data models is a problem for OSS integrations. There is no accepted overall common framework which would enable unified naming of resources.

Surprisingly, none of the operators mentioned OSS/J [5]. On the other hand several operators considered the eTOM [4] and ITIL [6] process standards to have real practical value. They used these process frameworks to structure the work and make it more efficient.

6.2   Research Efforts

In Figure 5 we can see the areas that the operators in this survey identified as the most important ones for future research.

It is well worth noting that for research alarm correlation is a key item, while it was not as prominent when the operators were asked to identify the key efforts and changes in the coming years. The opposite is true for service management and modeling, which were key items for more immediate change. One interpretation is

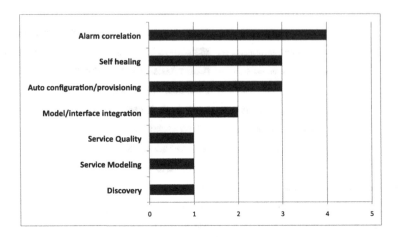

Fig. 5. Research efforts

that it is hard to foresee the challenges with the planned changes before we have attempted them. Many operators have struggled with alarm correlation for years without seeing any clear successes and are hoping for more research to help them. We might see the same thing happening with service management and modeling after a first wave of implementation efforts.

7 Discussion

7.1 OSS Research

Historically a lot of research has gone into alarm correlation. Looking at the current correlation rates it is not clear how successful these projects have been, many correlation projects are facing challenges trying to capture operator knowledge and transforming it into rules. Other methods for finding rules based on rule discovery, knowledge management, data-mining and self-learning networks are interesting, but seem to require further investigation to be of practical use.

Having service models in place would be a key to unlocking many other functions. The current industry practice of large UML models with loose structure does not seem able to cope with the requirements, more modular and semantically rich ways of doing service modeling are required.

Another basic area is that of formal interface definitions. The current integration costs can not be justified when we consider the fundamentally simple nature of the information that flows over the interfaces, integrating alarms should not be a complex and costly task. Semantically richer interface definitions would probably improve the situation, but this requires a focus on the semantics of the model and not only the syntax, protocol and software architecture.

Boutaba and Xiao [7] point to the following major enablers for future OSS systems:

- Policy-based network management, [8], [9]
- Distributed computing, [10], [11]
- Mobile agents, [12], [13]
- Web techniques, [14]
- Java, [15]

These are topics that we see in many network management efforts. However we see little correlation between these and those identified in this survey. Furthermore it partly illustrates the research's focus on software architectures rather then management.

7.2   Fulfilling the Future Needs of Operators with OSS

It is easy to talk about paradigm shifts but things change more slowly than we expect, nonetheless some major changes in OSS solutions are needed to help service providers to cope with the changing environment. Operators want to manage services rather than the network resources that are used to deliver services. This change in focus is driven by several factors; increased competition, more complex service offerings, distribution of services, and a market for Service Level Agreements.

One operator had this to say about the market for services:

> *The competition between companies pushes them to offer more and innovative services, they need to sell more services first, the want to go out before the others.*

Current network management solutions control and administer resources; physical resources are found, configured and monitored. However, from a customer point of view, services are bought, provisioned and billed.

One of the underlying challenges in a service centric solution is to maintain a model of the service topology. In contrast to the network resources services are abstract by nature, while it is often possible to automatically discover the network topology this is not necessarily true for the service topology.

Future solutions must rely on service repositories where different and systems publish their respective topology information with lightweight technologies, this will enable operators to maintain a centralized view of the topology which will be the future OSS foundation. Note that this improvement has to come without significant additional integration costs or complexity.

Moving forward in the direction identified in this survey will fail if there is no way to share the information model between OSS systems. The feedback we get from operators who apply SID [16] is that it works well as a design base for the OSS system but not as a service model to maintain the dynamic business services. Service modeling must be dynamic and have well-defined semantics, the current practice of static models and informal documents does not cope with a changing environment.

While OSS solutions have primarily been network oriented it now needs to change focus to customer care, since operators see a huge possibility to reduce costs in an automated customer care. The number of employees in mobile network customer care greatly outnumbers the OSS staff, therefore, solutions that help automate customer care activities will be a priority in the coming years.

Operators will also look for automated provisioning solutions including self-configuration of the network elements which helps avoid tedious parameter setting. The move from fixed-line services to broadband consumer services stresses this further since customers need to be able to buy, configure and troubleshoot their services with minimal support.

While we see these changes coming we need to realize that the integration of Telecom, IT and IP has not yet happened. Some of the operators have a somewhat naïve vision of a future when network administrators will only look at service views and SLA status.

None of our respondents reported positive results regarding the deployment of standards. Over the years we have seen great efforts to move from one protocol to another, from OSI-based solutions to CORBA and now Web Services. This journey is based on a desire to find a technology solution to an information problem, unfortunately OSS integration standards like OSS/J has not yet proven its cost effectiveness.

Alarm quality and alarm correlation is still an underdeveloped area, although research and industry initiatives go back decades [17] the current alarm flow at a standard network operations centre is fairly basic and often of low quality.

We did not get any real numbers on filtering and correlation rates, but the informal indications pointed to very low success rate which is consistent with what is reported by Stanton [18]. In many cases alarm messages go untransformed, unfiltered, and uncorrelated from the network elements to the network management system which leads to a chaotic situation that needs to be cleaned up before we can move into service and customer management. A representative answer was:

> [around] 40% percent of the alarms are considered to be redundant as many alarms appears at the same time for one 'fault'. Many alarms are also repeated [...]. One alarm had for example appeared 65 000 times in todays browser. Correlation is hardly used even if it supported by the systems, [current correlation level is] 1-2 % maybe.

Some operators chose to completely ignore alarm correlation, they considered it too expensive and complex to get good results. These respondents instead pointed to probing, statistics, and performance based solutions to get an overall picture rather then trying to automate root-cause analysis. It was also stressed that advanced alarm correlation projects are in many cases signs of bad alarm quality from the low-level systems.

Finally, we let an operator conclude this survey by pointing to ongoing challenging OSS improvements:

> Significant work underway to move to a self-service enabled environment for the customer. Whilst this is to improve the customer experience, this is also expected to dramatically increase operational efficiencies. Other

key improvements are, (1) [...] capability to enable growth and the rapid on-boarding of customers, (2) Improve flow-through provisioning and activations [...] to reduce manual intervention, improve service delivery timeframes and room for human error.

8 Conclusion

We hope that this survey can form the basis for prioritizing among research topics. The most important conclusion is probably that there is a great potential to further network management research by working closer with service providers. There is a gap between the current research efforts which typically focus on new software architectures and protocols and the telecom companies that has other priorities.

It is worth noting that after decades of research, alarm correlation is still the most prioritized research area. This can partially be interpreted as a failure, since no solution seems to be ready. Instead we see a new set of research challenges emerging, connected to self-healing, service activation and provisioning.

If research is to support the future focus areas for service providers we need to find solutions for service and quality management. Another observation is the failure of alarms as an indicator of service status, where we see a trend towards probe based solutions.

The operators gave a clear message on their desire to move from network and resource management towards customer and service management solutions. This comes as no surprise, as the trend has been clear for some time, but the path there needs attention. A new brand of OSS Solutions that are based on the service life-cycle rather then separate OSS components for different processes is needed.

References

1. Bransby, M., Jenkinson, J.: The Management of Alarm Systems. HSE Contract Research Report 166, 1998 (1998)
2. Stanton, N.: Human Factors in Alarm Design. Taylor & Francis, Abington (1994)
3. Hollifield, B., Habibi, E.: Alarm Management Handbook. PAS (2006)
4. TMForum: eTOM - Telecom Operators Map (2006)
5. TM Forum: OSS/J, http://www.tmforum.org/ossj/ (accessed August 14, 2008)
6. Office of Government Commerce: ITIL, http://www.itil-officialsite.com (accessed August 14, 2008)
7. Boutaba, R., Xiao, J.: Network Management: State of the Art. In: Communication Systems: The State of the Art: IFIP 17th World Computer Congress, TC6 Stream on Communication Systems, Montréal, Québec, Canada, August 25–30 (2002)
8. Strassner, J.: Policy-Based Network Management: Solutions for the Next Generation. Morgan Kaufmann, San Francisco (2004)
9. Lymberopoulos, L., Lupu, E., Sloman, M.: An Adaptive Policy-Based Framework for Network Services Management. Journal of Network and Systems Management 11(3), 277–303 (2003)

10. Tennenhouse, D., Wetherall, D.: Towards an active network architecture. In: DARPA Active Networks Conference and Exposition, Proceedings, pp. 2–15 (2002)
11. Chen, T., Liu, S.: A model and evaluation of distributed network management approaches. IEEE Journal on Selected Areas in Communications 20(4), 850–857 (2002)
12. Papavassiliou, S., Puliafito, A., Tomarchio, O., Ye, J.: Mobile agent-based approach for efficient network management andresource allocation: framework and applications. IEEE Journal on Selected Areas in Communications 20(4), 858–872 (2002)
13. Stephan, R., Ray, P.: Network Management Platform Based on Mobile Agents. Int. J. Network Mgmt. 14, 59–73 (2004)
14. Pavlou, G., Flegkas, P., Gouveris, S., Liotta, A.: On management technologies and the potential of Web services. IEEE Communications Magazine 42(7), 58–66 (2004)
15. Lee, J.: Enabling network management using Java technologies. IEEE Communications Magazine 38(1), 116–123 (2000)
16. TM Forum: Shared information data model (2005)
17. Steinder, M., Sethi, A.S.: A survey of fault localization techniques in computer networks. Science of Computer Programming 53(2), 165–194 (2004)
18. Stanton, N., Harrison, D., Taylor-Burge, K., Porter, L.: Sorting the Wheat from the Chaff: A Study of the Detection of Alarms. Cognition, Technology & Work 2(3), 134–141 (2000)

On-Demand Multicast Streaming Using Collaborative Prefix Caching*

John Paul O'Neill and Jonathan Dukes

School of Computer Science and Statistics
Trinity College Dublin, Ireland
{jponeill,jdukes}@cs.tcd.ie

Abstract. Increasing mass-market acceptance of on-demand streaming services motivates us to seek new innovations in the way we deliver media content over networks. An architecture is proposed in which edge-resources in a peer-to-peer network assist in the provision of fully-interactive on-demand streaming services based on multicast. This approach represents a synergy between multicast batching, proxy prefix caching and collaborative caching of media content. The approach differs from other work in its use of long-term caching of content across streaming sessions. The proposed approach has been evaluated using a highly detailed network simulation that models real-world network (IPv6) and streaming (RTSP) protocols and the Pastry overlay network. Results demonstrate that substantial reductions in server bandwidth can be achieved with low client storage and bandwidth overhead.

1 Introduction

On-demand, Internet-based media streaming services are gaining mass-market acceptance as an alternative to traditional broadcast services for television and radio. The emergence and popularity of services such as BBC's iPlayer [1] and Hulu [2] is evidence of this. The strain that the popularity of these services places on network infrastructure has also been reported [3]. These factors motivate continued effort to seek new innovations in the delivery of media content.

This paper describes an approach to the delivery of on-demand media streams, in which edge-resources in a peer-to-peer network assist in the provision of on-demand streaming services based on multicast. The approach represents a synergy between a number of techniques, including multicast *Batching* [4], *Proxy Prefix Caching* [5] and collaborative caching [6]. These techniques can be combined to varying degrees, according to the behaviour the content provider wishes to see in the network.

Recent renewed interest in multicast support for delivery of multimedia content [7] has prompted a re-examination of its use in on-demand streaming applications. Multicast streaming has the potential to offer significant savings in the

---

* This work was supported by the Irish Research Council for Science, Engineering and Technology. The authors would like to acknowledge the support of the Grid Ireland Operations Centre personnel.

T. Pfeifer and P. Bellavista (Eds.): MMNS 2009, LNCS 5842, pp. 27–40, 2009.

resources consumed by the delivery of popular streams. The challenge, however, is to service multiple clients with a single multicast stream, while still providing each client with full, independent, interactive control over the streams it receives. In particular, clients should experience low-latency when requesting playback of a new stream or moving to a new offset in an existing stream. *Patching* [8] has been proposed in the past as a means of addressing this challenge.

The use of peer-to-peer networks in applications such as PROMISE [9], Split-Stream [10], and the Multimedia Distribution Service proposed by Zhang et al. [11] has also received much attention. Applications such as these are based solely on the use of overlay networks and do not rely on central servers that store and supply all of the content, thereby removing the likelihood of a bottleneck occurring at any point in the network.

In contrast with these approaches, the architecture proposed here uses multicast as the primary delivery mechanism between servers and clients. Clients collaborate in a peer-to-peer network to cache and serve *prefix* streams containing the beginning of recently accessed streams. Delivery of these prefix streams can begin immediately to achieve low stream start-up latency, while delivery of multicast streams can be delayed to allow multiple clients to be *batched* into a single multicast stream, thereby reducing server bandwidth utilisation.

A detailed simulation of the proposed architecture has been developed. This simulation models real-world network (IPv6), stream control (RTSP) and multicast control (MLD and PIM-SSM) protocols and the Pastry [12] peer-to-peer overlay network. The simulation has been used to evaluate the hybrid architecture and demonstrate its effectiveness in reducing bandwidth utilisation between servers and localized groups of collaborating clients (e.g. on a local area network or in a neighbourhood). The combination of multicast and peer-to-peer techniques can achieve this reduction while using only a small proportion of each client's storage and bandwidth resources. The approach also allows service providers to achieve a balance between the use of multicast and reliance on client resources.

2   Background

The simplest way of implementing an on-demand streaming service that gives clients interactive control over stream playback is to provide each client with a dedicated, independent stream. Server and network resource requirements may be reduced in a simple manner by grouping together two or more client requests arriving over a short period of time and servicing those requests using a single multicast stream, an approach that has been referred to as *Batching* [4]. This approach, however, results in significantly higher stream startup latencies, since client requests must be delayed until a number of requests can be batched together. Furthermore, servicing multiple clients with a single multicast stream will result in the loss of independent, interactive client control over stream playback. *Patching* [8] was proposed as a way of using multicast to reduce network and server resource requirements, while still achieving low stream startup latencies.

Alternatively peer-to-peer architectures such as Joost [13], PPLive [14] and PPStream [15] offer a decentralized means of distributing on-demand content. Huang et al [16] have demonstrated that these architectures are becoming increasingly popular and that peer-to-peer on demand streaming is as viable as BitTorrent style download.

The use of peer-to-peer overlay networks in conjunction with multicast has been proposed by Lee et al. [17] and Ho et al. [18]. The architecture proposed here, however, differs significantly in the way in which cached content is managed, located and used. Both of these existing architectures use a central server to locate buffered content and select peers to service new client requests, rather than the decentralised approach proposed here. Furthermore, the collaborative prefix caching approach that is proposed here caches content for long periods across multiple streaming sessions, thereby allowing more extensive use of peer resources.

In the proposed architecture, *patch* streams of a defined maximum length are supplied by peers, rather than by the server. As a result, parallels can be drawn between this scheme and the *Proxy Prefix Caching* scheme proposed by Sen et al. [5]. Rather than relying on dedicated infrastructure to cache and serve prefix streams, however, peer resources are used to implement a collaborative, decentralised cache.

The collaborative prefix cache builds on the *Squirrel* decentralised peer-to-peer web cache proposed by Iyer et al. [6]. Instead of caching and serving small web objects, however, peers in the proposed architecture provide streams of cached multimedia content. The changes that result from this difference are discussed in Section 3.3.

The main advantage of the hybrid architecture is that it provides a reduction in bandwidth utilisation for the server, without causing clients to become fully dependant on peer-to-peer resources. By using peer resources at the edges of the network to supply cached prefix streams, the server is given an opportunity to delay the provision of streams, and thus group together numerous requests for the same content item and serve these requests with a single multicast stream.

3   Peer-Assisted Multicast

The challenge when implementing a multicast streaming service is to maximise the sharing of multicast streams while retaining low stream start-up latencies. The *Patching* scheme described in Section 2 achieved this by using a centralized server to provide both the multicast *batch* streams and the *patch* streams necessary to provide low-latency and client interactivity. A different approach is taken here, illustrated in Figure 1, in which clients collaborate to provide each other with the prefix streams necessary to facilitate low stream start-up latencies, leaving centralized servers to implement what effectively becomes multicast *Batching*.

Like Squirrel, it is assumed that collaborating clients are close together. Clients cache the prefix of streams that are required locally. When a client requests a stream, it first determines whether the prefix is available in the local

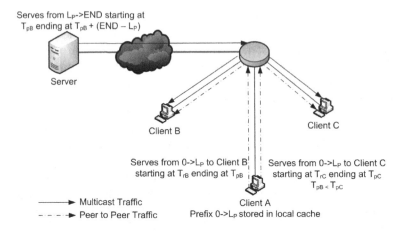

Fig. 1. Peer-Assisted Multicast. Clients B and C retrieve cached prefixes from Client A and the remainder of the stream from the server. The server needs to start providing the remainder by the time Client B has finished receiving the prefix.

cache, in which case only the remainder of the stream must be retrieved from the server. Otherwise, the client determines whether the prefix is available in the collaborative peer cache, in which case it retrieves the prefix from a peer and the remainder of the stream from the server. If the prefix is not available from either the local cache or the collaborative peer cache, the entire stream is retrieved from the server.

This approach will have the greatest effect on the server and network resources required to provide the most popular content streams, as the potential for multicast sharing for these streams is highest. The benefit for resource utilisation resulting from serving unpopular content will be significantly smaller since the server only benefits by not having to supply stream prefixes that clients can obtain from local or peer caches. Increasing or decreasing the prefix length will result in a server obtaining greater or lesser benefit respectively from the use of multicast.

3.1 Server Behaviour

A server can expect two types of request: those that must be served immediately and those that can be served at a future time. Requests that must be served immediately are those requests from clients who were unable to locate the prefix in either their local cache, or in the collaborative peer cache. As these requests must be served immediately, it is unlikely the server will be able to batch a number of these together, so the possibility of multicast sharing is minimal.

The second type of request is generated from clients who have located the prefix in either their local cache or a peer's cache. While these clients are viewing the prefix, the remainder of the content does not need to be served until the prefix is finished (allowing for some network delay). This window, between the

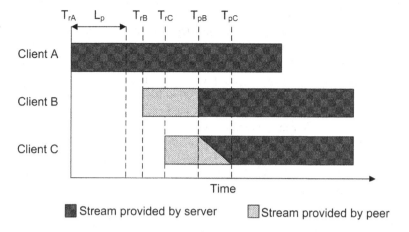

Fig. 2. Clients B and C retrieve cached prefixes from Client A and the remainder of the stream from the server

request arriving at the server and the required start time as specified by the client, allows the server to batch together other requests for the same content that arrive during this window.

Figure 2 illustrates the behaviour of the protocol. In this example, Clients A, B and C request the same stream. Client A was unable to locate the prefix in either its local cache or the collaborative cache so the client sends a request to the server at time T_{rA} which requires immediate playback of content. Once Client A has received the stream prefix of length L_p, it can supply that prefix to other clients. At time $T_{rB} > (T_{rA} + L_p)$, Client B issues a request for the stream. As the prefix is now stored in the collaborative cache, Client B requests the prefix from Client A and informs the server that it requires the content from L_p until the end of the stream, and that it must begin receiving the stream by T_{pB}. At time $T_{rC} < T_{pB}$, Client C sends a request identical to the request sent by Client B, except that in this case the stream needs to be served by T_{pC}. As there is already a request pending for this content, the server can satisfy both T_{pB} and T_{pC} by serving a multicast stream at $MIN(T_{pB}, T_{pC})$. Client C will need to buffer the stream from the server, and begin playback from the buffer at time T_{pC}.

3.2   RTSP Implementation

The simulation of peer-assisted multicast, described in Section 4, models the use of the RTSP [19] protocol for control of all multimedia streams in the system. For streams served by one peer to another using a unicast transport mechanism, the application of RTSP is straight forward. For streams served by a server using a multicast transport mechanism, however, the use of RTSP must be considered in more detail. A description of the use of RTSP to implement multicast *Patching* has been described previously by the authors [20]. Here, the focus will be on the most salient aspects of the use of RTSP to implement peer-assisted multicast. (It is assumed that an appropriate transport protocol, such as RTP, will be used for the delivery of unicast and multicast streams to clients.)

RTSP requires that the client and server participating in a session agree on the transport parameters including, in particular, the multicast address to which the client must subscribe, during the SETUP phase of the session. The server, however, must assign the client to a multicast batch without knowing when the client will issue a PLAY request, what range the client will request or what time the client expects playback to begin.

When the server receives a PLAY request, it is possible that the multicast batch to which it originally assigned the client is no longer suitable. To determine whether this is the case, the server checks whether the first packet in the range requested by the client has already been sent to the multicast address to which the client has subscribed. If this is the case, the server responds using the RTSP "Request Time-out" response and the client renegotiates the transport parameters with a new SETUP request.

In the case where the first packet in the range requested by the client has not yet been sent to the multicast address, the server then compares the playback start time requested by the client with the scheduled start of the current batch. If the scheduled start time is later, the server brings it forward to satisfy the start time requested by the client.

3.3   Collaborative Prefix Caching

Like the Squirrel decentralised web cache [6], clients in the proposed collaborative prefix cache collaborate in a peer-to-peer network to implement a cache of recently accessed content. Also like Squirrel, the Pastry [12] overlay network has been chosen as the substrate for the collaborative cache. This approach exploits temporal locality in the same way as a centralised cache but avoids the need for additional infrastructure. The differences between the collaborative prefix cache and the original Squirrel approach arise from the need to store and supply potentially lengthy, high-bandwidth media streams.

Both Squirrel and the collaborative prefix cache described here use key-based routing in a peer-to-peer network to locate content items. The authors of Squirrel explored two alternative approaches, which they termed *home-store* and *directory*. In both approaches, a request for a content item is routed through the peer-to-peer network to the *home node* whose identifier is numerically closest to the content item identifier.

In the *home-store* approach, each node is responsible for caching content items for which it is the home node. Thus, the cache at each node will contain both content items that were required locally and content items that were requested by other nodes and for which the node is the home node. Using the *directory* approach, home nodes are responsible for maintaining a directory of the nodes (as in Squirrel, these are termed *delegates*) that have a cached copy of the content items whose identifiers are closest to the node. Thus, each node only caches

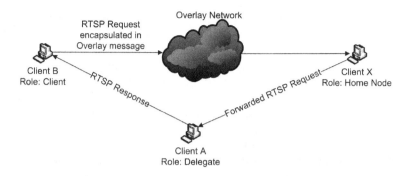

Fig. 3. Collaborative Cache Lookup

content items that were required locally. Figure 3 illustrates the roles played by peers in the location and supply of cached stream prefixes.

In their original work on Squirrel, the authors established that *home-store* performed better than *directory* with respect to its ability to both reduce external bandwidth usage (resulting from cache misses) and also balance load internally among participating nodes. However, since caching and serving high bit-rate media streams requires a significantly higher proportion of a client's bandwidth and storage resources, it is unreasonable to expect a client to retrieve, store and serve content that it does not itself require. Accordingly, a *directory* approach similar to that proposed for Squirrel is more appropriate for a collaborative prefix cache for media streaming applications.

The initial SETUP request issued by a client is treated in a similar manner to a HTTP GET request in Squirrel. This request may be conditional or unconditional, depending on whether the client has a fresh, cached copy of the requested stream prefix. The request is initially directed to the home node for the stream prefix, based on an identifier derived from the request URI.

The unconditional case is examined first. If the home node's directory contains one or more delegates with a cached copy of the requested content, the request is forwarded to a selected delegate. If the delegate's cached prefix is fresh, it will send an RTSP OK response to the client, establishing a new session. If the cached prefix is stale, the delegate will issue a conditional RTSP SETUP request to the server, the response to which will indicate whether the cached prefix has been modified. If the prefix has not been modified, the delegate will send an RTSP OK response to the client. If, however, the prefix is out of date, a new copy of the prefix must be retrieved from the server. The collaborative prefix cache differs from Squirrel at this point. In Squirrel, a delegate whose cached prefix has been modified will receive an up-to-date copy of the object from the server, in response to the conditional GET request. Retrieving a media stream that is not required locally, however, is likely to be a prohibitive use of client resources. Accordingly, the delegate issues an RTSP NOT FOUND response to the client and informs the directory that the prefix has been modified, causing it to be removed from the directory. The client will retrieve the entire stream from the server, caching the new prefix and eventually becoming the sole new delegate for the stream.

The case is now examined where a client has a locally cached prefix but the cached copy is stale. Again, the collaborative prefix cache behaves in a similar manner to Squirrel. The client issues a conditional RTSP SETUP request to the home node. Like Squirrel, the collaborative prefix cache maintains time-to-live information for each cached prefix. If the directory entry is fresh and the client's prefix has not been modified (we assume that this can be established through the use of Last-Modified timestamps) then the directory issues an RTSP NOT MODIFIED response to the client. If the prefix has been modified, then the request is forwarded to a chosen delegate and handled as described above. If the directory entry is not fresh, the client is instructed to contact the server to either validate its existing cached prefix or retrieve the entire stream from the server, thereby caching a new prefix. In either case, the client will update the directory with new information, allowing the directory to either validate all of the existing delegates or replace them with the requesting client as the new sole delegate.

When a client receives an RTSP OK response from a peer in response to a SETUP request, both it and the chosen delegate become participants in a new RTSP session. Although it would be possible at this point for the client and delegate to continue to communicate using the peer-to-peer network, a scheme in which the participants transfer to a more efficient, direct TCP connection is proposed. This has the effect of limiting the use of the peer-to-peer network to the location of home nodes and the occasional exchange of cached prefix metadata between delegates and home nodes.

Two approaches were considered to determine when clients advertise the availability of cached prefixes. In the first approach, clients wait until the entire prefix is cached before advertising the availability of the prefix to the directory node. Using this approach, the maximum delay until the server must begin streaming the remainder of the content is determined by the fixed prefix length. This in turn allows the server more time to batch requests together. The main disadvantage of this approach is that when the popularity of a content item increases suddenly (commonly referred to as a "flash crowd") there will be period of time during which peers are unable to provide prefix streams and hence the server will not be able to batch together requests.

Using an alternative approach, clients advertise the availability of a prefix as soon as they begin caching the stream and later update the directory when the entire prefix has been cached. If a client with an incomplete prefix is required to provide a prefix stream, it only provides the portion of the prefix that is currently cached. The receiving client must then obtain the remainder of the stream (from the end of the incomplete prefix to the end of the stream) from the server. Using this approach, the server has less time to group requests into a multicast stream. However, the approach also allows a larger pool of prefixes to be used when flash crowds occur.

Using both approaches, the prefix length represents the maximum any client will need to retrieve from the peer-to-peer network. This way clients will be rewarded with a more reliable stream from the server if they are viewing content for a sustained duration, instead of depending on content retrieved from the peer-to-peer network. If clients only view a short portion of streams, they will only be served by a peer stream.

Fairness is a consideration in any system that relies on the resources of peers to provide a service. To ensure fairness, we have chosen to limit each client to provide a single stream to another client at any time. If a client which is already providing a prefix is contacted by the directory node, then the client informs the directory that it has insufficient bandwidth and the directory contacts a different client to supply the stream. If all clients are providing content then the requesting client will need to retrieve the full stream from the server.

The use of a round robin delegate selection policy when providing complete prefixes will ensure fairness. For incomplete prefixes, a round robin selection policy would ensure fairness but could result in the use of short prefix streams. The longer the prefix a delegate can provide, the more beneficial it is to the system as a whole as servers are given more time to delay the start of multicast streams. For maximum benefit to the server, incomplete prefixes are only used if there are no complete prefixes available.

4   Performance Evaluation

The performance of the proposed hybrid architecture has been evaluated using the OMNeT++ [21] discrete event network simulation system. Real-world network protocols have been modelled to allow an exploration of the implementation of the architecture, in addition to its performance. An IPv6 network has been modelled, using the MLD [22] and PIM-SSM [23] protocols for multicast control. The main parameters used are listed in Table 1. These parameters have been chosen to subject the server to a mean load of 900 concurrent streams if no multicast is used. To provide a continous flow of requests a client population greater than this needs to be maintained. Although a cache TTL is used, it was assumed for these experiments that the content is never modified by the server. A Zipf distribution has been used to model the popularity of content items. The total duration of each simulation is 48 hours and the first six hours of each simulation have been ignored to allow the system to stabilize.

To investigate the sudden introduction of new, popular content to the system, akin to a "flash crowd", ten new items were added at regular intervals of six hours, with the first new items introduced eighteen hours into the simulation. These new items became the most popular items according to the Zipf distribution and the original content items were all reduced in popularity by ten places.

Figure 4 illustrates the effect of prefix length on the mean number of streams served concurrently by the server and by each client for the complete prefix selection scheme. The schemes which used incomplete prefixes produced similar results, which are omitted for brevity. Prefix length has an approximately linear relationship with the mean number of streams served by each client. The effect

Table 1. Experiment Parameters

Parameter	Range
Number of Content Items	5000
Mean Stream Length (seconds)	3600
Prefix Length (seconds)	0-1800
Cache Size (number of prefixes)	5
Network Size (number of clients)	1000
Request Rate (requests/second)	0.25
Zipf Skew Factor	1.0

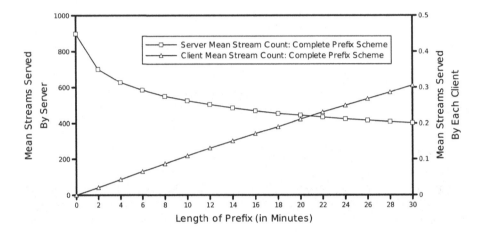

Fig. 4. Mean number of concurrent streams served by the server (left axis) and by any client (right axis)

of prefix length on the mean number of streams served by the server initially shows a sizable reduction for even a small increase in prefix length. As the prefix length increases, the server is able to serve more clients with each multicast stream, thereby reducing the number of multicast streams required. Further increases in prefix length have a diminishing effect.

The effect that varying prefix length has on the number of clients served by each multicast stream is linked to the popularity of the content. This can be observed in Figure 5, which shows that the majority of the benefit is seen for only the most popular content items, but that for these items, even relatively small prefix lengths result in a significant reduction in server bandwidth. (e.g. A six minute prefix allows the server to service a mean of ten clients with one multicast stream for the most popular content item.)

The effect of a flash crowd when using a prefix length of thirty minutes can be seen in Figure 6. If only complete prefixes are used, the server must deliver significantly more streams than the mean (solid horizontal line) for a sustained period of time. If a round robin scheme is used to select incomplete prefixes,

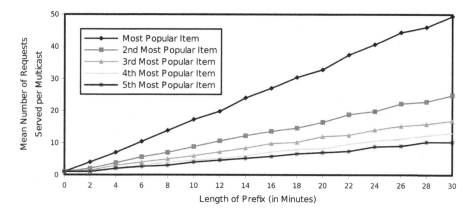

Fig. 5. Mean number of requests serviced per multicast stream for the five most popular content items

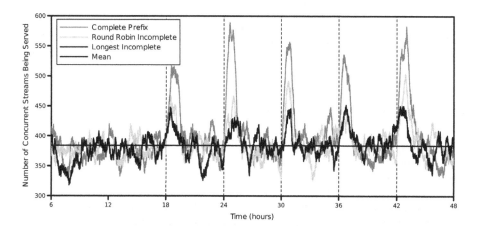

Fig. 6. Effect of flash crowds on the system. The timing of each flash crowd is illustrated with a dotted vertical line.

however, server load is reduced. If a scheme that selects the longest available incomplete prefix is used, then the effect of flash crowds is reduced further.

The effect on the main server of using incomplete prefixes is also illustrated in Figure 7, which shows the server behaviour around the peaks seen in Figure 6. The time at which the server is required to start each new stream to serve a batch of requests for one of the newly introduced content items is plotted against the cumulative number of such streams served. As can be seen, using complete prefixes requires the most time for the server to stabilise, since the server cannot batch together requests until a sufficient number of prefixes are available. Using the longest available prefix, however, allows the maximum time for requests to be batched together and, as a result, the server requires less time to stabilise.

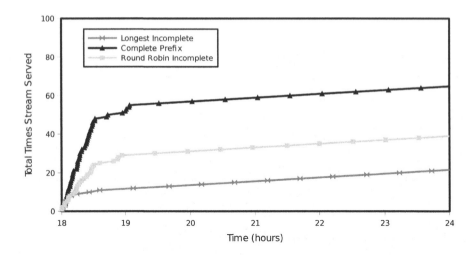

Fig. 7. Effect of new popular content

The rate at which the server provides stream of these popular content items eventually stabilises using all three policies, once there is a large enough pool of complete prefixes available in the collaborative cache.

5   Discussion and Conclusions

The use of peer-assisted multicast batching can significantly reduce server and network bandwidth utilisation by allowing servers to take advantage of the benefits of multicast streaming, without incurring high playback latencies or sacrificing independent client control over playback. To provide servers with the opportunity to batch multiple clients into a single multicast stream, clients implement a collaborative prefix cache containing the start of recently accessed streams. A peer-to-peer overlay network can be used to facilitate the location of cached content within the collaborative cache. This flexible approach gives service providers the ability to balance the benefits gained from multicast with reliance on client resources at the edges of the network. The work described in this paper differs from other proposals to combine multicast with peer-to-peer overlay networks in its use of a long-term, collaborative prefix cache.

A detailed simulation study of the use of collaborative prefix caching has been conducted, which allowed an investigation of its practical implementation in addition to its performance. The simulation model is based on the use of real-world network (IPv6), streaming (RTSP) and multicast control (MLD and PIM-SSM) protocols and on the use of the Pastry overlay network.

The results from the performance evaluation show that peer-assisted multicast can significantly reduce the server and network resources required to serve popular content items, while using only a small proportion of each client's storage and bandwidth resources. For example, using a prefix length of ten minutes yielded a reduction in the average number of streams served by the server of approximately 40%, while requiring an average of 9% of the client population to serve prefix streams concurrently. The results also show that a high degree of load balancing can be achieved with even a simple delegate selection scheme such as round-robin.

The effect of "flash crowds", which occur when there is a rapid increase in the demand for one or more content items, has been demonstrated by simulating the introduction of new popular content. Flash crowds have the largest effect when only complete prefixes are used, whereas a system based around using the longest available incomplete prefix suffers least from a flash crowd.

As with any system based on peer-to-peer technology, the effect of churn, which occurs when peers join and leave the network, must be a consideration as high levels of churn can destabilize a peer-to-peer network. Also, as this system allows peers to renege on requests if they are already providing a stream, it is open to abuse by a malicious peer not wishing to contribute resources to the system. This behaviour is commonly referred to as free loading. The ability of the hybrid architecture to handle churn and freeloading will be the subject of future research. The detailed network simulation will also allow an evaluation the effect of network location on the performance of peer-assisted multicast batching.

References

1. BBC iPlayer, http://www.bbc.co.uk/iplayer/ (Last accessed July 13, 2009)
2. Hulu: http://www.hulu.com/ (Last accessed July 13, 2009)
3. Wakefield, J.: BBC and ISPs clash over iPlayer (April 2008), http://news.bbc.co.uk/1/hi/technology/7336940.stm (Last accessed July 13, 2009)
4. Dan, A., Sitaram, D., Shahabuddin, P.: Scheduling policies for an on-demand video server with batching. In: Proceedings of the 2nd ACM International Multimedia Conference, San Francisco, California, USA, October 1994, pp. 15–23 (1994)
5. Sen, S., Rexford, J., Towsley, D.: Proxy prefix caching for multimedia streams. In: Proceedings of the 18th Annual Joint Conference of the IEEE Computer and Communications Societies (INFOCOM 1999), New York, USA, March 1999, pp. 1310–1319 (1999)
6. Iyer, S., Rowstron, A., Druschel, P.: SQUIRREL: A decentralized, peer-to-peer web cache. In: Proceedings of the 12th ACM Symposium on Principles of Distributed Computing (PODC 2002), Monterey, California, USA (July 2002)
7. BBC Multicast, http://www.bbc.co.uk/multicast/ (Last accessed July 13, 2009)
8. Hua, K.A., Cai, Y., Sheu, S.: Patching: A multicast technique for true video-on-demand services. In: Proceedings of the 6th ACM International Multimedia Conference, Bristol, UK, September 1998, pp. 191–200 (1998)
9. Hefeeda, M., Habib, A., Botev, B., Xu, D., Bhargava, B.: PROMISE: peer-to-peer media streaming using collectcast. In: MULTIMEDIA 2003: Proceedings of the 11th ACM International Conference on Multimedia, pp. 45–54. ACM, New York (2003)

10. Castro, M., Druschel, P., Kermarrec, A., Nandi, A., Rowstron, A., Singh, A.: Split-stream: High-bandwidth multicast in cooperative environments. In: Proceedings of the 19th ACM Symposium on Operating Systems Principles (SOSP 2003), October 2003, pp. 298–313 (2003)
11. Qin Zhang, Y.: Peer-to-peer based multimedia distribution service. IEEE Transactions on Multimedia 6(2), 343–355 (2004)
12. Rowstron, A., Druschel, P.: Pastry: Scalable, decentralised object location and routing for large-scale peer-to-peer systems. In: Guerraoui, R. (ed.) Middleware 2001. LNCS, vol. 2218, pp. 329–350. Springer, Heidelberg (2001)
13. Joost: http://www.joost.com/ (Last accessed July 13, 2009)
14. PPLive: http://www.pplive.com/ (Last accessed July 13, 2009)
15. PPStream: http://www.ppstream.com/ (Last accessed July 13, 2009)
16. Huang, Y., Fu, T.Z., Chiu, D.M., Lui, J.C., Huang, C.: Challenges, design and analysis of a large-scale P2P-VoD system. SIGCOMM Comput. Commun. Rev. 38(4), 375–388 (2008)
17. Lee, C.H., Gui, Y.Q., Jung, I.B., Choi, C.Y., Choi, H.K.: A peer to peer prefix patching scheme for vod servers. In: Proceedings of the 3rd International Conference on Information Technology: New Generations, Las Vegas, Nevada, USA (April 2006)
18. Ho, K., Poon, W., Lo, K.: Enhanced peer-to-peer batching policy for video-on-demand system. In: International Symposium on Communications and Information Technologies (ISCIT 2006), September 2006, pp. 148–151 (2006)
19. Schulzrinne, H., Rao, A., Lanphier, R.: Real time streaming protocol (RTSP). IETF RFC 2326 (April 1998)
20. O'Neill, J., Dukes, J.: Re-evaluating multicast streaming using large-scale network simulation. In: Proceedings of the First International Conference on Intensive Applications and Services (April 2009)
21. Varga, A.: The OMNeT++ discrete event simulation system. In: Proceedings of the European Simulation Multiconference (ESM 2001), Prague, Czech Republic (June 2001)
22. Vida, R., Costa, L.: Multicast listener discovery version 2 (MLDv2) for IPv6. IETF RFC 3810 (June 2004)
23. Bhattacharyya, S.: An overview of source-specific multicast (SSM). IETF RFC 3569 (July 2003)

Quality Adaptive Peer-to-Peer Streaming Using Scalable Video Coding

Osama Abboud*, Konstantin Pussep, Aleksandra Kovacevic, and Ralf Steinmetz

Multimedia Communications Lab,
Technische Universität Darmstadt,
Merckstr. 25, 64283 Darmstadt, Germany
{abboud,pussep,sandra,steinmetz}@kom.tu-darmstadt.de
http://www.kom.tu-darmstadt.de/

Abstract. P2P (Peer-to-Peer) video streaming has attracted much attention recently. However, streaming over P2P is still best effort and suffers from lack of adaptation. Therefore, video streaming over P2P either works or not. In this paper, we propose a P2P streaming system with an inherent support for adaptation. By leveraging scalable video coding, our system is able to adapt to different requirements and constraints that heterogeneous peers have in today's Internet. We make a subtle distinction between initial and progressive quality adaptation, which allows for precise adaptation to various parameters of the system and the P2P network. Our decision-taking algorithms for quality adaptation help not only in perfectly matching QoS to resources but also in bringing the P2P network to self organization.

Keywords: P2P, video streaming, SVC, adaptation, QoS.

1 Introduction

Video streaming has recently become the most traffic intensive application in the Internet. Studies [1] show that streaming a video is becoming preferred over video file sharing. One reason behind this, is that a video is usually viewed only once, therefore streaming helps in reducing storage space requirements. In addition, streaming allows for the convenient *watch while you download* experience.

Current technologies for streaming are based on either the client/server or the Peer-to-Peer (P2P) architectures. As an example of client/server streaming, Youtube [2] is a popular medium for viewing user generated content. However, although YouTube provides good performance with high availability rate, it only supports low quality videos. Moreover, YouTube inflicts enormous costs [3]. P2P, on the contrary, allows for a cost efficient solution for video delivery to potentially large audiences. It also provides desirable traits such as self organization

---

* This work was funded by the Federal Ministry of Education and Research of the Federal Republic of Germany (support code 01 BK 0806, G-Lab).

T. Pfeifer and P. Bellavista (Eds.): MMNS 2009, LNCS 5842, pp. 41–54, 2009.

and resource scalability [4]. However, P2P-based streaming is faced with several challenges, such as churn and the lack of support for peers with weak resources. Moreover, high definition video streaming is still an open challenge. Weaknesses of many P2P streaming systems come from static selection of streaming parameters that are based on average peer resources. This selection might work if all systems in the network would have equal resources, which is not true due to the heterogeneity of the Internet. Internet devices are heterogeneous not only in their resources, but also in the type of connections they have. Therefore, bandwidth, delay and reliability vary drastically, rendering current P2P video streaming techniques best effort, i.e. they either work or not.

A possible solution to the problem of supporting streams with different qualities is achieved by creating a different video file for each quality level and therefore different overlays or swarms. However, this solution is not only inefficient due to data duplication across overlays, but also limited with respect to the level of possible collaboration between strong and weak peers across different overlays. To overcome these challenges, we investigate advanced adaptation mechanisms that are efficient and have potential for an overlay-wide collaboration. In addition, we aim at supporting adaptation for heterogeneous devices of the Internet ranging from handheld mobile devices to high-end computer machines.

Our main contribution is a P2P video streaming system based on Scalable Video Coding (SVC) with an inherent support for adaptation. We make use of a mesh-based streaming architecture that is applicable to both live streaming and video-on-demand. The key feature of our design is that it allows for adaptation to resources with three degrees of freedom. Receivers can have different

- Screen sizes and resolutions,
- Connections with variable downlink bandwidth and delay, and
- Processing capabilities.

This paper is structured as follows, Section 2 states the problem statement of this paper. Background of SVC are explained in Section 3. Our proposed architecture for P2P streaming is presented in Section 4. In Section 5, we present some simulation results. Section 6 provides related work. Finally, we conclude this paper in Section 7.

2   Problem Statement

Every device connecting to the Internet has specific resource characteristics, which includes different processing power, screen resolution, and bandwidth. However, video streaming is a demanding application and works only when minimum resource requirements are met. Many devices simply do not meet these requirements. This problem can be overcome if the quality is reduced, hence streaming capacity requirements are lowered, which leads to support for more devices, but at the expense of streaming lower quality. Increasing the quality, on

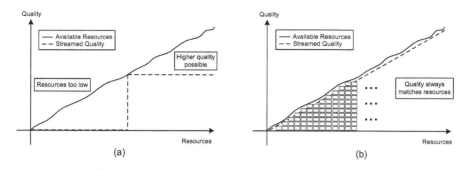

Fig. 1. Comparison of video streaming: (a) without quality adaptation, (b) with quality adaptation

the other hand, increases capacity requirement, but then a wide set of devices are unable to participate. This aspect is depicted in Figure 1.

In this paper we consider the problem of how to stream a video to a device adaptively by identifying the highest quality level supported by its available resources. Here we consider two types of resources:

- Peer resources such as screen resolution, processing power[1], and bandwidth.
- P2P overlay resources such as active neighbors, throughput, and network condition.

We propose an architecture that supports low scale mobile devices and high definition streaming at once. Our quality adaptation mechanisms help in introducing Quality of Service (QoS) into P2P video streaming by taking device resources and network state into account. Hence, we define a set of requirements and constraints with which a device can adapt to different scenarios and therefore achieve best performance.

3   Scalable Video Coding

SVC, which is based on the H.264/MPEG-4 AVC standard [5], allows for scalability by encoding a video stream into multiple layers or sub-streams each with different quality information. The lowest layer, called *base layer*, is always needed for decoding the video. With more enhancement layers received, better video quality is available. SVC is based on three modalities or flavors of scalability: spatial scalability, temporal scalability, and quality scalability. Quality scalability is also called Signal-to-Noise Ratio (SNR) scalability, both terms will be used interchangeably throughout this paper. Now we give a brief overview over SVC, more information can be found in [5] [6].

---

[1] In mobile devices, processing power directly translates to battery life, hence using processing-power-aware quality adaptation allows for a tradeoff between energy requirements and quality.

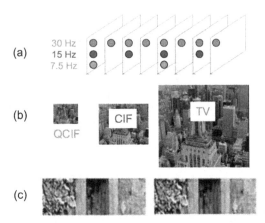

Fig. 2. Scalability variations: (a) temporal scalability, (b) spatial scalability, (c) SNR scalability [6]

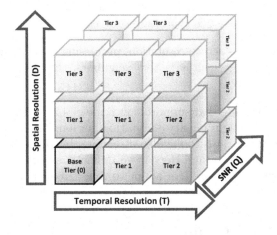

Fig. 3. SVC basic chunk structure: one chunk contains many blocks in the different dimensions of scalability

The different dimensions of scalability offered by SVC are as follows:

– Temporal scalability is based on providing different frame rates for a video stream as shown in Figure 2a. This is achieved through structuring picture and motion estimation dependencies such that complete pictures can be dropped from the bitstream while still providing the possibility of decoding the video stream.
– Spatial scalability is based on providing different resolutions for a video stream as shown in Figure 2b. This is achieved through the usage of lower resolution pictures to predict data of higher resolutions pictures.

– SNR scalability is based on providing different quality levels for a video
  stream as shown in Figure 2c. This is achieved through hierarchical construction of quantization coefficients for each picture.

To allow for streaming, an SVC stream is divided into chunks. Each chunk
contains layers in the three dimensional quality space. The smallest quality unit
is called a *block* as shown in Figure 3. A block will be used as basic unit for
fetching and distributing video data across the network.

4   Quality Adaptive Streaming

Now we present the core concepts behind our quality adaptive streaming architecture. Quality adaptation based on the SVC design is basically performed
during layer selection, which is responsible for making a decision on best matching spatial, temporal and SNR layers. Based on this decision, block selection
requestes the blocks needed to stream the selected layers. Our proposed architecture for quality adaptive video streaming is presented in Figure 4.

Quality adaptation mechanisms for layer selection fall into two broad categories: *Initial Quality Adaptation* (IQA) and *Progressive Quality Adaptation*
(PQA). When a peer wants to start viewing a video, it first invokes the IQA
module, which chooses the quality level best suited to the static resources of
the peer. After peer discovery, which locates all peers streaming same or lower
quality, peers are selected and put in the active senders set. The peer selection
module interacts with the underlay awareness module in such a way to optimize
the overlay based on various metrics. After successful connection establishment
with provider peers, streaming starts filling the video buffer. During streaming a
control loop has to assure proper adaptation to changing conditions. Therefore,
the PQA module is responsible for reacting to and overcoming any changes in
network condition and available throughput. When necessary, block selection is
updated in order to support an increased or decreased quality level.

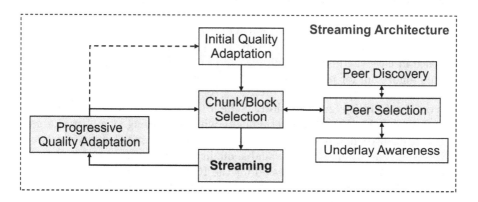

Fig. 4. The quality adaptive P2P streaming architecture

4.1   Quality Adaptation: Layer Selection

We now discuss in more detail the structure of the IQA and the PQA modules that are responsible for layer selection.

Initial Quality Adaptation. The architecture of the IQA module is presented in Figure 5. When the IQA module is invoked, it performs evaluation of current resources and requirements in order to match them with achievable quality. This module mainly handles static parameter, such as screen resolution, bandwidth, and processing power.

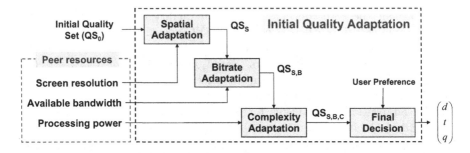

Fig. 5. Initial quality adaptation structure

First an initial quality set QS_0 is populated which contains all possible combinations for spatial, temporal, and SNR scalability. Therefore

$$QS_0 \triangleq \{(d, t, q) : \forall d = 0 \ldots D, t = 0 \ldots T, q = 0 \ldots Q)\}$$

where D, T, and Q are the total number of layers in the spatial, temporal, and SNR dimensions. Each row in this quality set would then represent one quality combination that can be used by the peer.

The IQA works by filtering this initial quality set based on the previously stated peer resources. Therefore, the spatial, birate, and complexity adaptation modules filter out all incompatible rows in QS_0 based on screen resolution, bandwidth, and processing power respectively. Final decision is performed using user preference in case the filtered quality set $QS_{S,B,C}$ has more than one row. Our proposed algorithm for initial quality adaptation is shown in Algorithm 1.

Progressive Quality Adaptation. The PQA architecture is presented in Figure 6. The PQA is executed periodically while streaming as a part of a control loop to ensure smooth adaptation. This module adapts to changes in network conditions in order to maximize available quality at the receiver. Other than using resources information as discussed for the IQA, the PQA relies on real-time overlay status reflected from current throughput and block availability. This allows the peer to quickly react to changes in the P2P network, such as peer churn or a sudden drop in throughput.

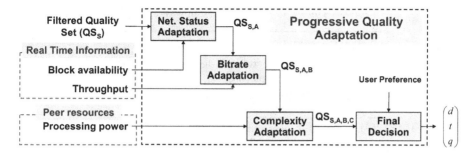

Fig. 6. Progressive quality adaptation structure

Only temporal and SNR adaptation are handled by the PQA because additionally changing the resolution frequently introduces unwanted artifacts. Therefore, the PQA starts from the pre-filtered set QS_S. The network status, birate, and complexity adaptation modules filter out all incompatible rows in QS_S based on block availability, throughput, and processing power respectively. Here, the block availability indicator provides information about layers that are available in the P2P network. User preference here is also used to make the decision in case $QS_{S,A,B,C}$ has more than one row.

Complexity Adaptation. The role of the complexity adaptation module is to take processing requirements for decoding into consideration and to match it with available processing resources. This prevents the video decoder from overloading weak mobile devices. For this end, we need to calculate processing requirements for each layer combination in QS_0. This module uses a complexity

---

Algorithm 1. Initial quality adaptation algorithm

Input: Quality level set QS_0
Output: Quality level t, d, q fulfilling constraints
foreach *row QS_i in QS* **do**
   | **if** $QS_i.SpatialLevel \leq$ *Screen resolution* **then**
   | └ $QS_S.append(QS_i)$;

foreach *row $QS_{S,i}$ in QS_S* **do**
   | **if** $Complexity(QS_{S,i}) \leq$ *Processing power* **then**
   | └ $QS_{S,B}.append(QS_{S,i})$;

foreach *row $QS_{S,B,i}$ in QS_S* **do**
   | **if** $Bitrate(QS_{S,B,i}) \leq$ *Bandwidth* **then**
   | └ $QS_{S,B,C}.append(QS_{S,B,i})$;

if *$QS_{S,B,C}$ is not empty* **then**
   | Filter $QS_{S,B,C}$ based on user preference
   | **return** t, d, q of single row of $QS_{S,B,C}$;
else
   └ **return**"Error: resources too low for base stream"

Table 1. Symbols for analytical complexity model [7]

Notion	Description
C_I, C_P, C_B	Average macroblock decoding complexity of I-/P-/B-picture
C_S, C_Q	Average macroblock decoding complexity at spatial/quality enhancement layers
$T/D/Q$	Total layer number for temporal-/spatial-/quality-scalability
$t/d/q$	Layer index for temporal-/spatial-/quality-scalability
M	Number of macroblocks per picture
α	Portion of pictures that are I-pictures

estimator that works by mapping every set of quality levels (spacial, temporal, and SNR) into processor cycles required for decoding the video stream.

To estimate the required complexity for each row in QS_0, we use an analytical model following the approach of Zhan *et al* presented in [7]. Based on definitions in Table 1, decoding complexity of an SVC stream can be calculated.

In SVC, an I-frame is a picture which can be decoded independently. This is not the case for P- and B-frames, which are a prediction of other frames in the stream. The smallest predicion unit in a frame is called a *macroblock*. Assume that C_I, C_P and C_B estimate the average complexity for decoding a macroblock in I-, P-, and B-pictures respectively. Moreover, we suppose that α is the portion I-pictures in the video and that M macroblocks exist per picture. Then the complexity for decoding scalable streams having T, D, and Q temporal, spatial, and SNR layers respectively is given by:

$$C_{\text{Decoding}} = M_0 \left(\alpha C_I + (1 - \alpha)C_P + (2^T - 1)C_B \right) +$$
$$\frac{8^{D+1} - 1}{7} 2^T M_0 Q C_Q + 4\frac{8^D - 1}{7} 2^T M_0 \left(C_S + C_B \right). \quad (1)$$

This equation is applied to all rows in the initial quality set QS_0 to calculate the complexity of decoding all possible video streams.

4.2 Block Selection

As stated in Section 3, a video file is divided into chunks. Based on the SVC design, each video chunk is further divided into blocks as depicted in Figure 7. Block selection is an important part of our streaming architecture, since it is behind making a decision on which blocks to request. This module works by assigning a probability for each block and chunk based on its importance.

In this paper, we take a multi-coefficient modeling approach for block selection. Note that here only the blocks of layers selected by the IPQ and PQA are considered. Therefore the calculated priority is always finite. The priority of a block in the video file is given by

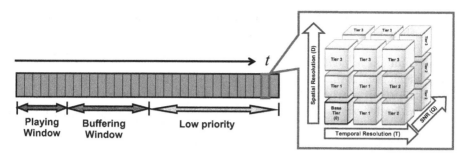

Fig. 7. File and SVC chunk structures

$$\text{Priority}(\text{Block}(t, D, T, Q)) = -A\,t - B(a\,D + b\,T + c\,Q). \qquad (2)$$

Chunk priority is separated into two parts, a temporal part and a per-chunk part. This allows for a separation between urgency due to playback and due to importance to the stream. Increasing the temporal and per-chunk parameters decreases the chunk priority factors A and B respectively. Within each chunk, the parameters a, b, c define the different weights for the different blocks within each chunk. Simply put, the priority decreases with time, and is highest for the base layer, and decreases for increasing enhancement layers in any dimension. The interesting thing about such a model, is that the different weights can be different depending on the peers resources and requirements. For example, if a peers is more interested in smoother playback the parameter A is increased. If higher quality is preferred when long buffering times are not an issue, B is increased, and so forth.

4.3   Peer Discovery: Neighbor Set Management

This section describes the required support for scalable video coding in the signaling component. Our architecture utilizes a tracker-based approach known from BitTorrent and utilized by many IPTV systems. Here, the tracker manages the information about all peers participating in the swarm. Each new peer registers itself at the tracker and receives a list of potential neighbors. Peers renew their registration at the tracker periodically (to show that they are still alive) and obtain updated lists of participants.

In order to support the proposed layer adaptation mechanisms, the tracker protocol is realized as follows: the tracker manages the list of active peers together with the layers they are currently streaming. The clients send an announce request to the tracker when they: join the overlay (only base layer supported by default), perform the initial adaptation (shortly after joining), and perform the progressive adaptation. In the latter case, a minimum re-announce interval assures that the tracker is not contacted too often. Since the layer adaptation is not done at a timescale smaller than a few seconds, the impact is uncritical.

Information about the currently streamed layers is crucial since clients streaming an additional layer cannot do so if they don't have neighbors possessing blocks from the same layer. Additionally, the clients advertise the currently supported layers to their neighbors. They do so by two means:

- The common *bitfield* message is extended to support the higher granularity, which means that the message contains availability information of SVC blocks instead of whole chunks (that are different depending on the number of downloaded layers). Hence, the message contains a list of bitfields, one per supported layer, tagged with the layer ID. This way each peer can calculate useful blocks owned by its neighbors.
- Peers announce the supported layers to their neighbors. This is done during the connection establishment phase (handshaking) and later after the successful PQA (support of new layers, or discontinued support of some layers).

This way a peer can detect whether the required layers are supported by the current neighbor set. If the number of peers supporting a given layer falls below the threshold of, e.g. 4 peers, the peer contacts the tracker for additional new neighbors. The request contains the list of layers currently not properly supported by the neighbors. The tracker responds with a list of peers supporting these layers. Since the mechanism is bi-directional, the peers are eventually clustered according to their capabilities, while the seeders support both weak and strong peers.

4.4 Peer Selection

After assigning priorities to the different blocks in the chunk selection module, the peer selection module chooses peers to request needed chunks. In this paper, we make use of an underlay-aware peer selection strategy. Peer selection with underlay awareness can be defined as using underlay information to optimize some aspects of communication and therefore enhancing the performance of the streaming system. Different underlay metrics affect the overlay in various ways. For video streaming, it has been identified that bandwidth is the underlay metric with the greatest impact [8]. Therefore, whenever a peer has a choice between more than one provider peer, the one that can offer more bandwidth is selected. This also helps in creating a healthy clustering of the network based on streamed quality as discussed in Section 4.3. Therefore, fast peers will tend to get their blocks from similarly fast peers. Here again we extend the BitTorrent protocol to support information about bandwidth offered by every peer. This is achieved by requiring all registering peers to provide information about offered bandwidth.

5   Evaluation

Here we present a preliminary evaluation of our proposed quality adaptation mechanisms. We simulate changing parameters and see how the PQA reacts to them. We consider having 3 layers for both spatial and temporal scalability and 2 layers for SNR scalability. This leads to the total of 18 possible layer

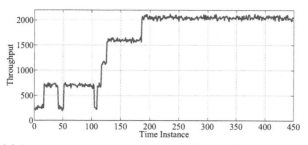

(a) Instantaneous throughput available at the peer (Kb/s)

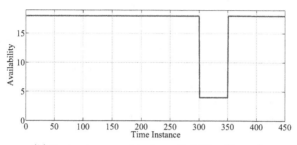

(b) Instantaneous block availability (Layer)

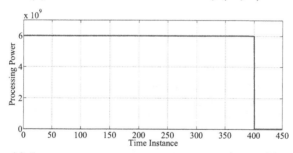

(c) Instantaneous peer processing power (cycles/s)

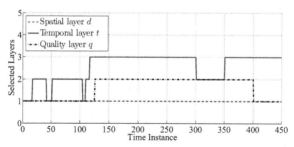

(d) Decision output of the PQA module

Fig. 8. Evaluation of the PQA module

combinations. We also suppose that the IQA has already decided on a basic spatial level, i.e. $d = 1$.

The PQA adapts to three parameters: block availability, throughput, and processing power. To evaluate how fast the PQA module reacts to the different parameters, we simulated a changing throughput using a Markov chain with transition matrix

$$P = \begin{bmatrix} 0.9 & 0.1 & 0 & 0 & 0 \\ 0.05 & 0.9 & 0.05 & 0 & 0 \\ 0 & 0.05 & 0.9 & 0.05 & 0 \\ 0 & 0 & 0.05 & 0.9 & 0.05 \\ 0 & 0 & 0 & 0.1 & 0.9 \end{bmatrix} \qquad (3)$$

This model is used for the first 250 time instances, then the throughput is fixed at 2 Mb/sec. The next step was to change the chunk availability to simulate peer churn. In this case, blocks of layer 5 to 18 are no longer available from time instant 300 to 350. Then we simulate a sudden drop in processing power at time instant 400. These test scenarios and the results represented by the instantaneous decision on d, t, and q are shown in Figure 8. The results show that our mechanisms are able to quickly react to different changes in the system to provide a persistent availability despite an unpredictable network and changes in peer resources.

6   Related Work

Many current video streaming systems are based on the client/server architecture with servers providing the video content. However, such systems either provide low quality content, or introduce costs high enough to prevent deployment when trying to provide high quality. To shift load from servers and to allow for reduced costs, streaming solutions based on P2P architectures have been considered, like BiToS [9] and Octoshape [10]. In such systems, users act as both producers and consumers of video content.

There exists two types of overlay topologies for video streaming, push-based multicast trees and pull-based mesh topology. In push-based solutions [11], peers are structured in a tree topology with content providers positioned at the top of the tree pushing video data down the tree towards the leaves. In pull-based systems [9], a peer actively requests parts of the video from peers that have already downloaded it thus forming a mesh topology. Mesh-based streaming solutions are characterized by lower overlay maintenance costs and higher flexibility in block selection.

There is a plethora of research on P2P systems with support for adaptation such as [12] [13] [14]. PALS [14] is a receiver driven P2P video streaming system with quality adaptation. However, PALS only considers single dimensional scalability (as the case for many layered streaming systems) and therefore cannot adapt to heterogeneous characteristics of peers. Baccichet et al. [13] use a prioritization mechanism and multicast trees to distribute SVC streams. Lee et al.

discuss in [15] issues related to deploying a P2P video streaming system based on SVC. These approaches differ from ours since we focus on using three dimensional scalability to adapt to different peer resources and network conditions using QoS-aware decision-taking algorithms.

7 Conclusion

In this paper, we considered quality adaptive video streaming to heterogeneous devices using a collaborative P2P architecture. By leveraging quality adaptation through SVC, our system can support heterogeneous peers while providing the highest supported quality to every device. Using SVC, which allows to combine video layers from various sources, flexible received quality is possible. Therefore, weak peers receive and process only lower layers, and strong peers are able to process and share more layers, and thus can consume better video quality.

It is crucial to estimate the achievable QoS from system resources to provide highest achievable quality without overloading the devices. We have considered adapting to both peer resources as well as network state in such a way to fully utilize system capabilities.

The distinction between initial and progressive quality adaptation is crucial in separating adaptation stages of a streaming session. The initial stage assures that static resources of a peer are considered and matched to prevent overloading. Progressive quality adaptation handles what is considered as a limiting factor for P2P video streaming systems, fluctuating throughput and churn. Moreover, using an underlay aware peer selection, our solution is able to better optimize the streaming performance. Our preliminary simulation results show that our mechanisms react quickly to various system changes while providing best quality that matches current resources and network state.

As future work, we plan to do more extensive evaluations of the proposed mechanisms. Moreover, we will investigate the dynamics of both chunk and peer selection. We also want to implement a prototype to validate our findings in realistic application scenarios.

Quality adaptation is the key for next generation multimedia distribution where more heterogenous devices are joining the Internet. Client/server systems' scalability issues and high costs require the switch to P2P. But without support for heterogeneity, P2P video streaming will not be widely deployed. Nonetheless, the possibility of supporting such a wide range of collaborating peers makes us believe that our vision is not so far off.

References

1. Dissecting the Gap Between Downloading and Streaming Video,
   http://www.ipsos-ideas.com/article.cfm?id=3804
2. YouTube - Broadcast Yourself, http://www.youtube.com
3. Huang, C., Li, J., Ross, K.W.: Can Internet Video-on-demand be Profitable? In: SIGCOMM 2007, pp. 133–144. ACM, New York (2007)

4. Jurca, D., Chakareski, J., Wagner, J.P., Frossard, P.: Enabling Adaptive Video Streaming in P2P Systems. IEEE Communications Magazine 45(6), 108–114 (2007)
5. Schwarz, H., Marpe, D., Wiegand, T.: Overview of the Scalable Video Coding Extension of the H.264/AVC Standard. IEEE Transactions on Circuits and Systems for Video Technology 17(9), 1103–1120 (2007)
6. The Scalable Video Coding Amendment of the H.264/AVC Standard,
   `http://ip.hhi.de/imagecom_G1/savce/`
7. Ma, Z., Wang, Y.: Complexity Modeling of Scalable Video Decoding. In: ICASSP 2008, USA, pp. 1125–1128. IEEE, Los Alamitos (2008)
8. Spoto, S., Gaeta, R., Grangetto, M., Sereno, M.: Analysis of PPLive through Active and Passive Measurements. In: HotP2P 2009 (2009)
9. Vlavianos, A., Iliofotou, M., Faloutsos, M.: BiToS: Enhancing BitTorrent for Supporting Streaming Applications. In: 9th IEEE Global Internet Symposium 2006 (2006)
10. Octoshap, `http://www.octoshape.com`
11. Liu, Y., Guo, Y., Liang, C.: A Survey on Peer-to-peer Video Streaming Systems. Peer-to-Peer Networking and Applications 1(1), 18–28 (2008)
12. Padmanabhan, V.N., Wang, H.J., Chou, P.A.: Supporting Heterogeneity and Congestion Control in Peer-to-Peer Multicast Streaming. In: Voelker, G.M., Shenker, S. (eds.) IPTPS 2004. LNCS, vol. 3279, pp. 54–63. Springer, Heidelberg (2005)
13. Baccichet, P., Schierl, T., Wiegand, T., Girod, B.: Low-delay Peer-to-peer Streaming Using Scalable Video Coding. In: Packet Video 2007, pp. 173–181 (2007)
14. Rejaie, R., Ortega, A.: PALS: Peer-to-Peer Adaptive Layered Streaming. In: ACM NOSSDAV 2003 (2003)
15. Lee, T.C., Liu, P.C., Shyu, W.L., Wu, C.Y.: Live Video Streaming Using P2P and SVC. In: Pavlou, G., Ahmed, T., Dagiuklas, T. (eds.) MMNS 2008. LNCS, vol. 5274, pp. 104–113. Springer, Heidelberg (2008)

Modeling of a QoS Matching and Optimization Function for Multimedia Services in the NGN

Lea Skorin-Kapov[1] and Maja Matijasevic[2]

[1] R&D Center, Ericsson Nikola Tesla, Krapinska 45, HR-10000 Zagreb, Croatia
[2] FER, University of Zagreb, Unska 3, HR-10000 Zagreb, Croatia
lea.skorin-kapov@ericsson.com, maja.matijasevic@fer.hr

Abstract. A key challenge for Next Generation Networks (NGN) is providing support for the negotiation and dynamic adaptation of Quality of Service (QoS) parameters. In this paper we propose a novel *QoS Matching and Optimization Function* (Q-MOF) to be included along the signaling path with the purpose of providing advanced service-level QoS matching and optimization logic for multimedia services being delivered to heterogeneous end users and access networks. The Q-MOF is introduced in the NGN architecture as a generic functionality, allowing for it to be reused by services requiring advanced QoS support. We illustrate Q-MOF applicability in a case study involving an audio/video streaming session between two users.

Keywords: QoS matching, QoS optimization, multimedia services, next generation network.

1   Introduction

With the Next Generation Network (NGN) aimed at offering end users personalized multimedia services across heterogeneous networks, a key issue is providing support for end-to-end (E2E) Quality of Service (QoS) negotiation and adaptation (QNA). During QNA, the requirements and capabilities imposed by various actors involved in service delivery (e.g., user, service provider, network provider, third party service/content provider) need to be coordinated [15]. At the service level, NGN standards specify requirements for entities at the rim of the network (e.g., terminals) to negotiate and select common codecs for each E2E session [1]. 3GPP has specified the IP Multimedia Subsystem (IMS) procedures for negotiating multimedia session characteristics between endpoints [3].

With the transition to media-rich services, we argue that providing personalized and optimal service quality implies more advanced negotiation mechanisms (beyond those specified) matching user preferences/capabilities against service requirements, network resource capabilities, and operator policy. Furthermore, in addition to codec negotiation, additional operating parameters (e.g., resolution, frame rate, etc.) may need to be coordinated.

Related work on QoS adaptation in IMS networks includes solutions for dynamically adapting multimedia content to fit network/system resource availability [12] and maximizing perceived QoS [5]. Research on multimedia session

T. Pfeifer and P. Bellavista (Eds.): MMNS 2009, LNCS 5842, pp. 55–68, 2009.

control and content adaptation is further being conducted in the DAIDALOS [18] and ENTHRONE [19] projects. While additional related work can be found on profile matching [9], decision-making for the optimization of service parameters [10][17], and the description of various service and transport configurations for service negotiation [7][13][8], limited solutions unite these aspects to support delivery of personalized multimedia services in the NGN. Our goal is to propose such a solution, with our focus being on service-level negotiation mechanisms.

We have previously proposed the high-level concept of a *QoS Matching and Optimization Function* (Q-MOF) to be included along the E2E signaling path in the service control layer of the NGN architecture [14]. The contribution of this paper is a detailed generic model of the Q-MOF supporting optimized service delivery and controlled service adaptation in light of changing resource availability, user preferences, or service requirements. Furthermore, what is missing in most current approaches is the specification and signalling of an optimal degradation path for multimedia services composed of multiple flows. Our solution is for the Q-MOF to calculate a *media degradation path* (MDP) that will be signaled to communication end points and to the network layer to aid in efficient service adaptation in light of changing network resource availability.

The paper is organized as follows. In Section 2 we describe the role of the Q-MOF in the standardized NGN architecture. In Section 3 we present a model of the Q-MOF, and specify the *Matching Process* and *Optimization Process*. Section 4 describes a case study illustrating Q-MOF applicability for an audio/video streaming session. A discussion and conclusions are given in Section 5.

2   Enhanced Multimedia QoS Control in the NGN

The ITU-T NGN release 1 architecture [1] (Figure 1) is based on the concept of independence between the transport stratum and service stratum. In the service stratum, service control functions are based on an IMS service environment and support the provisioning of real-time Session Initiation Protocol (SIP) based multimedia services. The application support functions and service support functions can impact sessions on behalf of services. During session negotiation, QoS requirements are extracted by service control functions (e.g., Proxy Call Session Control Function in IMS) and used to issue resource reservation and authorization requests to the resource admission control functional architecture (RACF).

In order to provide enhanced QoS control mechanisms, we propose for the Q-MOF to be introduced in the service stratum as a new application server (AS). The Q-MOF is designed to be included along the E2E signaling path, providing support for advanced QoS parameter matching and optimization logic within the QoS negotiation process. Actual service adaptation (e.g., transcoding) may be performed at communication endpoints or in the network.

While today's Internet model is based on a user-centric view of the network, the IMS model uses a more operator-centric approach. In an actual network implementation, we propose for the Q-MOF to be included in a Service Provider (SP) domain as a generic reusable functionality. In addition to providing a better

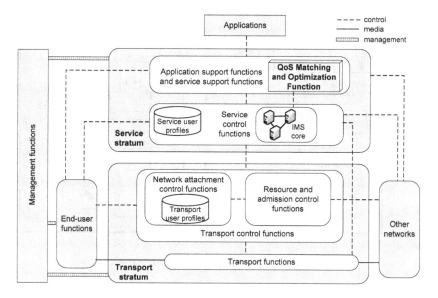

Fig. 1. Q-MOF in the NGN architecture

service to users, introducing enhanced QoS support in the network as a reusable service capability would benefit both the SP and third-party service/application providers. The SP would have additional means to control, differentiate, and appropriately charge the QoS a particular user receives for a given multimedia service. Third-party service/application providers would have to specify a service profile stating service requirements and options and would further be relieved from implementing complex QoS decision making functionality for each new introduced service, hence leading to simplified provisioning and possibly quicker time-to-market for new services requiring such mechanisms.

3   Modeling the Q-MOF

A multimedia service is composed of two or more *media components* (e.g., audio flows, video flows, graphics data, etc.). We assume that a multimedia service exists in one or more versions to meet heterogeneous user and network capabilities. We specify *service versions* as differing in the included media components (e.g., audio/video vs. only audio). Each media component may be configured by choosing from offered alternative *operating parameters* (e.g., different codecs, frame rates, resolutions, etc.). We refer to the overall *service configuration* as the set of chosen operating parameters for all included media components.

The Q-MOF functional architecture is shown in Figure 2. Upon a service request, input data is signaled by involved actors. Various sets of parameters/profiles that may be signaled include: end-user related parameters (e.g., capabilities, preferences, subscription data, context); service requirements, in terms of necessary

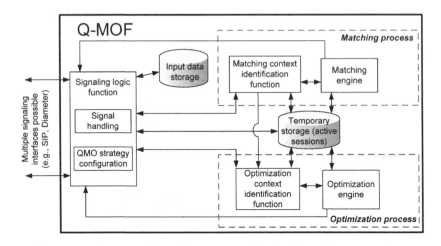

Fig. 2. Q-MOF functional architecture

resources (in the case of an adaptive service then adaptation capabilities need to be specified); network capabilities (e.g., specifcation of available QoS classes, available bandwidth); operator policies and pricing/charging data. An example of actors and input data is given in the case study. Input data is collected by the Q-MOF (either per-session or collected once and stored to be used for multiple sessions), and a *Matching Process* is invoked to determine a set of feasible service versions and operating parameters termed the *Feasible Service Profile* (FSP). The FSP is then offered to relevant entities in order to achieve an E2E agreement: an end user may accept, refuse, or modify the offered parameters, and network entities authorize resources. Negotiated and authorized parameters are passed to the *Optimization Process*, which calculates the optimal service configuration and resource allocation for all media flows. The optimal service configuration, and a number of alternative (suboptimal but feasible) configurations are ordered by descending utility and signaled to involved entities as an *Agreed Service Profile* (ASP). The ordered list of alternative configurations within the ASP is referred to as a *media degradation path* (MDP) to be used for efficient service adaptation.

In order to support the negotiation process, we assume a "one-stop responsibility" concept (adopted by the ITU-T in [2]) with a user's primary service provider as being responsible for coordinating the QoS negotiation process (via the Q-MOF), while further relying on the services of sub-providers in order to secure an E2E QoS. Therefore, we assume that necessary agreements exist along the multi-provider chain enabling the negotiation of session parameters.

We assume that the Q-MOF can implement multiple signaling interfaces (e.g., SIP, Diameter, etc.) to other services or entities (e.g., policy server, charging server, user/service profile repository). The Q-MOF may be applied for various business models, i.e., it can take into account parameters specified by different actors involved in the service negotiation process. In order for the proposed functionality to be applicable, it is assumed that the entities specifying various profiles and parameters agree on the semantics of those parameters that impact negotiation. In our previous work [16], we have specified a generic data specification model identifying the parameters specified by various actors impacting the QoS negotiation process, including user and service profiles.

Based on messages received during QoS (re)negotiation, the *Signaling logic function* decides when to invoke the *Matching Process* and the *Optimization Process* (Fig. 3). The matching and optimization algorithms are implemented independent of a particular service. With different services requiring different levels of QoS support (e.g., a mission critical telemedicine service vs. streaming music clips), the *QMO strategy configuration* function may decide on the complexity of the matching and optimization processes to be used. In general, the processes should be able to handle profiles/parameters of arbitrary complexity. For example, a particular user may have charging requirements specified in his/her profile that need to be considered while another user does not. Furthermore, providing advanced QoS support will not always be necessary (or desirable) due to increased processing complexity and signaling overhead.

Input data can be collected from entities for a given session, or can be collected once and stored by the Q-MOF to be used for multiple sessions. Data that needs to be stored is passed to either the *Input data storage* (stores data that is not session specific, such as service costs, general operator policy, etc.) or the *Temporary storage* (stores session specific data which is erased when a session is ended). During the course of service execution, the Q-MOF may receive various adaptation-triggering events indicating the need for renegotiation and adaptation. Based on user preferences or service requirements, the Q-MOF can also subscribe to various contextual events that may lead to adaptation, such as subscribing to user location information.

3.1   QoS Matching Process

The aim of the Matching Process is to parse collected input data and match service requirements against the capabilities/requirements of service users, and any additional imposed constraints (e.g., imposed by network policy) in order to determine feasible service parameters. The process is invoked through the *Matching Context Identification Function* (MCIF) which is responsible for determining a set of matching parameters $p_1, \ldots, p_k$ for a given service to be used as a basis for the actual matching process conducted by the *Matching Engine* (ME). Matching parameters represent those service requirements that need to be checked to make sure they can be met. An example of a matching parameter set would be {*min_bandwidth_downlink, min_bandwidth_uplink, media_required, codecs*}. The selection of matching parameters is based on requirements specified in the Service Profile and will depend on the type of service being established (i.e., different services may specify requirements in terms of different parameters). Parsing of the Service Profile to identify matching parameters may be done once for each new service rather than for each incoming user request.

Based on the identified parameter set $p_1, \ldots, p_k$, the ME conducts the actual matching process (Figure 4). The ME executes matching rules for each parameter

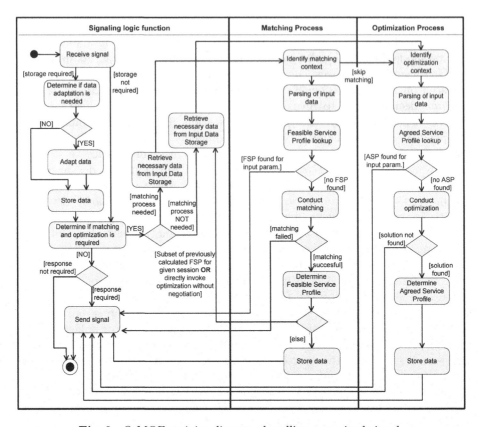

Fig. 3. Q-MOF activity diagram: handling a received signal

included in the matching parameter set. The rules are of the form: $if < p_i == p >$ $then <action>$. For example, $if < p_i == min\_bandwidth\_uplink>$ $then <check\ if$ $user\ capabilities\ and\ network\ constraints\ are\ greater\ than\ min\_bandwidth\_uplink>$.

After completing the matching, the ME will create an FSP that specifies all feasible service versions and operating parameters determined. After entities have agreed to the FSP, the FSP is passed on to the Q-MOF Optimization Process. If matching results indicate that requirements cannot be met, the Q-MOF will signal that no FSP can be found.

We note that in the case of an adaptation-triggering event received during service execution, the ME will execute matching rules only for updated parameters rather than repeating the entire process. The ME will compare new and old matching results to see if new results are a subset of old results. If they are a subset, there would be no need to repeat negotiation, and the Optimization Process may be directly invoked. If new matching results are not a subset of old results, a new FSP is determined, stored, and signaled to involved entities.

In networks with a large number of session requests, it may be too time-consuming to conduct the matching process for each new request. Assuming that input parameters to the matching process may often times be the same as

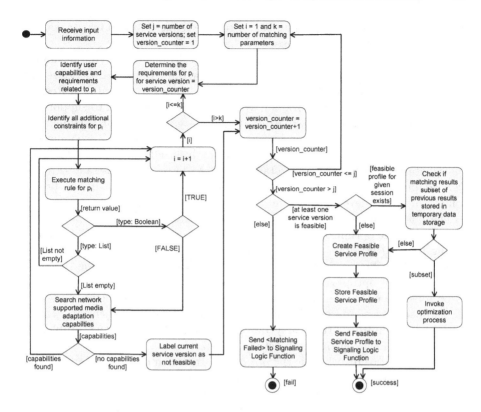

Fig. 4. Activity diagram for *Matching Engine*

previously signaled input parameters corresponding to an earlier session request (i.e., multiple users will often times have the same or similiar user profiles in terms of terminal/access network capabilities, preferences; operator policy may be the same across multiple users), we propose for the Q-MOF to store calculated FSPs for representative sets of input parameters which may be used for subsequent requests. With each new request for a given service, input data is parsed based on the matching parameter set for that service to determine if a request with the same relevant parameter values (or ranges of values) has already been processed. A hashing process may be used to encode parsed input parameters and enable efficient FSP profile lookup. If a previously calculated FSP already exists for the given input parameters, there is no need to invoke the ME and the previously calculated FSP is signaled.

3.2 QoS Optimization Process

The Optimization Process receives as input the negotiated FSP and produces the ASP. As in the case of matching, the Optimization Process can check whether a previously calculated ASP already exists for an equivalent negotiated FSP.

Hence, in the case of a large number of service requests, previously calculated optimization results may be reused.

Calculation of the ASP is based on the service profile specifying a mapping between a point in an Operating Space O whose dimensions constitute service-level parameters that are being negotiated (e.g., codec, frame rate); a Resource Space R indicating the (network and system) resources required to support that operating point; and a Utility Space U, which may consist of multiple dimensions representing both qualitative and quantitative quality measures. Such a mapping has been discussed previously in [17] and has been adopted in the MPEG-21 Digital Item Adaptation (DIA) standard [4] to be used for meta-data driven QoS adaptation. We adopt these mechanisms and apply them in the broader context of service-level (re)negotiation.

The *Optimization Context Identification Function* (OCIF) is responsible for determining the optimization objective, collecting necessary input data, and invoking the *Optimization Engine* (OE). The OE will then run the actual optimization algorithm(s), and determine the ASP based on calculation results. In determining the optimization objective, the OCIF can conclude that the problem to be solved is either a single-objective or multi-objective problem. As feasible media operating points may be mapped to multiple utility dimensions, the objective of maximizing utility may be considered a multi-objective problem. In this paper we focus on single-objective optimization.

The problem to be solved is the optimal distribution of constrained resources among multiple media flows. We assume a finite number of operating points per media flow. The goal is to choose exactly one operating point per media flow. For simplification purposes, we assume a one dimensional utility space corresponding to user perceived value. We consider total utility to be the weighted sum of the individual media flow utilities. Different user preferences and context information may be used for assigning weight factors (WF) and formulating the optimization problem. For preferences that are service or media flow specific, the Service Profile may provide the rules for assigning WFs (e.g., if $< pref == $ *"audio more important than video"* $ > then < audio_WF = 1$ and $video\_WF = 0.5 >$).

The general problem may be formulated as follows. We assume n different media flows, of which flows $1, \ldots, h$ are in the downlink direction and flows $h + 1, \ldots, n$ are in the uplink direction. The ith flow has p_i operating points. Required resources $\mathbf{r}$ for operating point j and media flow i are denoted as $\mathbf{r}_{ij} = (r_{ij1}, \ldots, r_{ijq}, \ldots, r_{ijk})$.

Assuming q different QoS classes, we specify $r_{ij1}, \ldots, r_{ijq}$ as corresponding to bandwidth assigned within different QoS classes (differing in delay, loss, jitter, and bandwidth guarantees). For a single operating point, we assume only one of the values $r_{ij1}, \ldots, r_{ijq}$ to be greater than zero, while all others are equal to zero. This is because only one QoS class is chosen per operating point for a media flow. We define variables $B_{downlink}$ and B_{uplink} to denote maximum available downlink and uplink bandwidth respectively, determined by user terminal capabilities and access network. They represent the resource constraints for $r_{ij1}, \ldots, r_{ijq}$. Additional resource constraints (other than bandwidth) related to the consumption of a particular resource across all media flows are expressed as $\mathbf{R} = (R_{q+1}, \ldots, R_k)$ (e.g., cost for all flows must be less than a specified amount). Resource constraints may also be added regarding resource consumption per flow and expressed as $\mathbf{R}_i = (R_{i1}, \ldots, R_{ik})$ (e.g., cost for a media flow must be less then a specified amount). The utility value for operating point j and media flow i is denoted as $u_i(\mathbf{r}_{ij})$. Weight factors w_i are assigned to utility values to indicate the relative importance of media flows. We include 0-1 variables x_{ij} to make sure that exactly one operating point is chosen per media flow.

Below we show formulation for the case of multi-flow resource constrained utility maximization. The problem is formulated as a multi-choice multi-dimension 0-1 knapsack problem (MMKP). Given a set of media flows, each with a number of specified operating points, the best operating point per flow is selected.

$$max \sum_{i=1}^{n} \sum_{j=1}^{p_i} w_i x_{ij} u_i(\mathbf{r}_{ij}) \tag{1}$$

such that

$$\sum_{i=1}^{k} \sum_{j=1}^{p_i} \sum_{y=1}^{q} x_{ij} r_{ijy} \leq B_{downlink} \tag{2}$$

$$\sum_{i=k+1}^{n} \sum_{j=1}^{p_i} \sum_{y=1}^{q} x_{ij} r_{ijy} \leq B_{uplink} \tag{3}$$

$$\sum_{i=1}^{n} \sum_{j=1}^{p_i} x_{ij} r_{ijy} \leq R_y, \ y = q+1, \ldots, k \tag{4}$$

$$\sum_{j=1}^{p_i} x_{ij} r_{ijy} \leq R_{iy}, \ y = 1, \ldots, k; \ i = 1, \ldots, n \tag{5}$$

$$\sum_{j=1}^{p_i} x_{ij} = 1, \ i = 1, \ldots, n \tag{6}$$

$$x_{ij} \in \{0, 1\}, \ i = 1, \ldots, n; \ j = 1, \ldots, p_i \tag{7}$$

The Q-MOF may implement different optimal solution algorithms and heuristics (for finding near optimal solutions for cases with a large number of variables) for solving the formulated problem (e.g., such as those proposed in [10]).

While we have focused on generic problem formulation, we note that a different approach to formulating the presented optimization problem (out of scope for this paper) may be to use tools specified as part of the MPEG DIA standard, namely Usage Environment Description tools, Universal Constraints Description tool, and AdaptationQoS tools. A decision-taking framework based on these tools and supporting media adaptation is described in [11].

4   Case Study

We illustrate Q-MOF functionality using a prototype **Audio/Video Call** (AVC) service allowing two end users to engage in an audio/video call. The service is implemented in a laboratory IMS testbed (details on testbed can be found in [14]). The Q-MOF has been added as a SIP AS along the E2E SIP signaling path and is invoked by the IMS Serving Call Session Control Function (S-CSCF). User and service profiles are specified using XML and included in SIP signaling. Furthermore, we have defined a policy file composed of IMS operator policy and access network policy to be used as input for QoS negotiation.

The service is offered in two versions: (1) *AVC 1* with conversational audio and video; and (2) *AVC 2* with only conversational audio. We assume the uplink direction as being from the call initiating user (User A) to the terminating user (User B). The AVC service matching parameter set $(p_1, \ldots, p_{12})$ is shown in Table 1. The AVC service specifies both network and processing (resolution) resource requirements.

We further illustrate a case of invoking the Optimization Process when the chosen service version is *AVC 1*. Operating parameters, resource vectors and corresponding utilities are specified in the service profile and summarized in Table 2 (parameters and resource vectors for uplink flows are identical and ordered the same as for downlink flows). For illustration purposes, we assume a specification

Table 1. Matching parameter set for AVC service

Matching parameters for AVC service	Service requirements (version *AVC 1*)	User A capabilities	User B capabilities	Operator constraints
p_1 = media_components	audio, video	audio, video, data, image, model	audio, video, data, image, model	User A and B: audio, video, data, image, text
p_2 = codecs	audio : mpeg, gsm; video : mpeg, h263	audio: mpeg, pcm, gsm; video: mpeg, mjpeg, h263	audio: mpeg, pcm, gsm; video: mpeg, mjpeg, h263	notAllowed : audio, G729, audio G723
p_3 = minBandwidth_DL	46	1200	1300	1400
p_4 = maxDelay_DL	150	150	150	N/A
p_5 = maxJitter_DL	10	N/A	N/A	N/A
p_6 = maxLoss_DL	1	N/A	N/A	N/A
p_7 = minBandwidth_UL	46	800	1000	1400
p_8 = maxDelay_UL	150	150	150	N/A
p_9 = maxJitter_UL	10	N/A	N/A	N/A
p_{10} = maxLoss_UL	1	N/A	N/A	N/A
p_{11} = resolution_local	176x144	1024x768	N/A	N/A
p_{12} = resolution_remote	176x144	N/A	1024x768	N/A

Table 2. Oper. parameters, resource vectors and utilities for AVC DL flows

Media flow	Operating parameters	Resource vectors	Bandw. [kbps] r_{ij1}	Cost [monetary_unit/s] r_{ij2}	Utility $u_i(\mathbf{r}_{ij})$
audio DL	codec: GSM, sample rate: 8000, bits per/samp: 8	r_{11}	21	210	0.5
	codec: MPEG, sample rate: 22050, bits per/samp: 16	r_{12}	34	340	0.80
	codec: MPEG, sample rate: 44100, bits per/samp: 16	r_{13}	64	640	1.00
video DL	codec: H263, res: 176x144, framerate: 5	r_{21}	25	900	0.20
	codec: H263, res: 176x144, framerate: 15	r_{22}	90	900	0.4
	codec: MJPEG, res: 176x144, framerate: 5	r_{23}	370	3700	0.5
	codec: MJPEG, res: 176x144, framerate: 10	r_{24}	400	4000	0.6
	codec: MJPEG, res: 176x144, framerate: 15	r_{25}	781	7810	0.7
	codec: MJPEG, res: 352x288, framerate: 5	r_{26}	1015	10150	0.8
	codec: MJPEG, res: 352x288, framerate: 15	r_{27}	1400	14000	0.9
	codec: MJPEG, res: 352x288, framerate: 30	r_{28}	2000	20000	1

of utility in the range of [0,1]. A different approach may be to specify utility in terms of a Mean Opinion Score (MOS) on a scale from 1 to 5, often used to provide a numerical indication of subjective user perceived quality.

The number of feasible operating points is as follows: audio downlink (DL) ($p_1 = 3$), video DL ($p_2 = 8$), audio uplink (UL) ($p_3 = 3$), and video UL ($p_4 = 8$). We assume that cost is based on amount of traffic and assigned QoS class. We therefore calculate cost as *bandwidth_class_q* [bit/s] · *price_class_q* [monetary_unit/b]. For the conversational audio/video QoS, we assume a hypothetical price of 10 [monetary_unit/bit].

For the optimization problem we assume user preferences which indicate that audio is preferred over video and set an audio WF to 1 and video WF to 0.7. The following constraints are determined based on user profiles: maximum DL bandwidth 1200 kbps, maximum UL bandwidth 800 kbps, and maximum cost 20000 [monetary_unit/s] (corresponds to User A's budget, assuming that User A will cover all costs). The result of the optimization is an ASP including an MDP. The MDP is composed of one optimal and four suboptimal service configurations, as shown in Table 3. We combine certain configurations and convert calculated bandwidth values to bandwidth ranges for media flows with continuous utility along those ranges (in this case video UL and video DL).

Table 3. Resource configurations for the AVC MDP

Resource configuration	Audio DL	Video DL	Audio UL	Video UL	Objective value
1 (optimal)	r_{13}	r_{26}	r_{33}	$[r_{43}, r_{44}]$	$[2.909, 2.980]$
2	r_{13}	$[r_{24}, r_{25}]$	r_{33}	r_{44}	$[2.840, 2.909]$
3	r_{13}	r_{26}	r_{33}	r_{42}	2.840
4	r_{13}	r_{25}	r_{33}	r_{43}	2.839
5	r_{13}	r_{23}	r_{33}	r_{44}	2.77

Table 4. Processing times for Matching Process

Matching results	Service establishment [s]	Update) [s]
Feasible service versions	0.531	0.683
No feasible service versions	0.245	0.670

For experimentation purposes, the Q-MOF was run on a Pentium IV PC with 2.4 GHz and 512 MB RAM. Signaled profiles are parsed using a Simple API for XML (SAX) parser. Measurements showing the Q-MOF matching processing time (including profile parsing) are given in Table 4 and correspond to: (a) initial service establishment, and (b) an update received during an active service indicating a change in the value of one matching parameter, e.g., decrease in user bandwidth. Both cases correspond to the situation when the ME is invoked. Results show that in the case when the ME finds no feasible service versions, processing time is significantly reduced as there is no FSP being created. Processing time is greater for the update scenario than for initial service establishment due to the comparison with previously found matching results for the given session.

Results showing the Q-MOF optimization processing times including MDP calculation are given in Table 5. We use the GLPK (GNU Linear Programming Kit) [20] simplex-based solver and MIP problem solver to search for an optimal solution. Measurements are conducted for different numbers of active media components and operating points. We added additional hypothetical active media streams to the FSP in order to see the effects on processing time. The number

Table 5. Processing times for Optimization Process

No. of active media components (n)	No. of oper. points $\sum_{i=1}^{n} p_i$	No. of feasible combinations $\prod_{i=1}^{n} p_i$	No. of found cfgs.	No. of chosen MDP cfgs.	Proc. time (single execution) [s]	Total proc. time [s]
2	6	9	7	7	0.016	0.264
4	22	576	9	7	0.016	0.383
4	44	9216	7	7	0.016	0.430
6	76	23592	16	7	0.031	1.933

of found service configurations corresponds to the number of times that the optimization algorithm was run. Found solutions where neither the total UL nor DL bandwidth decreased as compared to a previously found solution were not included in the MDP. Those solutions that were included in specifying the MDP are referred to as chosen MDP configurations. The total processing time for the optimization process includes parsing of the FSP and is significantly greater than processing time for the optimization algorithm (refers to single algorithm execution in searching for the optimal MDP configuration assuming profiles have been preciously parsed). It is clear that execution times greatly increase with the number of active media components. For cases in which a greater number of parallel streams are present, heuristics for providing fast and near optimal solutions may be used [10]. Another option is for the Q-MOF to conduct optimization procedures offline and store solutions offering certain combinations of feasible service parameters for groups of end users with common characteristics.

5   Discussion and Conclusions

The functionality proposed in this paper has focused on service-level QNA mechanisms for the NGN architecture. The novel contribution is the model of a Q-MOF based on matching restrictive user, service, and network requirements, policies and constraints, with the goal of maximizing utility. The proposed approach is applicable for the NGN architecture as discussed in Section 2. Furthermore, the Q-MOF may serve to enhance network-initiated QoS control mechanisms, such as those adopted in the 3GPP Release 8 Evolved Packet System [6]. Considering an IMS-based network architecture, the Q-MOF may be introduced at the application signaling level to determine optimal service resource and authorization requests which are then passed to the network.

Regarding scalability issues, it is clear that for a large number of users, running the matching and optimization procedures separately for each service session may be too time consuming and costly. We have therefore proposed for the Q-MOF to store service configuration solutions calculated in advance for particular combinations of constraints (as opposed to per user/per service request basis). While the presented case study serves to illustrate Q-MOF functionality, future work will focus on testing scalability of the proposed solution in cases involving a large number of parallel user sessions. Future research will explore the possibility for categorization of users and service requests in making domain-wide optimization decisions. Furthermore, research will focus on QoS negotiation models in cases involving multiple providers in service delivery.

References

1. ITU-T Recommendation Y.2012. Functional requirements and architecture of the NGN release 1 (2006)
2. ITU-T Recommendation E.860. Framework of a service level agreement (2002)
3. 3GPP TS 23.228: IP Multimedia Subsystem (IMS); Stage 2, Release 8 (2008)

4. Information Technology - Multimedia framework (MPEG-21) - Part 7: Digital Item Adaptation, ISO/IEC 21000-7 (2004)
5. Boula, L., Koumaras, H., Kourtis, A.: An Enhanced IMS Architecture Featuring Cross-Layer Monitoring and Adaptation Mechanisms. ICAS, Spain (2009)
6. Ekstrom, H.: QoS control in the 3GPP Evolved Packet System. IEEE Comm. Magazine 47(2), 76–83 (2009)
7. Guenkova-Luy, T., Kassler, A.J., Mandato, D.: End-to-End Quality-of-Service Coordination for Mobile Multimedia Applications. IEEE J. Selec. Areas Commun. 22(5), 889–903 (2004)
8. Handley, H., Jacobson, V.: SDP: Session Description Protocol. IETF RFC 2327 (1998)
9. Houssos, N., et al.: Advanced Adaptability and Profile Management Framework for the Support of Flexible Service Provision. IEEE Wireless Communications, 52–61 (August 2003)
10. Khan, S.: Quality Adaptation in a Multisession Multimedia System: Model, Algorithms and Architecture. PhD Thesis, Univ. of Victoria (1998)
11. Mukherjee, D., Delfosse, E., Kim, J.-G., Wang, Y.: Optimal Adaptation Decision-Taking for Terminal and Network Quality of Service. IEEE Trans. on Multimedia 7(3), 454–462 (2005)
12. Ozcelebi, T., Radovanovic, R., Chaudron, M.: Enhancing End-to-End QoS for Multimedia Streaming in IMS-Based Networks. In: ICSNC, pp. 48–53 (2007)
13. Rosenberg, J., et al.: SIP: Session Initiation Protocol. IETF RFC 3261 (2002)
14. Skorin-Kapov, L., Mosmondor, M., Dobrijevic, O., Matijasevic, M.: Application-level QoS Negotiation and Signaling for Advanced Multimedia Services in the IMS. IEEE Comm. Magazine 45(7), 108–116 (2007)
15. Skorin-Kapov, L., Matijasevic, M.: A QoS Negotiation and Adaptation Framework for Multimedia Services in NGN. In: Proceedings of ConTEL 2009, Zagreb, Croatia, pp. 249–256 (2009)
16. Skorin-Kapov, L., Matijasevic, M.: A Data Specification Model for Multimedia QoS Negotiation. In: Proc. ACM Mobimedia (2007)
17. Wang, Y., Kim, J.-G., Chang, S.-F., Kim, H.-M.: Utility-Based Video Adaptation for Universal Multimedia Access (UMA) and Content-Based Utility Function Prediction for Real-Time Video Transcoding. IEEE Trans. on Multimedia 9(2), 213–220 (2007)
18. IST DAIDALOS - EU FP6, http://www.ist-daidalos.org/
19. IST ENTHRONE - EU FP6, http://www.ist-enthrone.org/
20. GLPK (GNU Linear Programming Kit), http://www.gnu.org/software/glpk/glpk.html#TOCintroduction (last accessed November 10, 2008)

iBE: A Novel Bandwidth Estimation Algorithm for Multimedia Services over IEEE 802.11 Wireless Networks

Zhenhui Yuan, Hrishikesh Venkataraman, and Gabriel-Miro Muntean

Performance Engineering Laboratory, School of Electronic Engineering
Dublin City University, Ireland
{yuanzh,hrishikesh,munteang}@eeng.dcu.ie
http://elm.eeng.dcu.ie/~munteang/,
http://elm.eeng.dcu.ie/~hrishikesh/HomePage.htm

Abstract. Recently, multimedia streaming services over IEEE 802.11 based wireless networks have increased dramatically. This results in manifold increase in the bandwidth requirement, especially for high-quality multimedia services. Given the bandwidth constraint in the wireless networks, one of the most critical factors in improving the end-to-end performance of multimedia application is the fast and accurate estimation of bandwidth. This paper proposes a novel bandwidth estimation algorithm, iBE. The significant feature of iBE is that it relies on multimedia packets only from the application layer. In addition, iBE recognizes the dynamic fluctuations of the wireless channel quickly, which in-turn enables iBE to be used for real-time services. The experimental results demonstrate that the accuracy of the bandwidth estimated by iBE is significantly superior to other methods like Spruce. Secondly, even in high traffic conditions, the bandwidth estimated by iBE is very close to the actual measured bandwidth, unlike the other state-of-the-art methods.

Keywords: Wireless networks, bandwidth estimation, multimedia service.

1 Introduction

The popularity of multimedia-based services such as live multimedia streaming, Video-on-demand (VoD), IPTV, etc in the wireless networks has been exponentially increasing. In case of a wired network, the network capacity and the bandwidth is not a major constraint [1]. However, in a wireless network with continuous and dynamic fluctuations in the wireless channel, there are several challenges in case of streaming video and other data traffics [2]. Multimedia streams require large amount of bandwidth which is usually not freely available. Hence, the wireless network operators are greedy for more bandwidth, in order to simultaneously serve voice and video traffic to a large umber of users [3]. Unfortunately, with an increasing number of users in the wireless network, the quality of the multimedia applications fluctuates rapidly due to the decrease in

T. Pfeifer and P. Bellavista (Eds.): MMNS 2009, LNCS 5842, pp. 69–80, 2009.
© IFIP International Federation for Information Processing 2009

the per-user network capacity. In addition, the mobility of the user [4], dynamic fluctuation in the wireless channel [5] and cross traffics [6] also deteriorates the quality of the multimedia services.

Previous works such as "WBest" [7], [8] and "Spruce" [9] provides somewhat efficient solution to estimate bandwidth in the network. However, these methods rely on additional probing traffics which create a negative influence on the real-time service due to the introduction of extra bandwidth cost. This in-turn results in the end users having to pay additional cost just for estimating the bandwidth of the network. Demircin and Van Beek proposed a new on-line application-layer bandwidth measurement method [10] based on block-ACK mechanism of 802.11e. However, 802.11e protocol has been only used in the recent years and it increases the complexity of the original 802.11 MAC architecture (like 802.11b/g) which is more popular in current commercial market. Additionally, IEEE 802.11e increases the implementation cost and the real-time constraints have become a lot tighter [11].

This paper proposes a novel intelligent bandwidth estimation algorithm (iBE) for multimedia delivery over IEEE 802.11 wireless networks. iBE makes use of the information related to multimedia packets delivery at the application layer only. iBE estimates the bandwidth from the data packets transmitted over the wireless network; and does not utilize any resource for itself. Hence, iBE estimates the bandwidth very accurately. Apart from estimation accuracy, another major benefit of iBE is that it leads to a simpler implementation and lower computation than the other state-of-the-art methods like Spruce and WBest.

The paper is organized as follows. Section 2 shows the related work in bandwidth estimation methods. In Section 3, detailed description of iBE is provided. Section 4 and Section 5 presents the simulation setup and the result analysis respectively. Finally, Section 6 concludes the paper.

2   Related Work

Recently, bandwidth estimation techniques have drawn widespread interests in network management arena. Current research on bandwidth estimation algorithms could be classified into three categories [9], [12]: packet dispersion measurement (PDM), probe gap model (PGM) and probe rate model (PRM). The PDM techniques, such as the packet pair or packet train, estimates network capacity by recording the packet inter-arrival time. Extensive research works have been carried out based on the PDM technique, and several bandwidth estimation techniques have been proposed - "Nettimer" [13], and "bprobe" [14]. However, the main disadvantage of PDM-based technique is that they have very low accuracy when applied to the wireless networks.

Commonly used bandwidth estimation techniques like "Spruce" and the recently proposed "IGI" [15] are based on PGM. The basic principle of PGM is that the server sends a probe packet pair with time dispersion, T_{in}, and after successful transmission, the receiver records a changed dispersion time, T_{out}. The value, $T_{out} - T_{in}$ would be the time for transmitting cross traffics under the condition that a single bottleneck link is assumed. The cross traffic rate, BW_c, could be written as $BW_c = (T_{out} - T_{in}) \times C/T_{in}$, where C is the capacity of the network. Hence, the estimated available bandwidth would be $C - BW_c$. However, the main disadvantage of PGM is that it assumes that the network capacity is known. Hence, a faster estimation could be done along with an increase in the accuracy of estimation. In reality, however, the network capacity is not always known beforehand.

The PRM techniques such as "pathChirp" [16] and "pathload" [17], estimate bandwidth using three kinds of traffic rates: sender-side probing rate (C_s), receiver-side probing rate (C_r) and available bandwidth (BW). If it is considered that C_s gets increased to a level bigger than (BW), then C_s would exceed C_r as a result of packet delay at bottleneck link due to queuing mechanism inside routers. Hence, it is critical to find out such level at which C_s starts to become bigger than C_r, and this C_s would be measured as available bandwidth.

3   The Novel Intelligent Bandwidth Estimation Algorithm

3.1   Background

The basic idea of iBE is to make use of the difference between the packet's transmission time and reception time at MAC layer. In IEEE 802.11 b MAC protocol [18], the receiver sends acknowledge (ACK) packet for each frame successfully transmitted as shown in Fig. 1.

The RTS/CTS mechanism of MAC layer reduces frame collisions brought by the hidden terminal problem [19]. Even though RTS/CTS packets introduce additional overhead, the throughput loss introduced by RTS/CTS is less due to the smaller packet size (44 bytes and 38 bytes in our simulation) as compared to multimedia packets in the application layer. Inter-frame spacing (IFS) in MAC mechanism reduces the probability of conflict among different packets, thus proving an efficient use of wireless bandwidth. In addition, it should be noted that the control signals (RTS, CTS and ACK) and IFS (SIFS, SIFS) take some amount of bandwidth resources.

The key principle of iBE is to efficiently use packet delay during transmission. Since the waiting time in MAC buffer doesn't constitute the actual bandwidth, as shown in Fig. 1, only the delay in transmitting raw multimedia data is considered. An illustration of various types of delay is shown in Fig. 2.

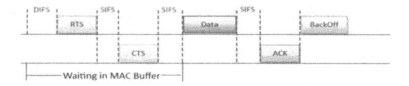

Fig. 1. Packet Sequence in 802.11b MAC Layer

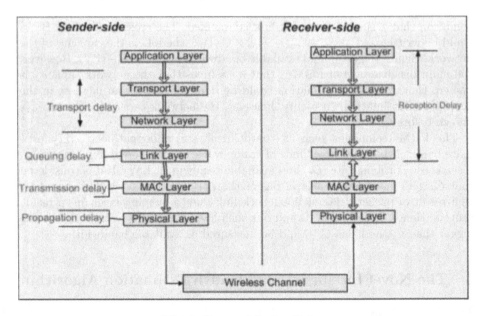

Fig. 2. Types of Packet Delay

Transport delay exists both at sender and receiver side. It is the delay incurred due to reassembling of an incoming or outgoing packet that would be transferred to lower layer (MAC) at sender side and higher layer (application) at receiver side. Transport delay is determined by system processing capability which is independent of wireless bandwidth. Another type of delay is reception delay which is the time taken for receiving a packet. Queuing delay indicates how long a packet have to wait in queues (IFQ) until it gets access to the wireless channel and transmission delay is the delay at the physical layer due to the bit by bit transmission of the packet by the sender. The transmission delay is a function of the packet's length and the transmission rate of link. Finally, the propagation delay is the time taken by one binary bit in a packet traveling the wireless link from sender to receiver. It is deterministic and depends on the distance between the sender and the receiver as well as medium of the link (such as fiber optics, wireless link, etc).

3.2   Overview

In order to get a more realistic bandwidth, iBE puts time stamps at MAC layer to calculate bandwidth; since packets buffering time (Queuing delay) and processing delay in upper layers do not reflect the wireless bandwidth [5]. A burst of multimedia packets is chosen as a sample (S_i), where i implies the picked sample. The sample size could be computed by:

$$S_i = packet\_recvd_i \times PS_i \qquad (1)$$

where $packet\_recvd_i$ is the number of multimedia packets received within a sample at client MAC layer. PS_i is the size of multimedia packet with MAC header. The time taken to transmit application data (T_i) is calculated as follows:

$$T_i = recv\_time_i - S\_time_i - (packet\_recvd_i - 1)$$
$$\times (3 \times SIFS + DIFS + Backoff_i + T_{ACK} + T_{RTS} + T_{CTS}) \qquad (2)$$

In eqn. (2) above, the $recv\_time_i$ and S_time_i imply the received time of last packet and the transmission time of first packet of $sample_i$ respectively. As discussed before, the time taken in MAC buffer such as SIFS, DIFS, TACK, TRTS and TCTS are subtracted from sample transmission time. Here T_{ACK}, T_{RTS} and T_{CTS} are time cost for transmitting ACK, RTS and CTS packets. Similarly the $Backoff_i$, which means the back off time between two consecutive packets, is subtracted. Back off time depends on current contention window size. Now, the instant bandwidth (instantBW) for a sample is calculated every 5 ms according to the equation(3):

$$instantBW = S_i/T_i \qquad (3)$$

It should be noted that the time space for periodic bandwidth estimation is chosen as 5 ms. The primary reason for selecting this value is to have a time space that is twice as the frame duration. A standard time frame chosen in the wireless systems (eg: 3G network like UMTS) is 10 ms. Hence, the 5 ms time space ensures that bandwidth changes every half the frame duration are accurately estimated. The instant bandwidth estimated is then sent to server as feedback indicating the current network condition.

4   Experimental Setup

iBE is modeled and evaluated using Network Simulator 2 (NS-2) version 2.29. Fig. 3 shows the simulation topology where servers send multimedia and cross traffic to clients via a wired network as well as a last hop wireless LAN (WLAN). Multimedia and background traffic share the bottleneck from the access point (AP) to the wireless clients.

Table 1 summarizes the NS-2 configuration used in our experiment. Two additional wireless update patches are deployed in the set-up: NOAH and Marco Fiero patch. NOAH (No Ad-Hoc) is used for simulating the infrastructure WLAN environment whereas Marco Fiero's patch provides a more realistic wireless network environment. As a result, in our experiment, we consider four bandwidth levels: 1, 2, 5.5 and 11 Mbps depending on the distance of the wireless devices from the AP. Fig. 4 shows the characteristic of the actual IEEE 802.11b network. The area with the dark color in Fig. 4 represents higher bandwidth than that with light color. For instance, the rate in the center area is 11Mbps, while the outside area is only 1 Mbps.

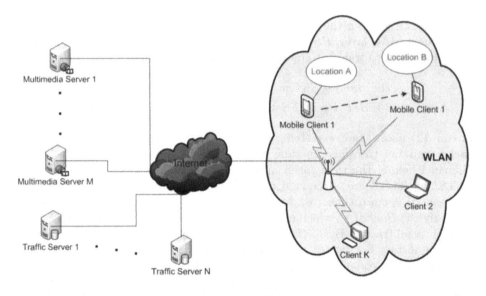

Fig. 3. Simulation Network Topology

Fig. 4. Dynamic Bandwidth around Access Point (IEEE 802.11b)

$W_{\min}$ and $W_{\max}$ are the minimum and maximum values of contention window. Basic rate, sending rate of control packets (ACK, RTS, CTS), is set as 1 Mbps.

In our experiment, six separate tests were conducted for estimating the bandwidth over different network conditions. Each test consisted of one to three unicast video traffics. The client were designed to move from t = 5s at the speed of 1 m/s. Variable network conditions were also realized by varying current traffic loads. This was done by generating CBR/UDP cross traffic using 1500 bytes packets. Additionally, the number of video traffic was scheduled to increase with each test. It should be noted that with an increase in the traffic load, the network becomes quite increasingly congested. The main aim of performing these experiments is to verify how iBE works under heavy and increasing traffic load.

Table 1. Simulation Setup in NS-2.29

Parameter	Description of Parameter
Transport Protocol	UDP
Wireless protocol	802.11b
Routing protocol	NOAH
Error Model	Marco Fiero patch
Wired Bandwidth	100 Mbps LAN
MAC header	52 bytes
Wmin	31
Wmax	1023
ACK	38 bytes
CTS	38 bytes
RTS	44 bytes
SIFS	10^{-6} sec
DIFS	50^{-6} sec
Basic rate	1 Mbps

5   Experimental Tests and Results

The performance study compares the measured bandwidth and estimated bandwidth (iBE and Spruce). The measured bandwidth is the actual bandwidth of the network that is measured and it indicates the maximum throughput that an application can obtain. The estimated bandwidth (iBE, Spruce) signifies the maximum end-to-end throughput achieved with cross traffic interferences.

Fig. 5 shows the comparison results of measured bandwidth (calculated from trace results of NS-2) and estimated bandwidth (iBE and Spruce) for periods from 0 to 200 seconds without cross traffic. Two different tests were conducted. The first Test consists of one server and one client using a topology similar to that presented in Fig. 3, whereas, Test two consists of two servers and two clients.

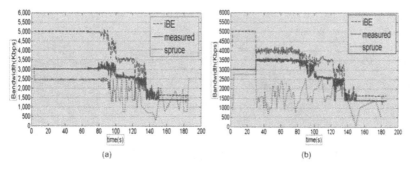

Fig. 5. Comparison of Estimated and Measured Bandwidth without Cross Traffic

The results of these two tests are shown in Fig. 5 (a) and Fig. 5 (b) respectively, for both Spruce and iBE. In case of Spruce, the probing traffic used CBR/UDP flow to send packets of 1500 bytes with the rate of 0.15 Mbps. In case of iBE however, there is no probing traffic. In addition, the Spruce traffic started at t = 3s, whereas that of iBE started at t = 2s. A video clip was transmitted to client via high speed (100 Mbps) wired network and IEEE 802.11b WLAN. In case of Test one, as shown in Fig. 5 (a), it was observed that the estimated available bandwidth dropped when the distance between mobile client and AP increased. Also, as shown in Fig. 5 (a), the bandwidth fluctuates at around 80s and 130s due to interference of incoming cross traffic. In order to assess the performance of bandwidth estimation, the concept of average estimated bandwidth has been introduced. The average bandwidth estimated by iBE and Spruce in Test one were 3.52 Mbps and 1.51 Mbps respectively, both of which were notably different from measured bandwidth value of 2.96 Mbps. However, there was a difference in the errors - 0.56 and 1.45 for iBE and Spruce respectively. Hence, it could be observed that, on an average, iBE generated fewer errors than Spruce although Spruce performed better in the first 80s of the simulation scenario.

With the same topology, in Test two, two video clips with the same size were sent to clients using unicast mechanism. The error of iBE and Spruce were 0.29 and 1.63 respectively, demonstrating that iBE outperforms Spruce in heavy traffic condition (two clients). In addition, for both one and two clients, iBE provided smoother estimated bandwidth during stable periods. In Fig. 5 (a) such period

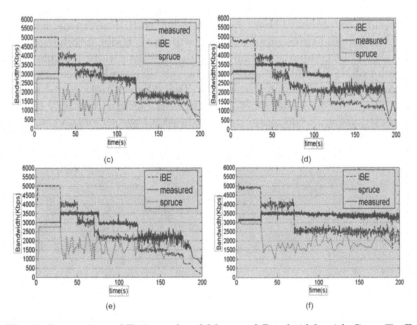

Fig. 6. Comparison of Estimated and Measured Bandwidth with Cross Traffic

lasted from 0 to 80s, 100 to 120s and 130 to 200s while in Fig. 5 (b), it lasted from 30 to 90s and 100 to 120s. Tests three, four, five and six, involve simulations with participation of constant bit rate over UDP cross traffic of different average bit-rates. This is a significant difference as compared to Test one and Test two. Results of these four tests are shown in Fig. 6. In Test three, two video servers start transmitting at t = 2s and t = 30s, and the cross traffic began at t = 50s, as shown in Fig. 6 (a). Fig. 6 (b) presents the results of Test four, which involves two video servers transmitting as in test three, but the two cross traffic sources started at t = 50s and t = 70s. Fig. 6 (c) illustrates the results of Test five, which involves an additional cross traffic source which starts at t = 80s. Test six adds an additional video traffic source to the network, which began delivering video at t = 50s. The results are presented in Fig. 6 (d). Overall, it can be observed from Fig. 6 (a) - Fig. 6 (d) that the performance of iBE was significantly closer to the actual measured bandwidth in all the four cases of Tests.

It is clear from the Fig. 5 and Fig. 6 that the bandwidth pattern estimated by iBE is similar to the actual measured bandwidth, though some delays are encountered in its estimation. This delay arises mainly due to the delay of the multimedia packets. However, it should be noted that the bandwidth estimated by iBE is always closer to the measured bandwidth than that of Spruce. Fig. 7 shows the average bandwidth for the six experiments (six Tests) as shown in Table 2. Table 2 itemizes the six experimental tests as well as the average bandwidth based on iBE, Spruce and actual measured bandwidth. The error columns in Table 2 show the difference between the measured bandwidth and estimated bandwidth (iBE and Spruce). For instance, in Test four, bandwidth error of iBE is 0.38 Mbps whereas that of Spruce is 1.05 Mbps, i.e., iBE is 63.8% better than Spruce. Additionally, the bandwidth error of iBE are 0.25 Mbps and 0.14 Mbps for Test five and Test six respectively, indicating 34.2% and 63.1% improvement when traffic load became heavier.

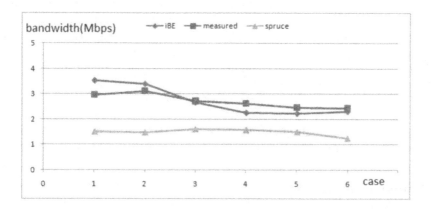

Fig. 7. Average Bandwidth based on Estimated and Measured Values

Table 2. Bandwidth Estimation for the Six Experiments

Sr. No.	Video Clients	Cross Traffic CBR/UDP	Measured BW (Mbps)	Estimated BW iBE (Mbps)	Estimated BW Spruce (Mbps)	BW Error Measured & iBE (Mbps)	BW Error Measured & Spruce (Mbps)
1	1	None	2.96	3.52	1.51	0.56	1.45
2	2	None	3.12	3.41	1.49	0.29	1.63
3	2	0.5 Mb/s 1.0 Mb/s	2.72	2.67	1.62	0.05	1.1
4	2	0.5 Mb/s 1.0 Mb/s	2.63	2.25	1.58	0.38	1.05
5	3	0.5 Mb/s 0.5 Mb/s 1.0 Mb/s	2.48	2.23	1.51	0.25	0.97
6	3	1.0 Mb/s 1.0 Mb/s 1.0 Mb/s	2.45	2.31	1.26	0.14	1.19

6   Conclusion and Future Work

This paper proposes a new intelligent bandwidth estimation algorithm (iBE) for multimedia delivery over wireless networks. The major benefit of iBE is that it uses multimedia application packets instead of extra probing traffic. This results in a much higher accuracy of the estimated bandwidth, as compared to the other state-of-the-art bandwidth estimation methods. In addition to accuracy, iBE provides a quick response, and at the same time, a smoother result with less variation in the estimated bandwidth. This is extremely beneficial for estimating the bandwidth real-time; which could be subsequently used for efficient resource allocation in dynamically changing wireless networks. The future work would focus on improving the accuracy of iBE and deriving mathematical models for achieving this higher accuracy. In addition, the performance of iBE would be verified under different network conditions and different wireless standards like IEEE 802.11e/g. It is anticipated that such an accurate estimation of the rapidly changing wireless bandwidth, would enable the network operators to use dynamic rate adaptive solutions for multimedia services in a much better fashion. This would in-turn enable high quality of experience for multimedia transmission in the next generation wireless networks.

Acknowledgments

The authors would like to thank China Scholarship Council and Irish research Council for Science Engineering and Technology (IRCSET) for their support.

References

1. Ngo, C.: A Service-oriented Wireless Home Network. In: IEEE Consumer Communications and Networking Conference, Las Vegas, Nevada, USA (January 2004)
2. Venkataraman, H., Haas, H., Yun, S., Lee, Y., McLaughlin, S.: Performance Analysis of Hybrid Cellular Networks. In: IEEE International Symposium on Personal Indoor Mobile Radio Communications (PIMRC), Berlin, Germany (September 2005)
3. Venkataraman, H., Sinanovic, S., Haas, H.: Cluster-based Two-Hop Cellular Networks. International Journal of Communications, Networks and Systems (IJCNS) 1(4), 370–385 (2008)
4. Mercado, A., Liu, K.J.R.: Adaptive QoS for Mobile Multimedia Services over Wireless Networks. In: IEEE International Conference on Multimedia and Expo, NY, USA, July 30 - August 2 (2000)
5. Muntean, G.M., Cranley, N.: Resource Efficient Quality-Oriented Wireless Broadcasting of Adaptive Multimedia Content. IEEE Transactions on Broadcasting 53(1), 362–368 (2007)
6. Robinson, B.P., Liberatore, V.: On the Impact of Bursty Cross-traffic on Distributed Real-time Process Control. In: IEEE International Workshop on Factory Communication Systems, Vienna, Austria (September 2004)
7. Li, M., Claypool, M., Kinicki, R.: WBest: A Bandwidth Estimation Tool for IEEE 802.11 Wireless Networks. In: 33rd Annual IEEE Conference on Local Computer Networks (LCN), Montreal, Canada (October 2008)
8. Li, M., Claypool, M., Kinicki, R.: Packet Dispersion in IEEE802.11 Wireless Networks. In: 2nd IEEE International Workshop on Performance and Management of Wireless and Mobile Networks, Tampa, FL, USA (November 2006)
9. Strauss, J., Katabi, D., Kaashoek, F.: A Measurement Study of Available Bandwidth Estimation Tools. In: The 3rd ACM SIGCOMM conference on Internet measurement, Miami Beach, FL, USA (October 2003)
10. Demircin, M.U., Van Beek, P.: Bandwidth Estimation and Robust Video Streaming Over 802.11E Wireless Lans. In: IEEE International Conference on Multimedia and Expo., Amsterdam, The Netherlands (July 2005)
11. Chung, S., Piechota, K.: Understanding the MAC Impact of 802.11e: Part 2, Silicon and Software Systems,
    http://www.commsdesign.com/showArticle.jhtml?articleID=16502136
12. Prasad, R.S., Murry, M., Dovrolis, C., Claffy, K.: Bandwidth Estimation: Metrics, Measurement Techniques, and Tools. IEEE Network 17(6), 27–35 (2003)
13. Lai, K., Baker, M.: Nettimer: A Tool for Measuring Bottleneck Link Bandwidth. In: USENIX Symposium on Internet Technologies and Systems, San Francisco, CA (March 2001)
14. Carter, R.L., Crovella, M.E.: Measuring Bottleneck Link Speed in Packet-switched Networks. Performace Evaluation 27-28(8), 297–318 (1996)
15. Hu, N., Steenkiste, P.: Evaluation and Characterization of Available Bandwidth Probing Techniques. IEEE journal on Selected Areas in Communications 21(6) (August 2003)
16. Ribeiro, V., Riedi, R., Baraniuk, R., Navratil, J., Cottrell, L.: Pathchirp: Efficient Available Bandwidth Estimation for Network Paths. In: Passive and Active Measurement Workshop, La Jolla, CA, USA (April 2003)

17. Jain, M., Dovrolis, C.: End-to-end Available Bandwidth: Measurement Methodology, Dynamics, and Relation with TCP Throughput. IEEE/ACM Transactions on Networking 11(4), 537–549 (2003)
18. IEEE 802.11, 1999 Edition (ISO/IEC 8802-11: 1999), IEEE Standards for Information Technology – Telecommunications and Information Exchange between Systems – Local and Metropolitan Area Network – Specific Requirements – Part 11: Wireless LAN Medium Access Control (MAC) and Physical Layer (PHY) Specifications (1999)
19. Xu, K., Gerla, M., Bae, S.: How Effective is the IEEE 802.11 RTS/CTS Handshake in Ad hoc Networks. In: IEEE Global Telecommunications Conference, Taiwan, China (November 2002)

A Cost Function for QoS-Aware Routing in Multi-tier Wireless Multimedia Sensor Networks

Stéphane Lohier[1], Abderrezak Rachedi[1], and Yacine Ghamri-Doudane[2]

[1] IGM - Université de Paris-Est Marne-la-Vallée, 75420 Champs sur Marne, France
[2] ENSIIE, 1Square de la résistance, 91025 Evry Cedex, France
lohier@univ-mlv.fr, rachedi@univ-mlv.fr, ghamri@ensiie.fr

Abstract. Wireless Multimedia Sensor Networks (WMSNs) are composed of small devices that are able to capture video or audio information and to transmit it over wireless channels. The development of wireless technologies, such as: WiFi, Bluetooth, Zigbee, and UWB, encourages the emergence of heterogeneous networks. However, only a few existing solutions take into account the constraints of multi-tier and multi-MAC wireless sensor networks. In this paper, we propose a cost function coupled to a new generic (i.e. independent from any MAC protocol) cross-layer routing protocol adapted to multimedia traffic over hierarchical and heterogeneous networks. The goal of our proposed protocol is to dynamically assess the routing process cost and the requirement of the multimedia application in order to ensure a sufficient quality of service (Soft QoS). Furthermore, the cross-layer approach is needed to use the physical and MAC parameters on the routing operation. Simulation results show that our solution is efficient and gives better results than classical protocols.

Keywords: WMSNs, heterogeneous network, cost function, cross-layer, QoS.

1 Introduction

The popularity of Wireless Sensor Networks (WSNs) is growing with the technological advancement that enables to design a small and smart device able to capture the multimedia information such as CMOS cameras and microphones [1]. This growing interest enables the development of particular wireless sensor networks called Wireless Multimedia Sensor Networks (WMSNs). Furthermore, WMSNs enable to enlarge WSNs application field: it can be used for multimedia surveillance systems against crime and terrorist attacks, car traffic monitoring in big cities or highways, environmental monitoring through acoustic and video data, etc.

Unlike classical WSNs, WMSNs have specific characteristics such as: 1) high bandwidth demand due to multimedia content, 2) specific QoS requirements that are dependent on the application, and 3) important power resource consumption due to high volumes of data to transmit (or forward) by battery-constrained devices. One should also note that due to the nature of WMSN applications, the node's mobility is not high. Obviously, WMSNs are more challenging than classical WSNs since additional constraints and parameters are introduced. That is why Akyildiz et al. [2] proposed and advocated for a multi-tier architecture. This architecture ensures the network

T. Pfeifer and P. Bellavista (Eds.): MMNS 2009, LNCS 5842, pp. 81–93, 2009.

scalability and enables the use of heterogeneous elements. These architectures provide an efficient cost-performance tradeoff while taking into account less expensive and resource-constrained scalar sensors and high power superior elements such as multimedia sensors. In this architecture, the network is divided into clusters. Each cluster elects a cluster head that has sufficient resources.

In this paper, we use the multi-tier architecture to ensure the scalability and the soft-based quality of services [2]. We focus on the routing process to increase the throughput and reduce the packet loss and the delay. Therefore, in order to optimize the resources and make the multimedia traffic routing more efficient, we propose a new routing protocol based on a cost-function called HQAX (Hierarchical QoS Aware Cross-layer routing protocol). The basic idea of this cost function is to take into account not only the routing parameters, but also the physical and MAC layers parameters such as the channel quality, the SNR, and the number of ACK failures. Our design is thus a cross-layer design enabling to take into account the physical and MAC layers parameters at the routing level. We show that with such a mechanism, we can improve the network throughput; reduce the packet loss and the delay in indoor environments. The impact of the environment on the communication channel quality is very significant. For instance, in the case of an outdoor environment, called free-space, the channel quality is better than when many obstacles are present inside a building. However, most applications of WMSNs, like building surveillance, are in an indoor environment. That is why we focus on such realistic scenarios to validate our proposed protocol.

After analyzing and studying WMSNs requirements and their potential implementation using multi-tier architecture, our contributions can be summarized in the three following points:

— Proposition of a new routing protocol (HQAX) based on a cost function in order to improve the throughput and to reduce the delay and packet losses.
— Definition of a cost function in order to optimize the resources and to make the multimedia traffic routing more efficient (the cross-layer approach is used for the cost function in order to take into account the physical and MAC layers parameters at the routing level).
— Implementation and evaluation of the proposed routing protocol in comparison with other existing protocols like AODV and OLSR which had been adapted to cope with the features and characteristics of multi-tier WMSNs.

The rest of the paper is organized as follows. In Section 2, we present the related works. In Section 3, we present and detail our proposed routing protocol. A description of our cost function follows in Section 4. In Section 5, we evaluate and compare our solution with existing routing protocols. Section 6 concludes the paper.

2   Related Works

Many routing protocols are proposed in literature. In proactive networks, Heinzelman et al. proposed a Low-Energy Adaptive Clustering Hierarchy (LEACH) for wireless sensor networks [3]. LEACH is a dynamic clustering protocol designed with energy constraint consideration. Lindsey et al. proposed an improvement of LEACH called Power-Efficient Gathering in Sensor Information Systems (PEGASIS) [4]. The basic idea of PEGASIS is to form a chain among the sensor nodes where each node will receive from and transmit to a close neighbor in order to reduce the energy consumption. These protocols focus on the dynamic clustering issue. Once the clusters are established and the cluster head role assigned, it is still necessary to ensure the quality of services required by multimedia traffic. Our objective is to target this second problem.

In the QoS-aware routing protocols class, we can quote some proposals for WSNs. One of them is the Sequential Assignment Routing (SAR) [5]. SAR creates trees routed from a one-hop neighbor of the sink by taking into account the QoS metric, the energy resource on each path and the priority level of each packet. However, the SAR protocol does not focus on the throughput maximization. Some other routing protocols also integrate the energy parameters in addition to other QoS parameters. An example of these is the SPEED protocol [6]. SPEED is a real-time communication protocol for sensor networks. The protocol provides three types of real-time communication services, namely real-time unicast, real-time area-multicast and real-time area-anycast. However, SPEED needs localization algorithms to achieve high scalability and avoid a flooding operation to discover new paths. Another protocol, proposed by C.G. Lee *et al.* and called Multipath Multi-SPEED Protocol (MMSPEED) [7], adopts a probabilistic approach to offer QoS assurance in wireless sensor networks. To do so, it uses a cross-layer approach between the network and the MAC layers. However, MMSPEED assumes that each node is equipped with a GPS chip which may not be a suitable assumption in WSNs, especially in indoor environments.

An energy-aware routing protocol in a cluster-based architecture is presented in [8]. It uses a cost function based on energy saving that is coupled with a source routing protocol. Unlike our approach, the topology is multi-gateway and non multi-tier (multi-MAC). Furthermore, the protocol is specific to the use of a TDMA MAC layer.

3 Hierarchical QoS Aware Cross-Layer Routing Protocol

3.1 Context

Figure 1 describes our proposal for a multi-tier architecture inspired by the work of I.F. Akyldiz et al. [2]. In this heterogeneous and hierarchical architecture, each tier corresponds to a category of video sensors with increased capabilities in terms of camera resolution, processing, storage and transmission. For the third tier, the sensors can be CMUCam (weak resolution of 160x255) coupled with microcontrollers allowing a minimum processing and not very greedy transmissions like in ZigBee, Bluetooth or UWB standards. The second tier can be made up of a webcam and microcontrollers with more processing, more storage and mixed transmissions, ZigBee and 802.11 for instance. The first tier is connected to the sink (multimedia server) and includes high resolution cameras coupled with laptops.

For each tier, our proposal is to organize the topology into clusters with a Cluster Head (CH), Cluster Routers (CR) allowing multi-hop routing when necessary, and Cluster Terminals (CT), only able to capture video information and to transmit it. In order to limit the interferences, the nearby clusters can use distinct transmission channels. The sensors at the various levels can be moved but are not permanently mobile.

Moreover, the processing essentially carried out in the CHs and towards the sink, includes specific operations like compression, data aggregation (images from different

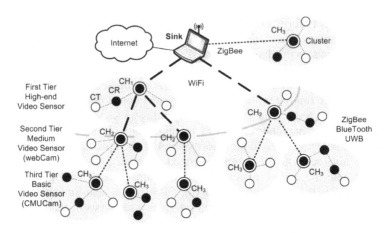

Fig. 1. Multi-tier Architecture of WMSN

scenes in the same flow) and data suppression (redundant images from various sensors). These different characteristics of the multi-tier WMSN architecture (clustered architecture, many-to-one flows, heterogeneous capabilities, and processing into the CHs) make us believe that a hierarchical routing is the most suited one.

3.2 The Goals of HQAX

The goal is not to propose an additional new routing protocol but rather to adapt existing solutions in order to have a QoS-aware routing protocol:

- linked to the application : the sensor networks are application-aware;
- based on a cross-layer cost function with routing, MAC and PHY parameters related to the multimedia feature of the flows;
- adapted to a hierarchical and multi-tier (multi-MAC) architecture;
- for many-to-one transmissions, and not for many-to-many like in current ad hoc network protocols like AODV or OLSR;
- generic, i.e. non related to a specific MAC layer but nevertheless compatible with the existing sensor routing protocols (ZigBee);
- with a limited overhead thanks to the combination of the cluster association and the route setup processes;
- easy to implement in the different devices of a real test bed.

The following sections describe our QoS-aware hierarchical routing inside clusters, whatever the tier is, and between the clusters of the various tiers. The QoS route setup is the first step of our solution. Indeed, the network organization must remain evolutionary according to the periodic requests from nodes to join or leave a cluster and to the needs of the sink-application which will select, starting from descriptors (fixed image, possible resolution...), the transmitting sensors as well as the characteristics of the transmitted flows (zone, resolution, compression ratio, cropping...). Thus, the objective here is not to constantly guarantee a QoS but to choose and receive pictures of a sufficient quality (soft QoS). The idea is thus to use the best available routes.

3.3 Intra-cluster QoS Routing

The QoS routing proposed in each cluster is proactive and includes 6 stages for the cluster self-organization and the route setup procedures (Figure 2). As indicated previously, we drew our inspiration from the existing solutions like ZigBee for the association process which is adapted to cope with the multi-tier feature of the WMSNs as well as with the QoS requirements of transmitted flows.

1. Each node self-determines its potential role (CH, CR or CT) in a cluster according to fixed or periodically re-evaluated criteria:

   — sufficient storage and energy (in comparison to specific thresholds for each role);
   — for CH: transmission capacity (presence of other devices corresponding to the tier) and computational capacity for aggregation, suppression, compression....

2. Each CH initiates a cluster (scan channels, select a channel, select a cluster id...).
3. CR and CT look for a cluster (Figure 3):

   — CR/CT broadcast a discovery message: Cluster_Discovery_Request (Scan Channels...);
   — response of the nearby CHs (and/or CR in the case of a multi-hop distance) with a Cluster_Discovery_Response (Cluster Description...).

4. Evaluation of a cost[1] C_{ij} for the links involved. This evaluation starts at stage 3 with the exchange of the *Cluster_Discovery*.
5. CR and CT choose a CH (or a CR) according to the previous QoS evaluation and join a cluster:

   — CR/CT send a message Cluster_Join_Request (Cluster id...);
   — response of the selected CH (or CR) with a Cluster_Join_Response (Cluster id, Network addresses...).

The associations of the CRs and the CTs are carried out in a recursive way: for the multi-hop routing, a CT out of the CH range has to wait for the association of a nearby CR to obtain an answer and thus join the cluster.

6. The CR informs its CH (or its nearby CR which is closer to the CH) about its router's role:

   — the CR sends a message Cluster_Router_Request (Cluster id...);
   — response of the CH (or CR) with a Cluster_Router_Response (Cluster id, Network address block...). In its response, the CH specifies the address block (or a sub-block in the case of a CR answering) which can be used by the requesting CR for its CT and its lower level CR.

After one or several exchange cycles, each CR or CT knows the address of its CH or its nearby CR (the one with the lowest cost towards the CH). Similarly, each CH or CR has a routing table for all its nodes. The routing is hierarchical: all data pass through the CH. According to the network dynamics, the various stages are periodically re-launched.

---

[1] The cost function integrating the QoS parameters is described in Section 4.

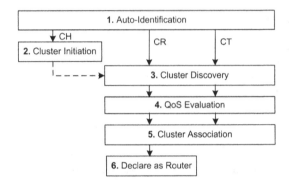

Fig. 2. Intra-cluster Routing Algorithm

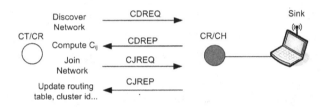

Fig. 3. Intra-cluster Association Process

3.4 Inter-tier QoS Routing

The routing between the CHs of various tiers (Figure 2) proceeds in 5 stages according to the same hierarchical and recursive principle:

1. The CH_3 (CH of third tier) broadcast a request to know the CH_2.
2. The CH_3 choose a CH_2 according to a cost estimated on the links.
3. The CH_2 broadcast a request in their turn on the corresponding interface to know the CH_1.
4. The CH_2 choose a CH_1 according to a cost estimated on the links.
5. The CH_1 broadcast a request to know the sink. In this last case, the cost is also computed to evaluate if, according to its location and environment, the CH_1 can get a sufficient QoS on the link towards the sink.

After sufficient exchanges, each CH_n knows the address of its CH_{n-1} and the sink (transmitted with the response to the broadcast). Each node in each cluster can thus transmit towards the sink and vice-versa (the sink knows the CH_1 which knows the CH_2…).

4 Utility Theory-Based Cost function

During the messages exchange of the discovery stage (between CT/CR and CR/CH or between CH_i and CH_{i+1}), the cost on each possible link is periodically estimated and compared (i) to a threshold to decide if it meets the conditions (noise, contentions…)

to get a sufficient QoS and (ii) with the costs on the other links to choose the most efficient CR/CH. The cost function on a link between two nodes i and j (j being the closest to the sink) can be expressed according to the chosen QoS metrics as follows:

$$C_{ij} = \sum_k c_k \times f_k(x_{ij}^k)$$

where x_{ij}^k is the value of metric k relatively to the link between two nodes i and j, c_k is the preference weight of metric k (where $\sum_k c_k = 1$), and $f_k(:)$ is a normalized function. In our case, we suggest choosing the five following metrics:

$$C_{ij} = c_1 \times f_1(delay_{ij}) + c_2 \times f_2(SNR_{ji}) + c_3 \times f_3(e_{ij}) + c_4 \times f_4(energy_i) + c_5 \times f_5(energy_j)$$

— $f_1(delay_{ij})$ is a function of the delay for a data packet transmitted from i to j;
— $f_2(SNR_{ji})$ is a function of the Signal/Noise Ratio assessed from j to i;
— $f_3(e_{ij})$ gives the error rate for the data packets transmitted from i to j;
— $f_4(energy_i)$ and $f_5(energy_j)$ give the remaining energy in i and j respectively.

The choice of weights c_1 to c_5 depends on the application and on the type of traffic (for instance, for streaming applications the delay is more important than the loss rate).

Besides, for "real time" applications, it is necessary to control the end-to-end delay. Rather than using higher level protocols like RTP and RTCP which involve an overhead, we can evaluate this global delay at the routing level, starting from the delay on each link and the knowledge of the route towards the sink, both data being provided by our routing protocol. The loss rate on a path from a CT towards the sink can also be evaluated, starting from the successive loss rates and the knowledge of the route.

The remaining question is related to the form to be used for the normalized $f_k(:)$ functions. To answer this question, the most suitable form can be found in the well-known concept of utility functions. Indeed, the utility theory correctly models the soft tuning of the perceived quality in modern networks.

The utility theory is used for multi-criteria selection which is a classical problem in economics and in many other fields. It is used to give a measure of the relative satisfaction from (or desirability of) the consumption of various goods and services. The use of the utility theory has been extended to many other fields where it is used as a scoring method that quantifies the score (suitability level, value, worth) of a particular choice compared to another one. In our current work, we suggest to use it to quantify the utility of using a link in a QoS-aware routing process. The utility of the link corresponds here to the cost function on the link between both nodes i and j. The utility theory is thus used as the basis of our cost function. The normalized function is introduced to express different characteristics of different units with a comparable numerical representation. Different normalized functions were used in literature to solve several QoS issues in communication networks. Among them, we can quote: the linear piecewise form [9], the logarithm form [10], the exponential form [10], and sigmoid forms [12, 13]. Among these, the most commonly used normalized functions are the sigmoidal (S-shaped) functions. Indeed, sigmoidal functions are well-known functions often used to describe QoS perception [13]. Thus we chose here to use these functions. More precisely, we consider the following analytic expression for the sigmoid form:

$$f(x) = \frac{(x-x_m)^\zeta}{1+(x-x_m)^\zeta}$$

where $x_m > 0$ and $\zeta \geq 2$ are tunable parameters, that differentiate the users' utilities. It is also assumed that the utilities are normalized to their highest limit, i.e. the asymptotic value of $f(x)$ for large x is considered to be equal to 1. This is only done for the sake of simplicity [13]. In other more complicated scenarios, different maximum utilities can also be considered.

5 Performance Evaluation

5.1 Context

To analyze the improvements registered by the HQAX protocol and the cost function, we implemented a set of simulations using the NS-2 simulator (version 2.33). The selected scenario implements a hierarchical multi-tier topology. Insofar as NS-2 is not conceived to bring together various interfaces and various MAC layers in the same node or in the same wireless network, only the 802.11 MAC layer will be used in the clusters of the different tiers. The objective being here to test the efficiency of the cost function integrated into our routing protocol, in comparison with current routing protocols, the simulations can be implemented without any real multi-MAC topology.

We chose to use the "shadowing" radio-propagation model, which is more realistic as it takes into account the shadowing and the fading effect that are common in indoor and outdoor environments with potential mobile obstacles. Moreover, to highlight the interest of the cost function, we chose the appropriate parameters for an indoor environment corresponding for example to a building surveillance application (see Table 1).

Table 1. Simulation Parameters

Nodes number	31
Simulation Area	135 x 84 meters
Simulation Time	20 seconds
Traffic Type, Packet size, Period	CBR, 1000 Bytes, 1.5 to 50ms
Radio-propagation model	Shadowing
Radio-propagation parameters	Reference distance=10m, β=5, σ=7dB
Transmission Range	25-50 meters

The simulated network includes 30 nodes and a sink distributed on a 135x84m area (see Figure 4). The role of each node (CH, CR or CT), which should depend on the available resources, is fixed at the beginning. The distances between the nodes are such that a CT_n or a CR_n has always the choice between at least two potential routes to join its CH_n. It is the same for a CH_n, during the association with its CH_{n+1}. Let us note that CH_2 or CH_3 can directly join the sink as this latter is assumed to have all MAC devices according to the use of multi-tier architecture. In addition, although the 802.11 MAC layer is common to all nodes, a CT (or a CR) can only join a CR or a CH at the same level. In this topology, all nodes can be multimedia sensors so all nodes are modeled as CBR sources. We tested several scenarios of sources activation with a number of CBR sources ranging between 1 and 30 (in this last case, all nodes are sources). The total duration of each simulation is 20s (sufficient in all cases to get a stable network) and the CBR sources are activated every 0.1s to avoid synchronized broadcast (in a multimedia sensor network, all cameras are seldom activated at the same time). In addition, in this type of applications (monitoring, surveillance ...), the nodes are often fixed or very slightly mobile. We thus chose a null mobility during the simulation.

The cost function implemented for the simulation is adapted to 802.11 devices and takes into account four parameters:

$$C_{ij} = c_1 \times f(delay_{ij}) + c_2 \times f(Pr_{ij}) + c_3 \times f(hops) + c_4 \times f(PLR_{ij})$$

— The delay on the link between nodes i and j is simply evaluated using a time-stamp transmitted to the CDREP association packet.
— The received power Pr is evaluated when receiving the CDREP packet. The number of hops is measured from the source to the sink.
— The *Packet Loss Rate* (PLR) is calculated on the node which transmits the CDREP packet and then transmitted in this same packet to the node having requested the association or to the node relaying the answer. The PLR is calculated from the MAC-MIB 802.11 information and then uploaded at the routing level:

$$PLR_{MPDU} = \frac{ACKFailureCount}{TransmittedFragmentCount + ACKFailureCount}$$

Coefficients c_1 to c_4 are optimized to get the best results in the selected context. To evaluate the HQAX performances and the associated cost function, we chose to compare it with the AODV and OLSR protocols which we adapted to a multi-tier architecture.

Concerning AODV, several reasons justify this choice:

— it is a standardized reference protocol for ad hoc networks and it is largely used in sensor networks: AODV is included in ZigBee [14];
— it is a generic protocol and it is not associated to a specific application or a particular access method as opposed to LEACH (based on dynamic clustering, energy saving and TDMA distribution) or SPEED (real time with geo-localization assumptions);
— AODV is implemented in the most common simulators like NS-2, as opposed to some specific WSN protocols.

In addition, the choice of OLSR (the implementation used here for NS-2 is UM-OLSR [15]) enables to compare HQAX to a proactive reference protocol in which the relay nodes (MPR) are elected according to the number of neighbors. For these simulations, AODV and OLSR were adapted, including cross-layer interactions with the MAC layer, to respect the multi-tier architecture (AODV-mt and OLSR-mt on the following figures). These adaptations are made so that: a CT_n/CR_n can only join a CR_n or a CH_n; a CH_n can directly join the sink or must pass by CH_{n+1}; a CT does not relay a route request broadcast; a CT cannot be elected as an MPR (in the case of OLSR).

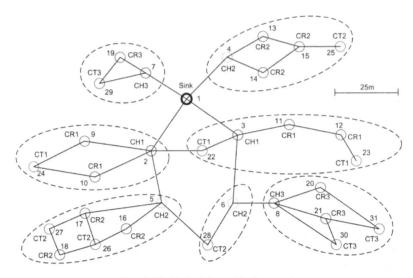

Fig. 4. Multi-tier hierarchical scenario

5.2 Results

Figure 5 presents the evolution of the average end-to-end delay for the CBR packets on all routes towards the sink, when the number of sources varies from 1 to 30. The results are slightly better with OLSR but with a much higher loss rate (Figure 7): the delays on the intermediate links between CR and CH can be shorter because many packets are lost on the way. For AODV, the average delay fluctuates between 3 and 8 ms showing a great dependence on the number of sources and the geographical distribution of nodes. Finally, HQAX presents a stable average delay, whatever the number of active sources, and relatively low if we take into account the number of packets actually transmitted. This shows the efficiency of the cost function which integrates the delay on the links.

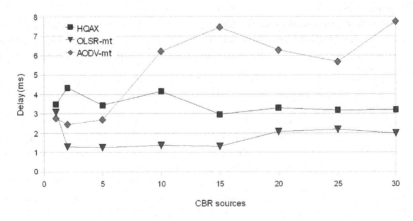

Fig. 5. Average Packet Delay / Number of CBR sources

Figure 6 shows the evolution of the average global throughput for all active CBR sources. The results are very close for a low number of sources and are slightly better for HQAX for more than 5 active sources. The evaluation in the cost function of the received power and of the loss rate during the association process makes it possible to reduce the risk of contentions on the selected links.

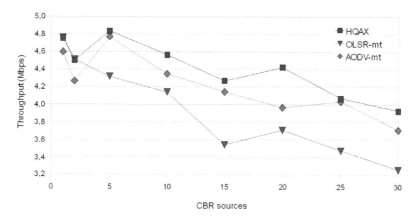

Fig. 6. Average Global Throughput / Number of CBR sources

In Figure 7, the packet loss rate for all active routes increases very quickly with OLSR, mainly because of a bad load balancing on the MPR which are elected according to the number of neighbors and not to the hierarchical organization of the network. AODV enables, with its error packet transmission mechanism, to mitigate the loss duration but at the expense of the overhead (see Figure 8). Whatever the number of sources, the loss rate remains lower than 1% with HQAX. This confirms the interest to upload at the routing level the number of non-received acknowledgements which is computed at the MAC level.

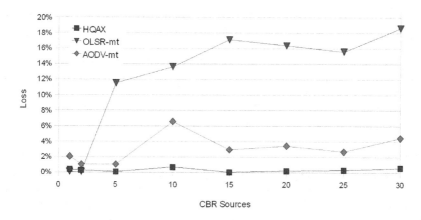

Fig. 7. Packet Loss / Number of CBR sources

The relative overhead of control packets (Figure 8) remains lower than 5% with OLSR and HQAX. Let us remind that for OLSR, the frequencies of Hello and TC messages are optimized for a not very dense and not mobile context. This overhead is much more important with AODV starting from 10 active sources. Although AODV is modified for our multi-tier architecture, the unsolved contentions can be numerous and the error messages can lead to broadcast new requests, creating a strong overhead.

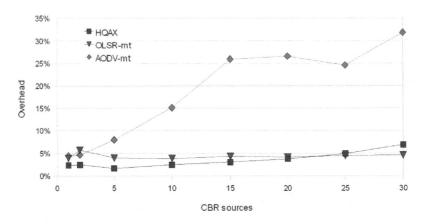

Fig. 8. Control Packet Overhead / Number of CBR sources

6 Conclusion and Perspectives

In this paper, we presented a solution including a reactive routing protocol associated with a cost function adapted to a heterogeneous and hierarchical WMSN architecture divided into clusters. This solution enables the sink to collect multimedia flows from different kinds of sensors, in the various tiers, with a sufficient quality of service. The advantages of this solution are on one hand its generic feature: it does not depend on a specific MAC layer or a particular access method, and on the other hand, the fact that it is compatible with the existing link and routing layers used by wireless sensor networks: the MAC parameters used in the cost function are generic and exist in both 802.11 and 802.15.4 MIBs; furthermore, the reactive routing approach used in HQAX is compatible with that used in ZigBee.

Our simulation study shows the efficiency of this solution, particularly in terms of throughput, loss rate, and control packet overhead. This first evaluation campaign will have to be confirmed by real test-bed experiments. Such a test-bed should integrate various devices corresponding to the different WMSN tiers (WiFi and ZigBee enabled sensors). The generic and compatibility features of our proposal should facilitate such an implementation. This experimental evaluation constitutes the target of our future work.

References

1. James, D., Klibanov, L., Tompkins, G., Dixon-Warren, S.J.: Inside CMOS Image Sensor Technology, Chipworks White Paper,
   `http://www.chipworks.com/resources/whitepapers/`
   `Inside-CMOS.pdf`
2. Akyildiz, I.F., Melodia, T., Chowdhury, K.R.: A survey on wireless multimedia sensor networks. Journal of Computer Networks 51(4) (2007)
3. Heinzelman, W., Chandrakasan, A., Balakrishnan, H.: Energy- Efficient Communication Protocol for Wireless Microsensor Networks. In: Proceedings of the Hawaii International Conference on System Sciences, January 4-7. IEEE Press, Los Alamitos (2000)
4. Lindsey, S., Raghavendra, C.S.: PEGASIS: Power-Efficient GAthering in Sensor Information Systems. In: IEEE Aerospace Conference Proceedings, pp. 1125–1130 (2002)
5. Sohrabi, K., et al.: Protocols for self-organization of a wireless sensor network. IEEE Personal Communications 7(5), 16–27 (2000)
6. He, T., Stankovic, J.A., Lu, C., Abdelzaher, T.: SPEED: A stateless protocol for real-time communication in sensor networks. In: The Proceedings of International Conference on Distributed Computing Systems, Providence, RI (May 2003)
7. Lee, C.-G., Ekici, E., Felemban, E.: MMSPEED: Multipath Multi-SPEED Protocol for QoS Guarantee of Reliability and Timeliness in Wireless Sensor Networks Full text. IEEE Transactions on Mobile Computing 5(6), 738–754 (2006)
8. Younis, M., Youssef, M., Arisha, K.: Energy-Aware Routing in Cluster-Based Sensor Networks. In: The Proceedings of the 10th IEEE/ACM International Symposium on Modeling, Analysis and Simulation of Computer and Telecommunication Systems (MASCOTS2002), FortWorth, TX (October 2002)
9. Ormond, O., Muntean, G., Murphy, J.: Economic model for cost effective network selection strategy in service oriented heterogeneous wireless network environment. In: Proc. of NOMS 2006, Canada (2006)
10. Ormond, O., Muntean, G., Murphy, J.: Network selection decision in wireless heterogeneous networks. In: Proc. of IEEE 16th Intl Symposium on Personal, Indoor and Mobile Radio Communications, Berlin (2005)
11. Wang, H.J., Katz, R.H., Giese, J.: Policy-enabled handoffs across heterogeneous wireless networks. In: IEEE Workshop on Mobile Computing Systems and Applications (1999)
12. Pal, S., Das, S., Chatterjee, M.: User-Satisfaction based Differentiated Services for Wireless Data Networks. In: Proc. of IEEE International Conference on Communications (ICC), vol. 2, pp. 1174–1178 (2005)
13. Badia, L., Lindstrom, M., Zander, J., Zorzi, M.: An economic model for the radio resource management in multimedia wireless systems. Computer Communications 27(11), 1056–1064 (2004)
14. ZigBee Specifications, ZigBee Alliance (December 2006), `http://www.zigbee.org`
15. Implementation of OLSR for NS,University of Murcia (Spain),
    `http://masimum.dif.um.es/?Software:UM-OLSR`

QoE Assessment of VoIP in Next Generation Networks

David Rodrigues[1], Eduardo Cerqueira[1,2], and Edmundo Monteiro[1]

[1] University of Coimbra, Department of Informatics Engineering,
3030-290 Coimbra, Portugal
[2] Federal University of Para, Rua Augusto Corra, 01, 66075-110, Belém, Brazil
drod@student.dei.uc.pt, {ecoelho,edmundo}@dei.uc.pt

Abstract. The Voice over Internet Protocol (VoIP) services are currently present in our personal and professional activities and will be key services in Next Generation Networks (NGN). Hence, in order to keep and attract new customers, the quality of delivery for VoIP services needs to be measured and optimized to ensure Quality of Service (QoS) and Quality of Experience (QoE) support to users in future multimedia networking systems. This paper presents the requirements to assess the quality level of VoIP services in NGN and analyzes the limitations of the well-known E-Model and Perceptual Evaluation of Speech Quality (PESQ) metrics for quality evaluation of VoIP services. Additionally, a new QoE metric, named Advanced Model for Perceptual Evaluation of Speech Quality (AdmPESQ), is proposed to overcome the limitations of current proposals concerning packet loss and packet delay awareness and to improve the VoIP assessment process. Performance evaluation was carried out based on simulation experiments to show the benefits of AdmPESQ in assessing the impact of VoIP services on the user's expectation.

Keywords: Quality of Service (QoS), Quality of Experience (QoE), Voice over Internet Protocol (VoIP), E-Model, Perceptual Evaluation of Speech Quality (PESQ).

1 Introduction

Voice over Internet Protocol (VoIP) services are now offered by different service providers and subscribed by a large number of fixed and mobile users in multimedia-aware networking systems. VoIP brings benefits for both service providers and customers. For service providers, operational costs are diminished due to the distribution of different services, such as voice and data, in a networking infrastructure with shared resources. For customers, VoIP presents the features of a traditional Public Switched Telephone Network (PSTN) phone, such as voice mail and conference, in a ubiquitous way as well as with quality level support and fair rates.

The quality level assessment for VoIP services in Next Generation Networks (NGN) with different Quality of Service (QoS) models (e.g., Differentiated Services (DiffServ) and IEEE 802.11e), wireless access technologies (e.g., from cellular to Wide Local Area Networks (WLAN)), mobility controllers (e.g., Mobile

T. Pfeifer and P. Bellavista (Eds.): MMNS 2009, LNCS 5842, pp. 94–105, 2009.

IP (MIP) and Hierarchical MIP (HMIP)) is still a challenging research goal [1]. Due to the real-time behavior of voice services, implementation of different network technologies and human perception characteristics, the quality level control of VoIP services must be performed taking into account both network/packet requirements, such as packet loss, delay tolerances and user-level requirements related with human perception [2], such as noise.

Due to the limitations of traditional QoS solutions regarding voice-awareness and human perception, Quality of Experience (QoE) assessment approaches have been introduced to estimate the quality level of VoIP services from the user point of view, as presented in the Telecommunication Standardization Sector (ITU-T) Recommendation P.800 [3]. In order to assure QoE support for voice services in NGN, VoIP quality assessment methods and metrics are required to estimate/monitor the quality level of services coded with different CODEC and transmitted over wired and wireless heterogeneous networks with links with different packet loss probability and delay. The output of an assessment solution can be used for both costumers, to know the real quality of the subscribed services, and providers, as input for future network management and optimization procedures such as resource reservation, mobility prediction and QoE routing, as well as for pricing schemes.

Most of the current assessment schemes for controlling the quality level of voice content assume random values for transmission parameters, such as packet delay and loss, as well as do not consider the CODEC types during the evaluation process[4], thus reducing their applicability for a controlled and limited number of scenarios. The basic idea behind assessment models in NGN are twofold: which metric must be used to estimate the quality level of VoIP services taking into consideration different CODEC types, loss and delay values, and how to communicate with other network entities and standards to collect and send voice information.

This paper studies QoE assessment schemes for quality evaluation of voice calls. Moreover, it analyzes the limitations of current QoE metrics with focus on two main standards presented in Section 2, E-Model and Perceptual Evaluation of Speech Quality (PESQ), by using both conceptual and simulation evaluation. Following, a new QoE-aware VoIP assessment solution to be used in next generation multimedia systems is proposed and validated in a heterogeneous scenario. The results show correct results for scenarios with different delays and loss rates, which is not provided by current metrics. The proposed scheme helps providers to develop or adapt management mechanisms to improve the quality level of VoIP services, as well as to enhance pricing schemes. Additionally, it allows costumers to know about the quality of the subscribed services.

The remainder of this paper is organized as follows. Section 2 discusses the actual QoE metrics used for VoIP evaluation. Section 3 proposes a new metric that combines the positive aspects of both E-Model and PESQ in order to give a better overall evaluation. Section 4 presents the simulation results and analyzes the Advanced Model for Perceptual Evaluation of Speech Quality (AdmPESQ) improvements. Conclusions and future work are summarized in Section 5.

2   Related Work

This section presents current studies of VoIP assessment schemes with focus on PESQ and E-Model, because they are widely used and well-known standards. A detailed description on VoIP subjective and objective metrics can be found in [2].

Subjective metrics assess how audio calls are perceived by users, where the Mean Opinion Score (MOS) is widely used. These assessment schemes are carried out by participants, who evaluate prerecorded audio signals with different impairments. ITU-T recommends the evaluation of voice taking into account three opinion scales: quality, effort and loudness[3]. Each opinion scale is expressed from 1 (worst result) to 5 (best result).

Objective metrics allow a quality evaluation from the user point of view by using mathematical models. Among several existing metrics, ITU-T introduces two main methods for objective evaluation of VoIP calls, named E-Model and PESQ. The E-Model is based on the concept that impairments which affects voice calls are independent[5]. Five factors are considered: the basic signal-to-noise ratio (Ro), which includes sources of noise such as the environment, the impairments which occur more or less simultaneously with the voice signal (Is), the impairments caused by delay (Id), the impairment introduced by the equipment (Ie_{eff}), such as losses, and the advantage factor (A)[6][7]. The A factor allows the compensation of impairment when there are other advantages of access to the user. Therefore, a conventional wired access has no compensation, while a wireless access in remote areas includes a high A factor. Each parameter is calculated separately and the final result is obtained by Equation 1, where R is the evaluation of the transmission on a scale from 0 (poor quality) to 100 (excellent quality).

$$R = Ro - Is - Id - Ie_{eff} + A \qquad (1)$$

The E-Model result can be mapped into MOS evaluation using Equation 2.

$$\text{MOS(R)} = \begin{cases} 1 & \text{if } R < 0 \\ R(R-60)(100-R)7 \times 10^{-6} + 1 + 0.035R & \text{if } 0 < R < 100 \\ 4.5 & \text{if } R > 100 \end{cases} \qquad (2)$$

Although the E-Model equation contain several variables, the amount of information required for its evaluation is minimal. Because they are essential to the calculation of Id and Ie_{eff}, the delay and packet loss are always necessary. However, the Is and Ro factors have a low variation and default values can be used. Regarding A, which is define by the advantages of access to the user, presents a constant or non-dynamic values. Therefore, the calculation of the R factor can be simplified according to Expression 3.

$$R = 93.2 - Id - Ie_{eff} + A \qquad (3)$$

Based on [6] and [8] recommendations, an extension to E-Model was proposed in [5] in order to include a new concept, called recency effect. The recency effect takes into account the moment (time) when the losses occur, where losses at the end of the call lead to further degradation compared to losses at the beginning of the conversation. However, the proposed solution does not take into consideration human psychological aspects related with the impact of losses on the user and is not suitable for QoE-aware multimedia systems.

Another important metric is called PESQ. PESQ evaluates the QoE of VoIP service by comparing the original and processed signals. This metric can be used in different environments, from analog to digital multimedia networks. PESQ evaluation includes factors of distortion due to channel/encoder, losses and jitter. The effects of delay, echo, loudness loss, sidetone and impairments related to two-way interactions are not reflected in the PESQ scores[9][10]. PESQ presents values from -0.5 (lower value) to 4.5 (higher value), although for most cases the output range will be a listening quality MOS-like score between 1.0 and 4.5. The PESQ score cannot be directly mapped to MOS, but can be approximated to it[11].

The E-Model and PESQ metrics have several drawbacks. On the one hand, the E-Model metric does not take into account packet loss proprieties during the content distribution, as shown by our simulation results in Section 4. On the other hand, the PESQ shows a good accuracy for different losses, but does not take into consideration the packet delay factor along the end-to-end communication path. Both metrics are implemented and evaluated by several proposals to control the quality level of VoIP services in networks[12][13][14]. However, the use of current PESQ and E-Model versions are not suitable for networking environments with variable packet loss and delay values as expected for NGN.

From the related work analysis it is concluded that both E-Model and PESQ metrics have key drawbacks and needs to be improved to operate in real networking systems. Therefore, this paper proposes a new metric for VoIP assessment that combines both E-Model and PESQ aspects as presented in Section 3.

3   Advanced Model for Perceptual Evaluation of Speech Quality (AdmPESQ)

In the face of network resource restrictions, voice delivery through NGN leads to unavoidable quality degradation and a solution to assess how good audio services meet the user's expectation is a key requirement for multimedia systems. The AdmPESQ proposal assesses the quality level of VoIP services along heterogeneous wired and wireless networks by using a new QoE metric for voice calls that extends PESQ and E-Model models.

AdmPESQ is a full reference metrics implemented at end-hosts to produce a final score about the VoIP quality level. Since the AdmPESQ voice assessment results can be used for optimization and mobility schemes, open interfaces are defined to allow a tight communication with existing standards and solutions. The use of interfaces increases the system flexibility and the inclusion (or change) of network control mechanisms or policies. Moreover, an interface with Real-time Control Protocol (RTCP) is used to collect information about the end-to-end delay along heterogeneous communication paths. Other interface with Session Description Protocol (SDP) (transported in Real-time Streaming Protocol (RTP) or Session Initiation Protocol (SIP)) is implemented to acquire information about the VoIP CODEC negotiated during the session establishment process.

As presented before, E-Model and PESQ metrics have several limitations to be used in heterogeneous networks with dynamic packet loss and delay parameters. To overcome the above limitations and to provide an efficient assessment model, AdmPESQ was designed. The proposed solution combines important characteristics of both E-Model and PESQ, namely the impact of delay during the evaluation process used by E-Model, with the impact of packet loss, packet loss concealment, transmission channel errors and jitter used by PESQ.

When all default values are used, the E-Model result is $R = 93.2$. However, the ITU-T Recommendation G.113 [15] suggests different values of Ie and Bpl depending on the CODEC used. Thus, for different codifiers, the E-Model is calculated by:

$$R = 93.2 - Ie_{eff} \qquad (4)$$

Because at this point only the impact of delay will be computed, losses will not be considered ($Ie_{eff} = Ie$) and therefore

$$R = 93.2 - Ie \qquad (5)$$

In order to take into account the delay, the Id must be added:

$$R = 93.2 - Ie - Id \qquad (6)$$

where

$$Id = Idte + Idle + Idd \qquad (7)$$

Since PESQ returns inaccurate values on the existence of echo, and therefore its use is not recommended in these conditions, only the Idd will be taken into account. Thus,

$$R = 93.2 - Ie - Idd \qquad (8)$$

where, for a given one-way delay ta, Idd is calculated by

$$Idd = \begin{cases} 0 & \text{if } ta \le 100 \\ 25((1 + X^6)^{\frac{1}{6}} - 3(1 + (\dfrac{X^6}{3})^{\frac{1}{6}} + 2) & \text{if } ta > 100 \end{cases} \qquad (9)$$

with

$$X = log_2 \frac{ta}{100} \qquad (10)$$

Then the ratio between $MOS(93.2 - Ie - Idd)$ and $MOS(93, 2 - Ie)$ is calculated in order to take into account the impact of delay on the user perspective. Finally,

AdmPESQ measures the overall quality by combining the delay impact and *PESQ* results:

$$AdmPESQ = PESQ\frac{MOS(93.2 - Ie - Idd)}{MOS(93,2 - Ie)} \tag{11}$$

where MOS is defined in Equation 2.

The *A* factor of E-Model is also added to take into account different users' tolerance and improve the AdmPESQ results:

$$AdmPESQ = PESQ\frac{MOS(93.2 - Ie - Idd + A)}{MOS(93,2 - Ie + A)} \tag{12}$$

With AdmPESQ better VoIP quality evaluation results are achieved than with pure E-Model or PESQ schemes (results are presented in Section 4). Only a single metric is needed to perform QoE-based assessment for voice services in NGN. Providers can also use AdmPESQ as a manner to optimize network management operations, detect network impairments and define QoE-based pricing schemes.

4   Performance Evaluation

To analyze the limitations of existing QoE metrics and the benefits of the Adm-PESQ metric in dynamic heterogeneous environments, several simulation experiments were performed using the Network Simulator 2 (NS2)[16] and the VoIP module developed by the Technical University of Berlin[17]. Additionally, bugs were fixed, an intelligent drop mechanism was added and the calculation of E-Model and AdmPESQ was introduced. The DiffServ and IEEE 802.11e QoS models were used to provide QoS assurance in wired and wireless links respectively as expected for NGN.

The topology was generated by Boston University Representative Internet Topology Generator (BRITE)[18]. The simulated scenario is composed by two networks with sixteen routers each. One network hosts the source and another hosts the wireless receiver. The propagation delay is assigned by BRITE according to the distance between each device. The bandwidth capacity of wired and wireless links is of 100 Mb/s and 11 Mb/s, respectively. The source transmits a VoIP flow coded with ITU-T G.729 [19] to a wireless receiver. The network load, loss and delay are randomly changed to simulated the characteristics of different networking scenarios. The default *Ie* and *Bpl* values for ITU-T G.729 codifier are used in accordance with the ITU-T Recommendation G.113.

4.1   End-to-End Delay Variation

The delay is an important parameter in real-time VoIP services and directly affects the quality of service from the user point of view. High delays induce high gaps between interlocutors responses and lead to discontentment. Several sources influence the delay, such as propagation, transmission, queuing and processing delay.

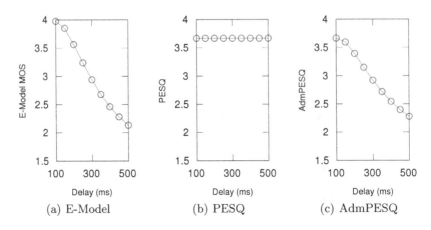

Fig. 1. QoE metrics variation with the increase of the delay

In order to analyze the impact of delay on user side and the performance of E-Model, PESQ and AdmPESQ metrics, several experiments were carried out in a scenario with assured bandwidth in the VoIP class (no loss) and the one-way delay varying. Since the E-Model can provide inaccurate predictions for values exceeding 500 ms, the delay ranges from 100 to 500 ms. Because there is no loss, for smaller values than 100 ms, the assessments are identical to the quality evaluation of 100 ms.

The behavior of E-Model and PESQ for different values of delay can be observed in Figure 1(a) and 1(b), respectively. The E-Model shows a continuous decrease on the VoIP quality level. Regarding PESQ, the values stay unchanged for the different values of delay, because the PESQ metric does not take into account this important parameter during the assessment process. The improvement of AdmPESQ is shown in Figure 1(c) when the delay parameter is considered to define the service quality level. When compared to PESQ, AdmPESQ has similar results for low delays values, but has a difference up to 60% when the delay is 500 ms. Because the impact of the delay on E-Model and AdmPESQ is calculated the same way, their variation are similar.

The variation of the E-Model and AdmPESQ metrics with the delay and the A factor is depicted in Figure 2(a) and 2(b), respectively. The A factor allows assessment models to take into account the tolerance of different users, which varies according to the access scheme used by them. In this context, PESQ performs poorly in dynamic and heterogeneous multimedia systems because it does not assume the existence of packet delay neither the A factor in a network.

4.2   Selective Loss Variation

The packet loss rate is another important metric to assessment models. Some losses are more harmful than others, depending on the time they occur and on the signal proprieties. This is clear in a situation when the interlocutor make

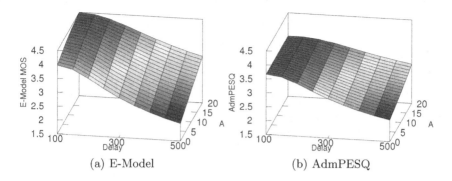

(a) E-Model   (b) AdmPESQ

Fig. 2. QoE metrics variation with the the delay and A

pauses in its speech. For example, if losses occur in periods of silence, they have low impact on the VoIP quality.

To verify the impact of various types of losses on the user experience, three experiments were performed and evaluated with E-Model, PESQ and AdmPESQ. The links have sufficient bandwidth in the VoIP classes in both wired and wireless interfaces and a constant delay of 100 ms was defined. In order to verify the impact of losses in different VoIP packets (packets with content related to silence periods and not) a random packet drop scheme was accomplished.

In the first scenario, a packet has a probability of 70% to be discarded, regardless of its content. In the second scenario, the drop is preferably done in packets that include voice content (no silence), according to Expression 13. Finally, the last scenario performs the drop of packets with silence content, and the probability defined in Expression 14.

$$\text{p(drop packet)} = \begin{cases} 0.9 & \text{if voice packet} \\ 0.1 & \text{if silence packet} \end{cases} \tag{13}$$

$$\text{p(drop packet)} = \begin{cases} 0.1 & \text{if voice packet} \\ 0.9 & \text{if silence packet} \end{cases} \tag{14}$$

Figure 3(a) illustrates the E-Model scores according to the number of losses occurred in the three different scenarios. The MOS calculated by the E-Model is directly influenced by losses, but the distinction between the various losses is not realized. Therefore, for each loss value, the E-Model only varies due to the different mean delays and fails in predicting the VoIP quality level in real networking environments.

As presented in Figure 3(b), PESQ performs well in scenarios with different type of packets dropped, because it uses a comparison between the sent and received voice signals. Regarding the scenario where the drop of packets containing silence is analyzed, the quality evaluation assessed by PESQ shows approximatively the same results through the different loss rates. The scenario where the loss probability is high in period of speeches shows the worst results. Finally, the

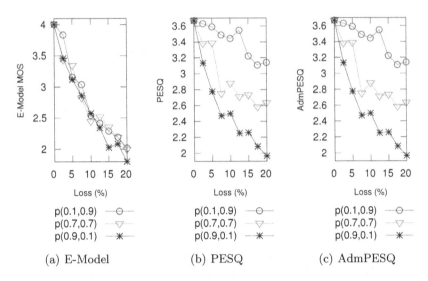

(a) E-Model   (b) PESQ   (c) AdmPESQ

Fig. 3. QoE metrics behavior for different values of losses and scenarios with different probability of discarding packets p(x, y), where x and y represent the discard probability of a packet containing voice and silence, respectively

scenario where the discard is realized totally randomly presents the intermediate values. AdmPESQ shows similar results compared to PESQ, as depicted in Figure 3(c). The AdmPESQ scores presents a significant difference relatively to E-Model when the discard focuses packets containing silence, presenting a more accurate assessment.

4.3   Load Variation

To verify the impact of the load variation on each QoE metric, several experiments were carried out with a fixed end-to-end delay of 150 ms and different loads causing a congestion up to 140% in the VoIP class in both wired and wireless links. With increasing of background traffic in a class, the number of packets present in queues also raises. This factor causes higher delays and jitters in VoIP services as shown in Figures 4(a) and 4(b), respectively. When the load is too high, the maximum number of packet in queues is exceeded, and some packets are discarded, as illustrated in Figure 4(c). Therefore a metric which combines both E-Model for delay and PESQ for loss performs better as presented by AdmPESQ.

Figure 5 depicts the behavior of E-Model, PESQ and AdmPESQ in the load variation scenario. For the increasing values of load, the E-Model shows a constant decrease in quality estimation process. This behavior is due to its mathematical model, which is focused on two metrics: the delay and loss. Since both metrics decrease, the E-Model also decrease steadily. However, the results can be incorrect because different types of packets are discarded. Regarding PESQ,

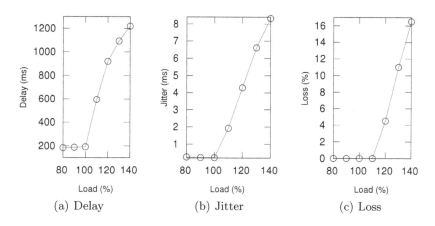

Fig. 4. QoS metrics variation with the load increase

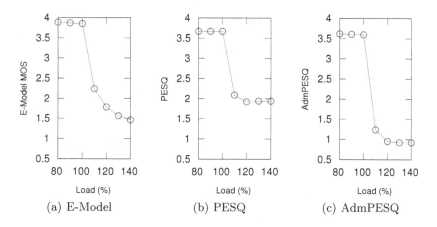

Fig. 5. QoE metrics variation with the load increase

the decline of its values is not linear. This because PESQ takes into account several factors of the audio signal. However, because it does not take into account the delay, it fails in predicting the overall VoIP quality level. Finally, AdmPESQ presents more accurate results than E-Model and PESQ, due to the combination of both metrics. When compared to PESQ, AdmPESQ has an accuracy up to 45% when the load is higher than 120%.

5   Conclusion

This paper analyzed the main limitations of well-known VoIP assessment metrics, namely E-Model and PESQ. In addition, a new metric, called AdmPESQ, was proposed to be used in NGN, where communication paths can have different packet loss and delay parameters. AdmPESQ combines the main attributes of E-Model and PESQ in a single metric, reducing the system complexity and optimizing the assessment process in hetereogeneous scenarios. The proposed solution can also be used for providers to adapt or develop new network resource and mobility controllers. Furthermore, simulation results demonstrate that AdmPESQ presents accurate results compared with E-Model and PESQ.

Future works will evaluate AdmPESQ in an experimental network and subjective QoE tests based on ITU-T recommendation will be performed to verify the efficiency of the proposed solution with real users.

Acknowledgment

The work presented in this paper is supported by the European Commission, under the Grant No. FP6-0384239 (Network of Excellence CONTENT).

References

1. Uemura, S., Fukumoto, N., Yamada, H., Nakamura, H.: QoS/QoE measurement system implemented on cellular phone for NGN. In: 5th IEEE Consumer Communications and Networking Conference, 2008. CCNC 2008, Las Vegas, NV, pp. 117–121 (2008)
2. Guguin, M., Le Bouquin-Jeanns, R., Gautier-Turbin, V., Faucon, G., Barriac, V.: On the evaluation of the conversational speech quality in telecommunications. EURASIP J. Adv. Signal Process 8(2), 1–15 (2008)
3. ITU-T p.800.1 : Mean opinion score (MOS) terminology (July 2006)
4. Sengupta, S., Chatterjee, M., Ganguly, S.: Improving quality of VoIP streams over WiMax. IEEE Transactions on Computers 57(2), 145–156 (2008)
5. Carvalho, L., Mota, E., Aguiar, R., Lima, A.F., de Souza, J.N.: An e-model implementation for speech quality evaluation in VoIP systems. In: Computers and Communications, 2005. ISCC 2005. Proceedings. 10th IEEE Symposium on, June 2005, pp. 933–938 (2005)
6. ITU-T g.107 : The e-model: a computational model for use in transmission planning (March 2005)
7. Bandung, Y., Machbub, C., Langi, A.Z.R., Supangkat, S.H.: Optimizing voice over internet protocol (VoIP) networks based-on extended e-model. In: IEEE Conference on Cybernetics and Intelligent Systems, Chengdu, China, September 2008, pp. 801–805 (2008)
8. Clark, A.D.: Modeling the effects of burst packet loss and recency on subjective voice quality. In: IP telephony Workshop, New York, NY, USA, April 2001, pp. 123–127 (2001)
9. ITU-T p.862 : Perceptual evaluation of speech quality (PESQ): an objective method for end-to-end speech quality assessment of narrow-band telephone networks and speech codecs (February 2001)
10. Rix, A.W., Beerends, J.G., Hollier, M.P., Hekstra, A.P.: Perceptual evaluation of speech quality (PESQ)-a new method for speech quality assessment of telephone networks and codecs. In: 2001 IEEE International Conference on Acoustics, Speech, and Signal Processing, 2001. Proceedings (ICASSP 2001), Salt Lake City, UT, May 2001, vol. 2, pp. 749–752 (2001)

11. Liang, H.M., Ke, C.H., Shieh, C.K., Hwang, W.S., Chilamkurti, N.K.: Performance evaluation of 802.11e EDCF in the ad-hoc mode with real audio/video traffic. In: 2006 IFIP International Conference on Wireless and Optical Communications Networks (April 2006)
12. Baratvand, M., Tabandeh, M., Behboodi, A., Ahmadi, A.F.: Jitter-Buffer management for VoIP over wireless LAN in a limited resource device. In: Fourth International Conference on Networking and Services, 2008 (ICNS 2008), Gosier, March 2008, pp. 90–95 (2008)
13. Peh, E.W.C., Seah, W.K.G., Chew, Y.H., Ge, Y.: Experimental study of voice over IP services over broadband wireless networks. In: 22nd International Conference on Advanced Information Networking and Applications, AINA 2008, Okinawa, March 2008, pp. 834–839 (2008)
14. Qiao, Z., Sun, L., Ifeachor, E.: Case study of PESQ performance in live wireless mobile VoIP environment. In: IEEE 19th International Symposium on Personal, Indoor and Mobile Radio Communications, PIMRC 2008, Cannes, September 2008, pp. 1–6 (2008)
15. ITU-T g.113 : Transmission impairments due to speech processing (November 2007)
16. The network simulator - ns-2 (May 2009), http://www.isi.edu/nsnam/ns/
17. Predicting the perceptual service quality using a trace of VoIP packets (May 2009), http://www.tkn.tu-berlin.de/research/qofis/
18. BRITE: boston university representative internet topology generator (May 2009), http://www.cs.bu.edu/brite/
19. ITU-T g.729 : Coding of speech at 8 kbit/s using conjugate-structure algebraic-code-excited linear prediction, CS-ACELP (2007)

NIDA: A Parametric Vocal Quality Assessment Algorithm over Transient Connections

Sofiene Jelassi[1,3], Habib Youssef[1], Lingfen Sun[2], and Guy Pujolle[3]

[1] Research Unit PRINCE, ISITCom, Hammam Sousse, Tunisia
[2] School of Computing, Communications and Electronics, University of Plymouth, UK
[3] Laboratory of Computer Science (LIP6), University of Pierre and Marie Curie, Paris, France
Sofiene.Jelassi@infcom.rnu.tn, habib.youssef@rnu.fsm.tn,
l.sun@plymouth.ac.uk, Guy.Pujolle@lip6.fr

Abstract. This paper presents NIDA, a Non-Intrusive Disconnection-aware vocal quality assessment Algorithm. NIDA accurately estimates vocal perceived quality over wireless data networks by discriminating the perceptual effect of a single random packet loss, 2-4 consecutive packet losses (burst) stemming from contentions, and discontinuity entailed by transient loss of connectivity. NIDA properly accounts for transient loss of connectivity experienced by mobile users over wireless data networks, stemming from vertical and horizontal handovers, or when users roam out of the coverage area of the associated infrastructure. To this end, a novel lossy wireless data channel model has been conceived based on a continuous-time Markov model. The channel model is calibrated at run-time based on a set of measurements gathered at packet layer using the header content of received voice packets. The perceived quality under each state is properly quantified, then combined in order to predict quality degradation due to wireless data channel features. Performance evaluation study shows that quality degradation ratings calculated using NIDA strongly correlate with quality degradation ratings calculated based on ITU-T PESQ intrusive algorithm, which mimics tightly subjective human rating behavior.

Keywords: Perceptual voice quality, Transient wireless connections, E-model.

1 Introduction

In recent years, Voice over IP networks, denoted as VoIP, becomes a popular service. Since its inception, huge strides have been made. Currently, VoIP has an increasing widespread popularity and used as alternative to traditional telephony in homes and enterprises. Unlike circuit-switched telephone networks, ordinary IP networks cater to applications a best effort service resulting in packet loss and variable network delay. These features significantly harm perceived quality of delay-sensitive service such as VoIP. These sources of disturbance negatively influence the perceptual quality in two ways, intelligibility of the speech sequence and interactivity. There are several ways to improve perceived quality over ordinary IP networks. Basically, the quality metric indicators can be improved in network- or application- centric ways. Network-centric approaches improve service quality by adequately upgrading core nodes to accommodate

T. Pfeifer and P. Bellavista (Eds.): MMNS 2009, LNCS 5842, pp. 106–117, 2009.

features of delay-sensitive services such as service differentiation and resource reservation [1]. In contrast, application-layer approaches improve service quality through an intelligent control of delivered media at sender and receiver sides [1]. It is highly desirable to evaluate the suitability of developed QoS mechanisms at users' level. Measuring accurately the perceptual vocal quality is pivotal from operators as well as customers' perspectives. In fact, perceptual quality can be used to rate service providers. Moreover, telecom operators can use assessment algorithms for management, maintenance, monitoring, planning, and diagnosis operations. On the other hand, subscribers can use perceived quality to select adequate access network under a given circumstance. Indeed, services over next-generation networks will likely be offered to users using a multitude of overlapping networks and terminals. In such a case, subscribers can select the configuration that responds to their preferences.

The assessment of voice quality at the user level can be performed subjectively or objectively. Subjective-based approaches derive the vocal quality using a set of human subjects which vote perceived quality under a given situation [2]. The vocal quality assessment is performed using a dedicated scale. The ITU has defined a standard subjective metric called the Mean Opinion Score (MOS) to quantify listing quality under ACR (Absolute Category Rating) subjective tests [2]. MOS scores vary from 1 (bad quality) to 5 (excellent quality). Certainly, subjective approaches are unable to rate at run-time the perceptual quality of live vocal conversations which confine their utility to a limited range of applications. Moreover, subjective approaches are time consuming, cumbersome, and expensive.

Rather than using human subjects to rate vocal quality, objective-based approaches estimate perceived quality using machine-executable algorithms running either on end- or mid- nodes [3]. There are several assessment algorithms reported in the literature which can be classed as *signal layer black box* and *parametric model glass box* categories [3]. Signal layer black box algorithms estimate the perceived quality by properly processing speech signals without knowledge of the underlying transport network and terminals features. In contrast, parametric model glass box algorithms require full characterisation of transport network and terminals to estimate perceived quality. Technically, parametric assessment algorithms are more attractive, especially over packet-based networks, due to their reduced complexity and their suitability to manage and monitor live packetized vocal service. This is made without acceding to speech sequences which is desirable for security reasons. However, parametric assessment algorithms are relatively less accurate than signal layer black box assessment algorithms.

In order to accurately estimate perceived quality based on parametric model paradigm, there is a need of rigorously defining appropriate input metrics, models, and combination rules. The ITU-T has standardized a parametric model-based assessment algorithm, called E-Model, which requires full characterization of underlying system (network and terminals) to estimate/predict perceived quality [4]. Suitable parameters, models, and combination rules have been defined and calibrated based on extensive conducted subjective experiences. ITU-T E-Model has been initially developed to evaluate perceived quality over wired Telecom networks. Since then, several revisions have been made by academics and industrials in order to increase its accuracy over a wide range of networks, especially over packet-based and wireless networks [4].

The main goal of this work is to properly build adequate objective models which are able to model and quantify the distortions encountered by VoIP-interlocutors over shared wireless data links. Besides traditional impairments incurred by users over packet-based networks, VoIP-customers over wireless data networks experience transient loss of connectivity stemming from either vertical or horizontal handovers, or when mobile users roam out of the coverage area of the associated network. It is well-recognized that such a disturbing event should be properly accounted for in the computation of perceived quality [5]. To properly include transient losses of connectivity in the vocal quality estimate, a novel lossy wireless channel model has been conceived based on a continuous-time Markov model. The conceived model incorporates three states which stand for a single random loss, 2-4 consecutive packet losses (a burst), and discontinuity. The channel model is calibrated at run-time using a set of network measurements gathered at packet layer. The perceived quality at the end of each assessment period is calculated through the combination of perceived quality in each state. To improve accuracy, the temporal location of transient loss of connectivity within an assessment period is considered in the calculation of the overall perceived quality. Performance evaluation study shows that our perceptual vocal quality algorithm, NIDA, produces well-correlated scores with ITU-T PESQ intrusive algorithm. Note here that conducting formal subjective MOS tests on a large scale is beyond any reasonable allocated time and budget. The ITU-T PESQ full-reference vocal assessment algorithm models accurately the subjective human rating behavior [3].

The remainder of this paper is organized as follows. Section 2 describes the principles of parametric models. Section 3 presents the novel wireless data channel model used to account for the different types of loss-related disturbances. In Section 4, we present how perceived quality is calculated under each state and how the overall perceived quality is produced. In Section 5, we compare the performance of NIDA against the ITU-T PESQ intrusive algorithm. We conclude in Section 6.

2 Principle of Parametric Perceptual Models

Parametric model glass box assessment algorithms estimate subjective speech quality using a set of input parameters gathered from the network and edge-devices. As illustrated in Figure 1, input parameters can be transformed to increase their correlation with subjective scores. Then, a combination rule, called also perceptual model, is used to estimate the Speech Quality Measure (SQM) metric, e.g., MOS.

As we can deduce, selection of pertinent input parameters, transformations, and perceptual models should be performed off-line. To this end, dedicated assessment frameworks for vocal quality modeling should be set-up. As illustrated in Figure 2, a

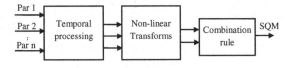

Fig. 1. Principle of parametric SQM, input parameters, and basic processing steps

large set of speech samples are processed by a system under test to produce degraded speech sequences under a given circumstance. The corresponding parameters for full system characterisation are properly recorded. The degraded speech sequences are evaluated either by human subjects or a signal layer assessment algorithm, which is deemed sufficiently accurate to mimic human behavior rating such as ITU-T PESQ. The system under test can be either a simulated or emulated voice transport system or an experimental test-bed.

Pertinent input parameters for full system characterization such as mean packet loss rate, loss pattern, delay, delay jitter, echo, side-tone, coding, packet loss concealment, and noises are closely dependent on the delivering systems and used terminals. In this work, we study packet-based vocal conversation over infrastructure-based shared wireless data networks such as IEEE 802.11, WiMAX, and Wi-Fi. The relevant sources of disturbance observed over data networks are packet loss, delay, and delay jitter. Moreover, over wireless networks, moving interlocutors encounter vertical and horizontal handovers, which are made to improve service quality and to assure service ubiquity.

In the context of ITU-T E-Model methodology, the effect of delay impairment factor (I_d) on perceptual quality, which influences interlocutors' interactivity, has been rigorously modeled in the literature [6]. In contrast, the effect of equipment impairment factor (I_e) on perceptual quality, which influences speech intelligibility, remains unsatisfactory under several situations [7]. This is due to the diversity of disturbing sources which include, among others, packet loss, de-jittering buffer management, coding switching, tandem configuration, and handovers. Moreover, rapid evolution of access and core networks as well as terminals entails complication in the development of accurate perceptual models. That is why I_e models need to be re-configurable and flexible as much as possible.

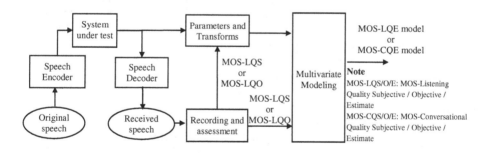

Fig. 2. Vocal assessment framework for non-intrusive quality modeling

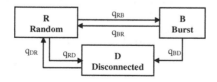

Fig. 3. Markov process model of packet losses over a wireless data channel

The main contribution of this work is the proposal of an adequate objective model that estimates the equipment impairment factor over a shared wireless data link. We are unaware of any similar work in the literature which targets the same goal.

3 Loss Modeling over Wireless Data Networks

It is well-recognized that packet loss behavior over cabled IP networks is bursty. That is why, a 2-state Markov model has been widely used in the literature in order to model and analyze packet losses over wide area IP networks [8]. The bursty loss behavior stems mainly from network congestion which still happens over shared wireless data networks. However, during certain periods of time, packet-based mobile receiver will likely incur random packet losses due to signal-related problems such as fading and interferences. In fact, in such a circumstance, link layer protocol attempts to recover lost voice packets through retransmissions which will entail additional transmission delays. In such a case, delayed voice packets will likely be ignored by the play-out process because they reach the receiver side after their playout instants. Moreover, mobile receiver incurs, during certain periods of time, transient losses of connectivity during handovers or when users roam out of coverage area of associated access point. It is important here to highlight the perceptual difference between a packet burst loss which lasts typically for 2-4 voice packets and disconnection which means that users will clearly hear a discontinuity in the rendered stream. In fact, a burst of 2-4 voice packets can be efficiently recovered by modern CODECs and users hearing brain [3].

To precisely account for wireless data networks behavior from users' perspective, we propose to model a wireless channel using a continuous-time Markov process (see Figure 3). The modeled stochastic process takes its values from the following 3-dimension state space: R (for random), B (for burst), and D (for disconnected). When in state R, packet losses are generated randomly according to a Bernoulli distribution. This behavior guaranties that packet losses occur in uncorrelated way for a given PLR (Packet Loss Ratio). However, when in state B, packet losses are generated in burst according to the traditional Gilbert/Elliot model [9]. The burstiness of packet losses is controlled using the ULP (Unconditional Loss Probability) and CLP (Conditional Loss Probability). When at state D, all sent packets are lost. q_{IJ}, where I and J $\in$ {R, B, D}, represents the transition rate from state I to J.

As illustrated in Figure 3, after a residence period in state B, the process will enter state R with probability $q_{BD}/(q_{BR} + q_{BD})$ and state D with probability $q_{BR}/(q_{BR} + q_{BD})$. The residence periods in states R, B, and D follow an exponential distribution with mean values equal to T_R, T_B, and T_D respectively. The mean residence time in each state can be computed as follows:

$$T_R = 1/(q_{RB} + q_{RD}) \qquad T_B = 1/(q_{BD} + q_{BR}) \qquad T_D = 1/q_{DR} \qquad (1)$$

4 Parametric Perceptual Models over Shared Wireless Data Channel

The main goal of parametric single-ended perceptual models consists of providing timely feedbacks about perceived quality at run-time of a live vocal session. The estimated perceived quality is included in QoS reports sent periodically to the sender or the policy enforcer nodes. For the sake of monitoring, the recommended assessment window lasts between 8 and 20 seconds [6]. The VoIP receiver gathers suitable measurements which can be transformed then combined to estimate perceived quality.

In order to develop suitable parametric perceptual quality estimate models, the modeling framework depicted in Figure 2 should be set-up. In our case, the impairments introduced by the system under test are rigorously modeled as in Figure 3. The level of introduced impairments can be finely calibrated according to the mean residence time and loss parameters in each state. In order to avoid useless extensive experiments which have been already made in the literature, we propose the following strategy:

- In states R, B and D, we use perceptual speech quality estimate models available in the literature.
- Perceived qualities under each state are meticulously combined to produce overall perceived quality at the end of an assessment period.

Surely, when perceptual models under R or B state are unavailable, the modeling framework described in Figure 3 can be used to develop such quality estimate models. In order to clearly illustrate our methodology, we give as guideline how to develop a perceptual model of ITU-T G.729 speech CODEC over wireless data channel. The G.729 CODEC is recommended over a wide range of configurations, especially over reduced capacity and lossy wireless channel [9, 10]. From [6], it has been shown that the equipment factor under random packet loss, I_{e-R}, is given by:

$$I_{e-R}(G.729, plr) = 11 + 40 \times \ln(1 + 10 \times plr) \tag{2}$$

where, plr represents the mean packet loss ratio encountered by the receiver during a random loss period. Note that (2) includes disturbances due to G.729 speech CODEC and mean packet loss ratio. In fact, distortion stemming from coding scheme can be obtained for a packet loss ratio set to 0, which is equal to 11 for G.729.

When in burst loss state, we use perceptual models presented in [11]. Authors indentify loss pattern and degree of burstiness by recording inter-loss gaps preceding loss bursts, in a series of (gap, burst) pairs [11]. The perceptual effect of each single pair is estimated using a perceptual model which accepts as input the gap and burst lengths expressed in packets. The perceived quality at the end of an assessment interval is derived through a weighted aggregation of produced scores. Specifically, authors show that the following expression accurately estimates speech quality:

$$MOS_B(\{gap_i, burst_i\}/1 \le i \le P) = \frac{\sum_{i=1}^{P}(gap_i/10) \times MOS_i(gap_i, burst_i)}{\sum_{i=1}^{P}(gap_i/10)} \tag{3}$$

where, gap_i and $burst_i$ are, respectively, the length of inter-loss and loss durations of ith (gap, burst) pair, MOS_i is the "base" quality model used for i^{th} (gap, burst) pair, and P represents the number of (gap, burst) pairs observed in burst state. Once MOS_B score is estimated, the equipment impairment factor under burst loss, I_{e-B}, can be calculated as follows:

$$I_{e-B}(G.729) = 93.2 - MOS2R(MOS_B(\{gap_i, burst_i\})) \tag{4}$$

where, MOS2R refers to the function which allows converting a quality score from the MOS domain to the rating factor domain [6, 8, 9]. The transient loss of connectivity significantly impairs the quality of users' experience. In fact, loss of connectivity entails service discontinuity which greatly degrades perceptual quality. In fact, beyond a certain threshold, such a temporary discontinuity will lead to the abrupt hang-up of voice sessions. Basically, service interruptions are entailed by horizontal (intra-) and vertical (inter-) network handovers. Typically, the procedure "make-before-break" is used during handovers for delay-sensitive services which reduces significantly the latency to change associated access point (AP). However, handover delay can be dependent on the actual cell load, AP search procedure, and authentication mechanism. Moreover, handover between Inter-network domains needs looking after IP address which could increase handover latency [12].

In [13], A. F. Duran et al. studied the effect of handover over wireless data networks on perceived quality. Important results are presented in the curve plotted in Figure 4a which shows the equipment distortion factor as a function of handover duration. In order to quantify the effect of handover on perceived quality at run-time, we build the following quality estimate model based on a logarithmic regression process applied on the set of obtained subjective scores:

$$I_{e-D}(G.729, T_D) = (6.1913 \times \ln(T_D) - 8.6216) \times L \tag{5}$$

where, T_D represents the handover/disconnection duration. The quality estimate model achieves a square correlation factor equal to 0.98. Note that discontinuity is only considered during active periods, where it influences perceived quality unlike silence periods. The coefficient L is a weighting factor used to account for handover location. In fact, earlier studies have shown that pertinent disturbing events occurring close to the end of a voice conversation disrupt more negatively users' experience [14]. According to a set of extensive subjective experiences made by France Telecom, we assign to L the value of 1, 0.9, and 0.78 when a handover occurs, respectively, at the end, middle, and beginning of an assessment period [14].

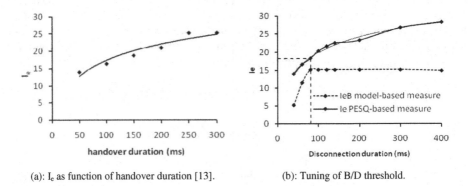

(a): I_e as function of handover duration [13].   (b): Tuning of B/D threshold.

Fig. 4. Discrimiation between effect of 2-4 packet loss and handover duration for G.729B speech CODEC

In Figure 4b, we plot speech quality as a function of disconnection duration introduced in the middle of a set of examined sequences. The speech quality is measured based on ITU-PESQ algorithm and predicted based on I_{e-B} model proposed in [11] using the framework depicted in Figure 2. These curves show clearly that I_{e-B} model is unable to accurately estimate the perceptual effect of disconnection. As we can see, the obtained results are well-correlated with subjective trials performed in [13]. Further details regarding empirical trials will be given later in the evaluation section. We experimented with several expressions to quantify the overall service quality degradation over wireless data channels at the end of a speech assessment period. Based on preliminary experimental results, the following model has been selected:

$$I_e(av) = \alpha_0 + \alpha_1 W + \alpha_2 W^2 \qquad \text{where} \qquad W = \frac{T_R \times I_{e-R} + T_B \times I_{e-B} + T_D \times I_{e-D}}{T_R + T_B + T_D} \qquad (6)$$

where, W corresponds to the experienced average equipment factor over time, and α_0, α_1, and α_2 are fitting coefficients obtained using polynomial regression. A series of equipment values are produced during a vocal conversation, which are averaged over time to quantify perceived quality at the end of service using ITU-T E-Model as follows [8]:

$$R = 93.2 - I_{e-weighted}(av) - I_{d-weighted} \qquad (7)$$

where, R is the rating factor varying between 0 (worst quality) and 100 (excellent quality), $I_{e-weighted}$ and $I_{d-weighted}$ represent, respectively, the weighted average over time of distortions due to equipment and delay. According to empirical subjective experiences, the mean of instantaneous perceived quality correlates well with subjective opinion scores given by humans at the end of a voice conversation [14].

5 Architecture of the Vocal Quality Assessment NIDA

As mentioned earlier, the developed vocal assessment tool is intended to evaluate voice service over transient connections at run-time of live voice conversations. This is performed by examining the header content of each received packet. As illustrated in Figure 5, our assessment approach, NIDA, examines received packets before and after de-jittering buffer. This allows, on the one hand, accounting for ignored packets at the de-jitter buffer, and on the other hand, reliably identifying channel connection state which is determined using a passive connectivity detector.

The packet loss process is only accounted for when communicating terminals are connected (see Figure 5). In such a case, the assessment voice algorithm classifies eventual lost packets under burst or random states as follows. If several successive voice packets are lost, then missing segments are accounted for in burst state. In such a case, NIDA updates the series of (gap, burst) pairs (see Figure 5). The value of gap corresponds to the number of consecutive played voice packets between last and current loss instances. The value of burst corresponds to the number of consecutive lost packets of the current loss instance. Note that gap and burst values are calculated according to the sequence numbers of examined packets. If a single packet loss happens, then NIDA checks the number of played packets before the loss occurrence.

Then, it classes the loss as random if the gap is greater than g_{min}, otherwise, it is classed as burst. This is made to consider frequent and temporally-close loss instances as burst loss. In random loss state, the mean packet loss rate and random period duration are updated.

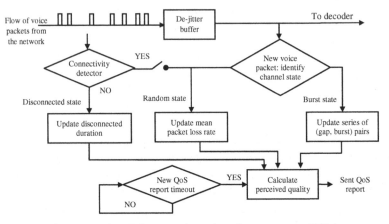

Fig. 5. Functional diagram of vocal quality assessment NIDA

The connectivity detector probes passively received voice packets in order to reliably identify channel connection state. The connectivity detector checks the sequence number of each in-sequence received packet. Indeed, out-of-order packets are seldom observed over infrastructure-based networks and can stem mainly from route switching. In contrast to play-out process, late voice packets are considered by connection detector process. In reality, delay can stem from congestion or reduced data rate switching when wireless interfaces enable multi-rate functionality. The temporary loss of connectivity is decided based on an empiric selected handover threshold. Specifically, we handle a loss instance in disconnection state when the loss duration is greater than 100 ms which corresponds to five 20-ms successive voice packets. Loss durations less than 80 ms are accounted for in burst state.

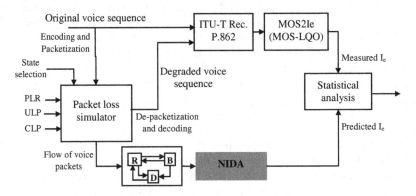

Fig. 6. Evaluation framework of NIDA

In order to detect the temporal location of a disconnected period in an assessment period, the lower and upper timestamp bounds of disconnected periods are recorded. In reality, it is likely to observe at most one disconnection instance during an assessment period, given the coverage range and human walking speed.

6 Calibration and Validation of NIDA

A set of emprical trials have been conducted in order to calibrate and validate the suitibility of NIDA to evaluate voice conversations over transient connections. To do that, we have developed the quality framework depicted in Figure 6. Actually, packet losses are generated according to channel model presented in Figure 3. The pertinent parameters of conceived packet loss model are the mean sojourn duration in each state which follows an exponential distribution. Moreover, the loss process parameters in random and burst states are given by users. The disturbance stemming from packet loss is measured based on the intrusive signal layer ITU-T PESQ algorithm. On the other hand, the flow of voice packets is examined by NIDA to predict perceived quality. In order to evaluate the accuracy of NIDA, the measured and predicted disturbances are statistically analysed in term of their degree of correlation and the Root Mean-Squared Error (RMSE).

The first series of trials aim at fine-tuning the parameter g_{min} used by NIDA to discriminate between random and bursty loss periods. This is done by introducing periodically single packet loss events to sixteen speech sequences spoken by eight male and eight female English speakers, taken from ITU-T P.Sup23 dataset. The inter-loss gap, g_{min}, was varied from 3 to 100 20-ms voice packets. The disturbance is measured using I_{e-R} speech quality model given in Equation (2). Figure 7a illustrates that a decrease of g_{min}, which induces an increase of burstiness, entails a reduction of the I_{e-R} model accuracy. This observation is somehow expected since the used model is only able to quantify the effect of random loss. According to our empirical measurements shown in Figure 7a, we set the value of g_{min} to sixteen 20ms-voice packets (320ms).

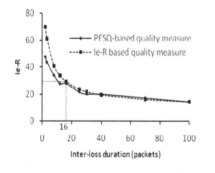
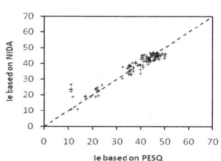

(a): Tuning of g_{min} value.   (b): Scatter-plot of I_e calculated based on PESQ and NIDA.

Fig. 7. Calibration and validation of NIDA

The second series of empirical trials is done to develop/calibrate and validate NIDA. The calibration is performed using the previous dataset, where speech sequences are distorted according to parameters summarized in Table 1. The validation dataset contains eight standard ITU-T 8s-speech samples, not used in the training dataset, spoken by four male and female English speakers. The mean duration of Random and Burst periods are set to 2 sec.

Table 1. Experienced empirical trials to calibrate and validate NIDA

State	Loss parameter	Level		Cardinality
		Modeling	Validation	
Random	$ULP_R^{(1)}$	0.02	0.03	1
Burst	$ULP_B^{(2)}$	0.15; 0.25	0.10; 0.20	2
	$CLP^{(3)}$	0.20; 0.50; 0.90	0.30; 0.60; 0.95	3
Disconnected	Mean (ms)	150; 250	120; 200	2
Total number of *scenarios*		($1{\times}2{\times}3{\times}2){\times}2$		24
Speech material		*Training dataset*	*Validation dataset*	
		8 females, 8 males	4 females, 4 females	
Number of measurements		192	96	288

[(1)] ULP_R: Unconditional Loss Probability in random state
[(2)] ULP_B: Unconditional Loss Probability in burst state
[(3)] CLP: Conditional Loss Probability in burst state

The results produced by the training dataset are used to derive fitting coefficients of the combination rule defined in (6). This statistical analysis indicates that the suitable fitting values are the following: $\alpha_0 = -17.017$, $\alpha_1 = 2.197$ and $\alpha_2 = -0.02$. The obtained model is used to predict equipment impairment factor of the validation dataset using NIDA (see Table 1). Figure 7b represents a scatter-plot showing the relationship between I_e values measured using ITU-T PESQ and predicted using NIDA for the validation dataset. This plot shows strong correlation between NIDA estimates and PESQ-based intrusive scores. Indeed, we found a correlation factor equal to 0.95 coupled with a Root Mean Square Error of 0.07. Finally, we note the presence of some outliers which deviate from the angle 45°. This deviation is located at loss region characterized by small and random loss behavior. In such a case, the effect of coding, which deviates from one sample to another according to the speech content, significantly influences the overall measured disturbance. Overall, NIDA exhibited excellent accuracy in evaluating, on a per-call basis, voice sequences with bursty losses and transient disconnections.

7 Conclusion and Future Work

This paper introduced NIDA, a Non-Intrusive Disconnection Aware vocal assessment algorithm. NIDA is intended to evaluate vocal quality over channels characterized by a transient loss of connectivity. To do that, a novel data channel model has been conceived based on a 3-state continuous-time Markov process. The perceived quality is quantified at run-time in each state, then properly combined at the end of an assessment period. NIDA discriminates between burst and disconnected periods in the calculation of perceived quality. Evaluation study showed that predicted measures produced by

NIDA strongly correlate with ratings given by ITU-T PESQ (R = 0.95). As such, the work has extended the current E-model for voice over wireless applications with a consideration of possible voice discontinuity during handover. As future work, we plan to model and evaluate more precisely the effect of large transient disconnection periods on perceptual quality. Moreover, we envisage increasing the accuracy of NIDA by including voicing features of handled voice frames.

References

1. Melvin, H.: The use of synchronized time in voice over Internet Protocol (VoIP) applications. Ph.D. Thesis, University College Dublin, Ireland (2004)
2. ITU-T Recommendation P.800: Methods for Subjective Determination of Transmission Quality (1996)
3. Rix, A., Beerends, J., Kim, D., Kroon, P., Ghitza, O.: Objective assessment of speech and audio quality: Technology and Applications. IEEE Transactions on Audio, Speech, and Language Processing 14(6), 1890–1901 (2006)
4. ITU-T Recommendation G.107: The E-Model a Computational Model for Use in Transmission Planning (2005)
5. Mobisense project: User Perception of Mobility in NGN. In: Proceeding of DTAG Workshop QoS and QoE monitoring, Berlin, Germany (2007)
6. Cole, R.G., Rosenbluth, J.H.: Voice over IP Performance Monitoring. Computer Communication Review, ACM Sigcomm 31(2) (2001)
7. Takahashi, A., Yoshino, H., Kitawaki, N.: Perceptual QoS assessment technologies for VoIP. IEEE Communication Magazine 42(7), 28–34 (2004)
8. Carvalho, L., Mota, E., Aguiar, R., Lima, A.F., de Souza, J.N.: An E-model implementation for speech quality evaluation in VoIP systems. In: Proceedings of ISCC 2005 (2005)
9. Hoene, C.: Internet telephony over wireless links, PhD thesis, Technical University of Berlin, Germany (2005)
10. ITU-T Recommendation G.729: Coding of speech at 8 kbit/s using conjugate-structure algebraic-code-excited linear prediction, CS-ACELP (2007)
11. Roychoudhuri, L., Al-Shaer, E., Settimi, R.: Statistical Measurement Approach for On-line Audio Quality Assessment. In: Proceedings of Passive and Active Measurement, PAM 2006 (2006)
12. Lakas, A., Boulmalf, M.: Study of the Effect of Mobility Handover on VoIP over WLAN. In: Proceedings of 3rd International Conference on Innovations on Information Technology, Dubai, UAE (2006)
13. Duran, A.F., Pliego, E.C., Alonso, J.I.: Effects of handover on Voice quality in wireless convergent networks. In: Proceeding of IEEE Radio and Wireless Symposium 2007, Long Beach, California, USA (2007)
14. France Telecom: Study the relationship between instantaneous and overall subjective speech quality for time-varying speech sequence: influence of a recency effect. ITU Study Group 12, Contribution D.139 (2000)

Voice2Web: Architecture for Managing Voice-Application Access to Web Resources

Jan Rudinsky[1], Tomas Mikula[1,2], Lukas Kencl[1], Jakub Dolezal[1], and Xavier Garcia[1,3]

[1] R&D Centre for Mobile Applications (RDC), Czech Technical University in Prague
Technicka 2, 166 27 Prague 6, Czech Republic
{rudinsj,kencl,dolezj8}@fel.cvut.cz
[2] Faculty of Mathematics and Physics, Charles University in Prague
Ke Karlovu 3, 121 16 Prague 2, Czech Republic
tomas.mikula@gmail.com
[3] Universitat Politecnica de Catalunya (UPC)
Jordi Girona, 31, 08034 Barcelona, Spain
xavi.garci@gmail.com

Abstract. Advances in voice-recognition platforms have led to new possibilities in deploying automated voice-interactive engines for Web content. We present Voice2Web, an architecture allowing to manage access to the resources of the World Wide Web using voice interaction. It rests on the VoiceXML standard and enables rapid composition of dynamic services querying the Web resources. We demonstrate its use on practical examples, discuss architecture implications and invite further platform experimentation.

1 Introduction

The rapidly advancing technologies of the Internet and the World Wide Web (WWW) have become indispensable for functioning of the developed and, increasingly too, the developing world. Yet barriers to access still exist — technological, financial, cultural and physical — for large portions of the world population. The mobile voice services technology has grown to even higher market penetration, and currently outnumbers Internet penetration in an approximately 2:1 ratio worldwide and a 5:2 ratio in the developing countries [1]. Potential voice interfaces to the WWW thus far outnumber the visual ones.

More natural multi-modal interfaces to WWW have many advantages: information provided orally occupies only a part of the brain, leaving remaining capacity and senses free for other tasks (such as visual input or body movement: sports, driving, etc.); people with visual impairment or other handicap would benefit from voice-based Web access; literacy constraints to Web access in the developing countries can be overcome; and better customer interaction would enhance Internet commerce sales and inspire novel automated voice services.

Speech is a natural form of communication for humans. The technological challenge is to manage a better interface for voice access to complex systems

T. Pfeifer and P. Bellavista (Eds.): MMNS 2009, LNCS 5842, pp. 118–131, 2009.

such as WWW. In this work we build on decades of research in automated speech recognition (ASR) and text-to-speech synthesis (TTS) [2] and the Voice Extensible Markup Language (VoiceXML) [3,4] and focus on the network service management architecture.

VoiceXML is a language for creating voice interfaces that use ASR and TTS. It is developing into a vital open standard, enabling rapid proliferation of new voice applications and services. Support by the VoiceXML Forum [5] and the key industrial players accelerates the adoption.

We focus on the problem of *designing and implementing an architecture for managing access of voice-interactive applications to the Web content via both the traditional and next-generation voice communication networks*. The expected architecture attributes are to be fast, manageable, modular, scalable and reliable and allow rapid prototyping of novel services. The logic of the user-interaction is driven by the natural logic of voice conversation, with the Web pages only providing the content (in contrast to the interaction being driven by the Web page structure).

The main contributions of this work are:

- a proposed novel modular *architecture* for building voice applications that use *voice-oriented logic* and *dynamically* access the *content of the World Wide Web*;
- working examples of such functionality;
- practical *experiments validating architecture feasibility*; and
- design of a novel *open VoiceXML Integrated Development Environment (IDE)*, allowing easy creation, sharing and replication of dynamic, WWW-interfacing voice applications. The IDE is Web-based, open to a world-wide developer community at [31] and provides instant setup of telephone and VoIP access to the voice applications.

The above proposed Voice2Web architecture thus represents a step towards a complete voice-services layer, functioning on top of WWW content.

The article is organized as follows: in Section 2 we discuss the related work, Section 3 describes the proposed architecture and Section 4 outlines voice-application dynamic Web access, including a real example. Section 5 describes the IDE, Section 6 presents practical results on experiments validating the architecture and Section 7 holds some concluding remarks and future outlook.

2   Related Work

Recent works develop the idea of the World Wide Telecom Web (WWTW) [10, 9, 12], a voice-driven ecosystem parallel to the existing WWW. It consists of interconnected *Voice Sites*, voice-driven applications created by users and hosted in the network [10], a *Voice Browser* providing access to the many voice sites [9] and the Hyperspeech Transfer Protocol (HSTP) [12] which allows for seamless interconnection of voice applications. Developing regions with large proliferation of phones but little Internet literacy are set to benefit. While WWTW supposedly exists in parallel to WWW, the authors envisage interconnection and interaction of the two systems, but do not (yet) offer architectural solutions of doing so.

Similarly, SpeechWeb [20] is composed of a collection of hyperlinked applications, accessed remotely by speech browsers running on end-user devices. Spoken commands activate the links, using a combination of markup languages. The related MySpeechWeb environment [21] enables development and web deployment of speech applications including the question/answer type applications, created by web forms. The process is completely based on the web-browser, with the constraint to the Opera 9.27 browser with the voice feature installed. In comparison, Voice2Web environment is accessible to end-users by a plethora of voice devices.

The concept of a Voice Portal was suggested in [11], but offering few suggestions as to the architecture. The authors present a system for operation with existing services (email reading, phone calling) and Internet interaction is correctly identified as having tremendous potential. Voice support (i.e. a VoiceXML server) may also be integrated directly into the Web server [8]. This offers greater control over the voice application, but restricts to only one content provider (Web server). In contrast, Voice2Web allows to create a wide range of services, without any Web alteration and accessing an arbitrary number of servers.

A similar concept of voice access to the Web content is represented by the design and implementation of an audio-wiki application [22], accessible via the Public Switched Telephone Network (PSTN) and the Internet. Based on VoiceXML and other W3C standards the system provides voice interaction with wiki web applications. In contrast, Voice2Web is focused on any-web access and thus broadens the target area.

The idea of web-driven *Voice Browsing* is to convert original Web content into VoiceXML dialogues, using VoiceXML templates and extraction rules written in XSLT. The work presented in [7] identified typical HTML patterns and designed a way to browse them using voice. Although similar to Voice2Web, it is based on the opposite logic of building a voice application around a Web page design.

Mobile Web browsing has been shown to be less convenient than desktop browsing [13], in particular Web page navigation and content location. Augmenting the interaction with voice may improve it. Conversely, pure voice-response systems have been shown to benefit from augmenting with a visual interface [14]. This motivates adding more modalities into the user-Web interaction.

Other research has focused on Web browsing by voice and its applicability for the handicapped or elderly. The HearSay audio Web browser [17, 18] allows to automatically create voice applications from web documents using VoiceXML and domain specific ontologies and templates. Recently a prototype of a telephony service for web-browsing via phone, TeleWeb [19], has been designed to combine the phone interface with intelligent browsing features (context-directed browsing, template-detection, macro-replaying) of the HearSay web browser. To improve the Web accessibility for visually impaired without the need to alter the original Web content, the concept of external metadata repository has been developed and shared among research institutions [23].

An architecture of Voice Web Pages implemented by .NET [24] offers the possibility of browsing web sites and playing related streaming media simultaneously. The concept however does not include voice-controlled browsing, as speech recognition is not implemented.

Others investigate utilizing voice for controlling the conventional Web browsers [15], or presenting a typical Web page using voice [16], reporting poor results, with voice-control often being much less productive or convenient. Contrary to Voice2Web, these applications are not initially designed for voice control and thus the results are suboptimal.

3   Voice2Web Architecture

3.1   Architecture Alternatives Discussion

Various alternatives exist for the architecture of voice access to WWW content. The architecture of a *thin, streaming client and strong server* performs all voice processing and executes application logic at the server and maintains a voice connection open throughout the conversation. Server-based solution allows for greater manageability and reliability (pending a network connection) with fast voice-processing and response times. It allows to rapidly introduce novel services and use all standard voice communication protocols, putting less requirements on end-users. The architecture may be easily scaled by adding more hardware resources and load-balancing on the server side.

A *thick client* may perform all of the ASR and TTS on the client and only send text messages over the network, or possibly the entire application may operate locally. While inherently scalable in terms of number of users, such architecture is significantly less manageable (requiring pre-installations and client application updates). Speech recognition and synthesis are strongly memory- and compute-intensive processes, with inadequate resources available in current mobile devices, thus affecting both their performance and power consumption.

While both architectures have their advantages, manageability, performance and scalability seems well addressed by the *thin, streaming client* and a *dedicated strong ASR, TTS and application-logic server.*

3.2   Voice2Web Architecture and Components

As a result of the above discussion, our proposed modular server-based Voice2Web architecture consists of the following components (see Fig. 1):

- Client - a mobile or fixed terminal for end-user interaction
- Telephony-system frontend for communication-channel unification
- Speech-recognition and synthesis engines
- Call-processing server (Voice Browser)
- Voice-application repository and development environment
- Web-interaction Proxy

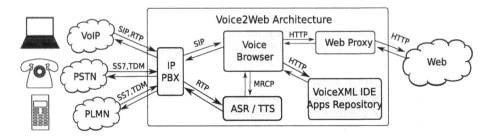

Fig. 1. Voice2Web architecture and function. A caller from the VoIP, PSTN or PLMN network is authenticated and a connection is unified by the IP PBX. Unified internal VoIP connection (SIP and RTP) is processed by Voice Browser according to VoiceXML retrieved from VoiceXML IDE and with help of ASR and TTS engines. To enable effective WWW access, the Web Proxy intermediates the connection to the Web.

The components are mutually independent as they are interlinked by standardized interfaces. Any component may appear multiple times ensuring system modularity, scalability and higher overall system reliability. Majority of the interface protocols are text based allowing easy monitoring and simplified system management.

The architecture should enable caller access by using any type of telephony network including traditional Public Switched Telephone Network (PSTN) and Public Land Mobile Network (PLMN) as well as Voice over IP (VoIP). A *multi-interface frontend telephony system* needs to be integrated, to unify inbound communication channels into a single internal channel. IP Private Branch eXchange (IP-PBX) is used for a small scale project while high-performance load-balanced servers should be used in larger scale networks. In our case Asterisk PBX [26] handles many analog and digital switched network signaling types and VoIP signaling and media protocols. All inbound protocols are converted into Session Initiation Protocol (SIP) and Real-time Transfer Protocol (RTP) internal protocol set. The PBX also performs user account and call management.

A server-side *call-processing* architecture is based on a voice application logic (dialogs). Voice Browser manages the dialogs with help of speech-recognition and speech-synthesis engines. The browser processes incoming calls by a set of predefined rules for call filtering, connection management and for linking traffic to a desired voice application. An increasingly popular W3C standard Call Control eXtensible Markup Language (CCXML) [30] is used to represent this ruleset. The dialogs, including user-machine communication and actions to be performed upon user's response, should be encoded in a human-readable form for easy development and should be platform-independent. This is met by using the W3C VoiceXML standard [4].

Voice Browser scalability may be achieved by DNS load-balancing [28], or a higher level of scalability may be achieved by implementing the Voice Browser as a service on top of multiple application servers. IBM WebSphere Voice Server [27] is an example of such distributed platfrom.

The *ASR and TTS engines* for speech recognition and synthesis should interoperate with the Voice Browser over a unified and open interface to ensure scalability. Media Resource Control Protocol (MRCP) [29] performs this function well. It has become the defacto standard for media resource management by a Voice Browser. MRCP conveys speech recognition results and synthesis progress to the Voice Browser, while input and output audio streams (setup by SIP) are exchanged directly between the end-client and the ASR/TTS engines via RTP.

The speech recognition system should recognize voice samples regardless of the speaker behavioral patterns, thus should not require any voice training. A presented solution is a speech recognition grammar based system which however brings a limitation in number of speech patterns included in the grammar.

A *repository of voice-application logic* can either be placed locally on Voice Browser or stored on a HTTP server. In our case the Web-based development environment VoiceXML IDE (see Section 5) serves as the source of voice applications, acting as an HTTP server.

Finally, voice-application access to the WWW is performed by a *Web Proxy*, which introduces benefits over direct Web access from VoiceXML (see Section 4).

4   Dynamic Voice-to-Web Access

4.1   Dynamic Data Instead of Dynamic VoiceXML

Web data are dynamic—may change over time. Prior to VoiceXML version 2.1, there were no means of integrating Web data directly. There was, however, the <submit> element, which *"is used to submit information to the origin Web server and then transition to the document sent back in the response."* [3] This document is commonly referred to as dynamic VoiceXML, due to its dynamic generation by the Web server. Dynamic VoiceXML has a few drawbacks: mixes application logic with data; unnaturally splits the application logic into two (or more) VoiceXML documents; must not be cached by the Voice Browser. This method, used e.g. in [7, 8], can now be considered legacy.

VoiceXML 2.1 introduces the <data> element, which *"allows a VoiceXML application to fetch arbitrary XML data from a document server without transitioning to a new VoiceXML document."* [4] Our applications use this novel approach to Web access, which avoids the above drawbacks.

4.2   Web Proxy

Web Proxy (WP) is an extra layer between VoiceXML and the Web (see Fig. 2). It acts as an HTTP server for VoiceXML applications and as an HTTP client for the Web. Although VoiceXML application can query the Web source directly, it is advantageous to use WP in cases when the application can benefit from its features: *substitutability* of Web sources, *preprocessing* and *caching* of Web documents. A typical example are information-providing services.

Substitutability of Web sources means that a voice application can transparently use any of configured websites as the source of data, while sending just

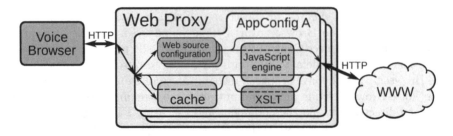

Fig. 2. Web Proxy schema. Upon the Voice Browser request, the Web Proxy decides which application configuration to use (here AppConfig A) based on the URL of the requested document. Then, it either serves the document from the cache, or requests it from a remote Web source. The request is formed based on the Web-source configuration, optionally using a JavaScript function. The response is processed by XSLT or a JavaScript function, optionally stored in cache, and returned to the Voice Browser.

one unified request to WP. The transformation of the request to WP into the request to the Web source is defined in the configuration of each Web source. Single-parametric requests can be transformed by a table that maps this parameter to a URI. More complex requests can be transformed by a JavaScript function. Currently, the Web sources are queried in the order defined in application configuration. If one fails, the next one is tried. An improvement could be to periodically reorder the sources based on their evaluated response time.

By preprocessing, uniform format of Web data is achieved, regardless of the Web source used. Furthermore, preprocessing typically results in a considerably smaller document, thus saving Voice Browser's processing time. The rules for preprocessing are specified for each Web source, either by XSLT or a JavaScript function. Using JavaScript for preprocessing also extends the domain of possible content source formats from just XML (required by both the <data> element and XSLT) to any reasonably structured text document.

The response of each request to WP can be cached for a specified *expiration time*, defined for each application. This saves requests to the Internet and processing time (cached documents are already preprocessed). Our implementation assumes that the cache can store documents for all possible requests to each Web Proxy application. This assumption is not unrealistic, as current voice applications can typically issue only a limited number of different requests. To support applications that can generate a large number of distinct requests, employment of a cache replacement algorithm (such as LRU) would be necessary.

Clearly, when the document is not cached, WP introduces some overhead. Disregarding other benefits of WP, let's calculate under what circumstances the average response time of WP is shorter than that of the Web. Expiration time (T_e) is application specific. The average response times of the Web (T_w) and WP for a cached (T_c) and uncached (T_u) document can be measured experimentally. We can safely assume $T_c < T_w < T_u$. We further assume exponential probabilistic distribution of intervals between requests. It can be shown that the expected response times of Web and WP are equal when the average interval between requests is $T_e(T_w - T_c)/(T_u - T_w)$. Thus, a shorter interval means that using the WP pays off.

4.3   Examples of VoiceXML Applications

The *Weather* application provides information about the weather around the world. It prompts the caller to choose a location and replies with the current weather conditions. Such application was proposed in [3]. It used the `<submit>` element to transition to dynamic VoiceXML containing the weather information. Our implementation, however, benefits from using the `<data>` element (see 4.1) to obtain the information from the Web Proxy (see 4.2) and, ultimately, from an existing Web page. Web Proxy obtains the information from one of the configured sources (Yahoo! Weather [32], Weather Underground [33]) and converts it to a uniform XML format. The application fetches the information from XML and says it back to the caller.

The *VoiceQuote* application helps to stay up-to-date on stock quotes. A user calls VoiceQuote and says a company name. Stock quote of the company is then retrieved from an available Web financial data provider (e.g. Yahoo) by Web Proxy. Finally, the quote is read back to the user (see Fig. 1).

5   VoiceXML Integrated Development Environment

VoiceXML Integrated Development Environment (*VXML IDE*) is a Web-based tool for development and management of voice applications, with emphasis on usability. Applications are designed in text or graphic mode. In text mode the developer writes the VoiceXML code directly, with the option to check the validity of the document by a VoiceXML validator. Graphic mode enables to create a voice application without knowledge of VoiceXML (see below). VXML IDE offers machine translation of voice applications to other languages (using third-party Web translators). Saved applications become *instantly available* to callers.

VXML IDE has a *three-tier architecture* with data, logic and presentation tiers (see Fig. 3). We further divide the logic tier into management and computation components. The presentation tier provides user interface (UI). As the

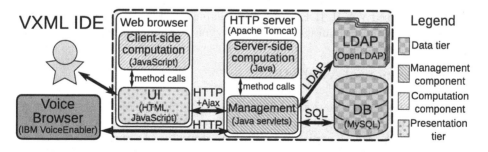

Fig. 3. VoiceXML IDE: the three-tier architecture

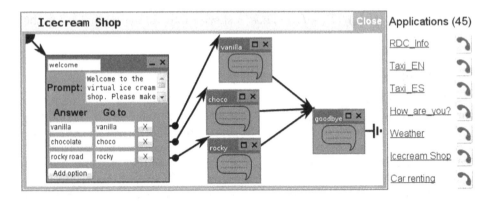

Fig. 4. VoiceXML IDE: graphic mode screenshot

VXML IDE is Web-based, it is coded in HTML and JavaScript and runs on the client. The data tier stores the user information and developed voice applications. Using LDAP directory for user information enables us to use VXML IDE user accounts in other applications, too (we use them for forum, bug-tracking system and Asterisk). For storing voice applications, relational database is a natural choice. The management component controls access to the resources of the data tier. It comprises several Java servlets within a HTTP server. The computation component performs tasks such as converting between textual and graphical representation of an application, translation of an application, or VoiceXML validation. To relieve burden from the server, an effort is made to put it mostly on the client. However, some computation is still needed on the server.

The graphical design of a voice application (see Fig. 4) consists of several graphical components, each representing a simple dialog. The call flow is illustrated by links between components. Internally, each component is a JavaScript object that implements a certain interface. Each component has methods to output its content as VoiceXML and to reconstruct (load) itself from a VoiceXML snippet. Turning the graphical design into VoiceXML then comes down to iterating over all the components and asking them for their VoiceXML output. To store the graphical design and to be able to return to it later, we extend VoiceXML by adding new elements and attributes that hold the graphical information.

The Web-based VXML IDE is openly available at [31] to the world-wide community, who are thus encouraged to indulge in voice-application experimentation!

6   Experimental Validation

In the experimental validation we focus on the promptness of the system interaction and the capacity issue. Section 3 discusses the attribute of scalability and reliability and Section 5 explains the rapid prototyping of novel services.

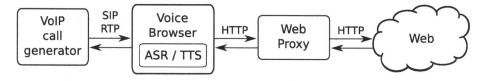

Fig. 5. VoIP call generator produces different amount of traffic load to stress Voice Browser and Web Proxy capabilities

6.1 Test Setup

The test setup is shown in Fig. 5. VoIP call generator (SIPp [25]) stresses the architecture with different traffic patterns. It produces signaling messages to manage variable amount of SIP calls and simultaneously generate streams carrying payload. It is also the point where the total response delay is measured. Generated traffic is received by the Voice Browser (IBM Voice Enabler), which makes use of ASR and TTS engines (IBM WebSphere Voice Server [27]). Voice Enabler governs the call connection and VoiceXML dialog processing. Web Proxy is used to retrieve Web information requested by voice applications. Part of the delay added by Web requests is measured separately.

The total response delay was derived by analysis of RTP streams as the interval between the caller query end instant (e.g. "London") and the initial time of response arrival (e.g. "Weather in London is.."). The Web delay was measured by analysis of HTTP packets between Voice Browser and Web Proxy, see Fig. 6.

The Voice Browser and the Web Proxy each run on a 2 GHz Intel Pentium 4 server with 2 GB RAM. The ASR/TTS engines utilize a 2 GHz Intel Xeon server with 2 GB RAM. All servers run OS Linux.

6.2 Delay Measurement

Ordinary Traffic Test. simulates the conditions of a typical load. The Weather application (see 4.3) with Yahoo! Weather as the Web source received 500 queries for weather conditions in a city randomly selected from thirty european capitals. The intervals between call arrival times were exponentially distributed with a mean of 1s. Test call scenario was approximately 10 seconds long.

Results of the total response delay per call are in Fig. 7. Two cases were studied: (1) calls where the weather information is retrieved via Web-Proxy

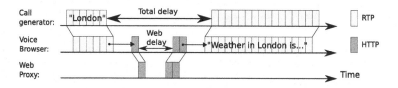

Fig. 6. Total response delay is measured as the time between the end of caller query in RTP and the start of Voice Browser response in RTP

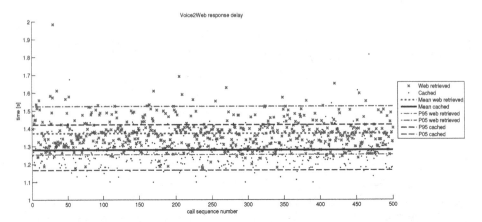

Fig. 7. Total response delay in case of Web-retrieved and cached information (500 values, mean and 5th and 95th percentile)

from the Web. The average delay is 1.37 seconds; (2) utilizing the Web-Proxy caching, where the average system response delay is 1.28 seconds. The cache can save hundred milliseconds per call for applications where information refresh interval is in the range of minutes (such as Weather). Table 1 discusses the Web-query part of the delay.

Call delay variation is caused by the non-deterministic speech recognition process (difference ~200 ms per word), Voice Browser grouping requests to ASR/TTS engines (up to 500 ms) and variable initial Web-response delay.

System Capacity Measurement. determines the throughput of our platform in the testbed environment. We maintained a constant number of parallel calls, initiating a new call every 1-2s (uniformly randomly) after any of the calls terminated.

Table 1. Web delay of the Weather application with Yahoo! Weather as the Web source. We measured average response time of Web Proxy when the requested document was cached (T_c) and uncached (T_u). We also measured the response time of direct queries to Yahoo! Weather (T_w) to determine when the expected response time of Web Proxy is shorter than that of the Web. If we set the expiration period of cache (T_e) to 10 minutes, we get (applying the formula from the end of Section 4.2) that the *threshold interval* between requests for one location is 55.54min. More frequent requests mean shorter expected response time of Web Proxy.

measured average response time of			expiration (T_e)	threshold interval
WP, cached (T_c)	WP, uncached (T_u)	Web (T_w)		
2.55ms	104.01ms	88.53ms	10min	55.54min

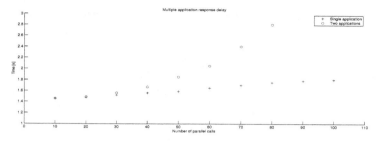

Fig. 8. Total response delay in dependence on the number of parallel sessions

First, multiples of tens of parallel calls using Weather application with identical query were generated. The total response delay increased almost constantly with a step of around 40ms per 10 increased sessions, as shown in Fig. 8. However, for values approaching 100 parallel calls, the fraction of rejected calls became significant, causing a lower increase in delay as more system resources remained available for the accepted calls. Second, two voice applications (Weather and VoiceQuote) with equal load share were tested. The effect of additional application was insignificant for lower number of concurrent calls. When reached the maximum of 80 parallel calls the total response delay almost doubled. The maximum number of parallel calls was determined by system capabilities and limited by hardware resources.

Summary. We evaluated the feasibility of an architecture for voice-application-managed access to the Web. From the human-computer interaction point of view the total response delay indicates a natural form of communication, where the interaction with the Web introduces only a small fraction of the delay that can be further reduced by caching. In the testbed environment we have reached the amount of 100 concurrent calls to single voice application with a per-call total response delay increase of about 15%. Measurements have indicated a dependence between the number of concurrent voice applications and the system response delay. The effect of multiple applications is insignificant for lower number of concurrent calls, however it can increase the delay by almost 100% in case of higher number of parallel calls in the testbed environment. This is likely caused by the increased delay in the Voice Browser and ASR/TTS engines due to multiple applications and could be avoided by application load-balancing or other scaling techniques.

7   Conclusion

Architecture discussion and experimental validation of the Voice2Web platform verifies its manageability and scalability. The platform enables rapid prototyping, replication, creation and immediate deployment of voice applications interfacing to the WWW. Performance scales well with the number of calls and improves with at least periodic cache use. Nevertheless, servicing multiple parallel voice applications may require increase in hardware capacity.

Practical realization of the Voice2Web management platform opens many possibilities, be it for specialized services for the communities of the handicapped or illiterate, or for commercial applications. Multi-lingual applications may be built and the Web-based IDE, openly available at [31], encourages experimentation and allows code-sharing among developer communities. An *open issue* remains designing an architecture for automating and managing the *reverse process of creating WWW content using voice.*

Validation of the architecture principles opens space for creation of a *multi-modal interaction management frontend to the resources of the World Wide Web*, allowing to build applications that respect or combine different modalities (voice, visual, haptic, etc.). Investigations of adding further modalities, such as visual avatars, 3D representations or visual pattern recognition, further contextual aspects, such as user location and behavior, as well as security and robustness considerations, are all part of the future activities of the project.

Acknowledgment

We wish to thank IBM Research for generous support of the project and Jan Kleindienst, Borivoj Tydlitat and Jan Sedivy for many thoughtful suggestions. We also thank CESNET for the generous lending of project equipment and Vodafone Foundation Czech Republic for the kind student scholarship support.

References

1. Mobile cellular and Internet user penetration worldwide, ITU 1997-2007 ICT Market Information and Statistics,
   `http://www.itu.int/ITU-D/ict/statistics/maps.html`
2. Roe, D.B., Wilpon, J.G. (eds.): Voice Communication Between Humans and Machines. The National Academies Press, Washington (1994)
3. Voice Extensible Markup Language (VoiceXML) Version 2.0, W3C Recommendation (March 16, 2004), `http://www.w3.org/TR/voicexml20/`
4. Voice Extensible Markup Language (VoiceXML) 2.1, W3C Recommendation (June 19, 2007), `http://www.w3.org/TR/voicexml21/`
5. VoiceXML Forum, `http://www.voicexml.org/`
6. World Wide Web Consortium (W3C), `http://www.w3.org/`
7. González-Ferreras, C., Cardeñoso-Payo, V.: Building Voice Applications From Web Content. In: Sojka, P., Kopeček, I., Pala, K. (eds.) TSD 2004. LNCS (LNAI), vol. 3206, pp. 587–594. Springer, Heidelberg (2004)
8. Vankayala, R.R., Shi, H.: Dynamic Voice User Interface Using VoiceXML and Active Server Pages. In: Zhou, X., Li, J., Shen, H.T., Kitsuregawa, M., Zhang, Y. (eds.) APWeb 2006. LNCS, vol. 3841, pp. 1181–1184. Springer, Heidelberg (2006)
9. Agarwal, S., Kumar, A., Nanavati, A.A., Rajput, N.: The World Wide Telecom Web Browser. Poster at WWW 2008, Beijing, China, April 21-25 (2008)
10. Kumar, A., Rajput, N., Chakraborty, D., Agarwal, S.K., Nanavati, A.A.: WWTW: The World Wide Telecom Web. In: NSDR, Kyoto, Japan, August 27 (2007)
11. Goldman, E.L., Panttaja, E., Wojcikowski, A., Braudes, R.: Voice Portals - Where Theory Meets Practice. Int. Journal of Speech Technology 4, 227–240 (2001)

12. Agarwal, S.K., Chakraborty, D., Kumar, A., Nanavati, A.A., Rajput, N.: HSTP: Hyperspeech Transfer Protocol. In: ACM Hypertext, Manchester, UK, September 10-12 (2007)
13. Shrestha, S.: Mobile Web Browsing: Usability Study. In: Proceedings of ACM Mobility, Singapore, September 10-12 (2007)
14. Yin, M., Zhai, S.: The Benefits of Augmenting Telephone Voice Menu Navigation with Visual Browsing and Search. In: Proceedings of ACM CHI:Managing Voice Input, Montreal, Quebec, Canada, April 22-27 (2006)
15. Hanson, V.L., Richards, J.T., Lee, C.C.: Web Access for Older Adults: Voice Browsing? In: Stephanidis, C. (ed.) HCI 2007. LNCS, vol. 4554, pp. 904–913. Springer, Heidelberg (2007)
16. Christian, K., Kules, B., Shneiderman, B., Youssef, A.: A Comparison of Voice Controlled and Mouse Controlled Web Browsing. In: ASSETS 2000, Arlington, VA, USA (2000)
17. Ramakrishnan, I.V., Stent, A., Yang, G.: HearSay: Enabling Audio Browsing on Hypertext Content. In: WWW 2004, New York, NY, USA, May 17-22 (2004)
18. Sun, Z., Stent, A., Ramakrishnan, I.V.: Dialog Generation for Voice Browsing. In: W4A Workshop at WWW 2006, Edinburgh, UK, May 23-26 (2006)
19. Borodin, Y., Dausch., G., Ramakrishnan, I.V.: TeleWeb: Accessible Service for Web Browsing via Phone. In: W4A2009 collocated with WWW 2009, Madrid, Spain, April 20-21 (2009)
20. Frost, R.A., Ma, X., Shi, Y.: A browser for a public-domain SpeechWeb. In: Proceedings of the ACM WWW 2007, Banff, Alberta, Canada (2007)
21. Frost, R.A., et al.: MySpeechWeb: Software to Facilitate the Construction and Deployment of Speech Applications on the Web. In: Proceedings of ACM SIGACCESS ASSETS 2008, Halifax, Canada (October 2008)
22. Kolias, C., Kolias, V., Anagnostopoulos, I., Kambourakis, G., Kayafas, E.: A pervasive Wiki application based on VoiceXML. In: Proceedings of PETRA 2008, Athens, Greece, July 15-19, ACM, New York (2008)
23. Kawanaka, S., Masatomo, K., Takagi, H., Asakawa, C.: Accessibility Commons: A Metadata Repository for Web Accessibility. In: SIGWEB Newsletter, Issue Summer, June 2009. ACM, New York (2009)
24. Guoqiang, D., Yaoyao, L., Lingchao, H., Jianping, W.: Design and Implementation of Voice Web Pages for Online Shopping Based on .NET and Streaming Media. In: Management of e-Commerce and e-Government, 2008, ICMECG 2008, Nanchang, China, October 17-19, 2008, pp. 226–229 (2008)
25. SIPp test tool and traffic generator, http://sipp.source.forge
26. Asterisk Private Branch eXchange, http://www.asterisk.org/
27. IBM WebSphere Voice Server, http://www-01.ibm.com/software/voice/
28. Gulbrandsen, A., Vixie, P., Esibov, L.: A DNS RR for specifying the location of services (DNS SRV). IETF RFC 2782 (February 2000), http://tools.ietf.org/html/rfc2782
29. Shanmugham, S., Monaco, P., Eberman, B.: A Media Resource Control Protocol (MRCP), IETF RFC 4463 (April 2006), http://tools.ietf.org/html/rfc4463
30. Voice Browser Call Control: CCXML Version 1.0, W3C Working Draft (January 19, 2007), http://www.w3.org/TR/ccxml/
31. Voice2Web VoiceXML IDE, http://bolek.feld.cvut.cz:8080/vxmlide/
32. Yahoo! Weather, http://weather.yahoo.com
33. Weather Underground, http://www.wunderground.com

A Robust Algorithm for the Membership Management of Super-Peer Overlay

Meirong Liu, Jiehan Zhou, Timo Koskela, and Mika Ylianttila

Media Team Oulu research group, Information Processing Laboratory,
Department of Electrical and Information Engineering
University of Oulu, Finland
P.O.BOX 4500 FIN-90014
firstname.lastname@ee.oulu.fi

Abstract. Peer-to-Peer technologies have been widely applied for multimedia applications. The super-peer based approach provides an efficient way to run applications by exploring nodes' heterogeneity. In P2P live video streaming, even though the number of stable nodes is small, they have significant impact on the performance of the network. Thus, we present a super-peer-based overlay design, where stable nodes are assigned as super-peers that organize client nodes. A gossip-based super-peer selection algorithm (GSPS) is proposed to identify the stable nodes to be chosen as super-peers and to manage the client nodes (namely the membership management). The basic idea of the GSPS is: first, a set of super-peer candidates for a node is built based on the gossip, then the role of this node is identified and the corresponding operations are executed. Simulation results show that the GSPS is efficient in managing the super-peer overlay and robust to the failure of super-peers.

Keywords: Peer-to-Peer, super-peer, gossip, robustness.

1 Introduction

The peer-to-peer (P2P) paradigm provides an effective approach to construct large-scale systems with high robustness, mainly due to their inherent decentralization and redundant structures [1] [2] [3]. Moreover, the P2P systems are able to utilize the resources distributed in a large number of machines connected to the system through the Internet. Therefore, much work focuses on building the P2P overlay, such as [3] [4] [5] [6] [7] [8]. In these research studies, Random walk and Graph theory are utilized for the construction of the overlay. For the management of the overlay, the diameter, and the degree are two important qualities to consider.

The super-peer-based overlay (such as Gnutella [9] and Kazaa [10]) provides an effective way to run applications by utilizing the heterogeneity of the peer nodes. Specifically, the super-peer approach does not have the disadvantage of the traditional client-server model (the single point of failure), resulting in the increased robustness [11] [12] [13]. Moreover, the nodes with low capacity are shielded from the massive query traffic by the super-peers, which improves the scalability of the system.

T. Pfeifer and P. Bellavista (Eds.): MMNS 2009, LNCS 5842, pp. 132–143, 2009.

Wang et al. [14] found that the number of stable nodes in P2P live video streaming is small, but these stable nodes make a significant contribution to the system performance. They presented a tiered overlay design for P2P live video streaming, where the stable nodes and the transient nodes are separated into two levels. Moreover, our previous work presented the P2P SCCM (Service-Oriented Community Coordinated Multimedia) paradigm [15], which leverages the roles of requestors, providers, and registry centre in the conventional SOA architecture as service peers for multimedia application. Those multimedia-intensive service peers are assumed to publish their services, access services provided by other peers through searching, and intermediately communicate with each other. The P2P SCCM uses super-peers to act as rendezvous peers that handle service indexing and identity mapping. Continuing the vision of the P2P SCCM, in this paper, we focus on how to manage the super-peer overlay, namely, how to select super-peers and rearrange the super-peer topology when some of the super-peers fail. To this end, we propose a gossip-based super-peer selection algorithm (GSPS) to identify stable nodes (the peers with high capacity) to act as super-peers and to manage client nodes. The capacity of a node is composed of the computational resource, the lifespan and the network connections [8] [14].

The basic idea of the GSPS is as follows. First, a set of super-peer candidates for a node is built based on the gossip communication, where this node exchanges information with its neighbors in order to select other nodes with higher capacity as the super-peers candidates. After that, if this node is in the list of the super-peer candidates, this node takes the role of a super-peer. Finally, the nodes execute the corresponding operations, joining a super-peer or recruiting a client node, according to their role. In the case of a disaster (i.e. the failure of a super-peer), the client nodes declare their state to be rebuilt and reconstruct their sets of super-peer candidates, selecting a new number of the required super-peers, and then join these super-peers. Simulations have been conducted and results show that the GSPS is efficient to manage the overlay, especially to select the super-peers. The GSPS is also robust to the failure of the super-peers. The terms node and peer are used interchangeably in the rest parts of the paper.

The remainder of this paper is organised as follows. In Section 2, the GSPS is presented to show how to select the powerful nodes to act as super-peers and how to manage the relation between the client nodes and a super node. How to handle the disaster of the super-peer failure is also considered. In Section 3, we show the evaluation results of the GSPS. In Section 4, we review the related work on the overlay management. The conclusion and future work are discussed in Section 5.

2   The Proposed GSPS Algorithm for Membership Management

In this section, the background of the communication method is first introduced, and then the GSPS algorithm is depicted. We assume that all the nodes are connected through an existing routed network. A node needs to store the identifiers of its neighbours in order to communicate with other nodes. Thus, each node can potentially communicate with other nodes directly or indirectly via other nodes. These neighbourhood relations constitute the topology of the overlay. Both the neighbours of a node and the overlay topology can change dynamically.

2.1 Background of a Gossip Communication Model

The gossip-based communication model in large-scale distributed systems has become a general paradigm for many important applications, which include information dissemination, aggregation, topology management and synchronization. We apply a gossip communication method called *Newscast* [16] to maintain a neighbor set of each peers in the network. The Newscast has been used for broadcast [17] and aggregation [17] [18] in several P2P protocols. In the Newscast, the state of a node is called a partial view, including a fixed-size set of descriptors of its neighbor peers. Two neighboring peers merge their partial views periodically to keep the freshest descriptors; thereby a new partial view is created. Peers always update their own, newly created descriptor into the partial view. By exchanging the partial view, old information is gradually replaced by new information. This approach enables the GSPS to rebuild neighbors of the nodes by excluding the crashed nodes.

2.2 Selecting Super-Peers and Client Peers

Building and maintaining a super-peer-based overlay topology are complex. On one side, the dynamic environment requires a robust and an efficient algorithm to self-organize and self-repair the super-peer overlay in the case of voluntary and unexpected events like joining, leaving and crashes [19] [20] [21]. On the other side, the nodes in the overlay are heterogeneous in their capacity [8]. We propose the GSPS to build and manage the super-peer overlay characterized by the minimum number of super-peers. Inspired by the method called VoRonoi Regions set up in the mobile network [22] and the clustering method [23], super-peers are first selected during the overlay construction.

We assume that the topology information such as the identifier, the capacity, the lifespan, the current role and the neighborhood of the participating nodes are disseminated through periodic gossip messaging. The notations used in the GSPS are given as follows for simplicity. Let n_i be a node in an N-node P2P network. Each super-peer maintains three sets: its neighbor sets, the client node set $S_c(n_i)$ and the set of the super-peer candidates. Each client node maintains the following information: its super-peer, its neighbors and the set of the super-peer candidates. Let $SP(n_i)$ denote the super-peer of the node n_i. To distinguish the capacity of each node, let c_{ni} represent the abstracted capacity of a node n_i. The abstracted capacity c_{ni} denotes the number of the client nodes that the node n_i can manage according to its resource property, if n_i takes the role of a super-peer. We assume each node n_i knows its capacity parameter c_{ni}, which could be computed on-the-fly in the application implementation. Let $Ld(n_i)$ denote the current load of n_i. For each node, there are two states: idle and rebuilt, e.g. State(n_i)={idle, rebuilt}. The idle state denotes that a node n_i joins the overlay but does not suffer from the failure of its super-peer. The rebuilt state denotes a node n_i joins the overlay but suffers from the failure of its super-peer. Specifically, if a client node n_i suffers from its super-peer's failure, n_i declares its state to be rebuilt. When the n_i with the rebuilt state is identified as a super-peer, the super-peer n_i possesses the state of rebuilt as well. The purpose of setting two states for the node n_i is to reorganize its super-peer candidates when its super-peer fails.

Input: A client node n_i
Operation:
if SP(n_i) is down and State(n_i) is idle **then**
    n_i changes its State(n_i) to be rebuilt;
    n_i removes its SP(n_i) from its set of super-peer candidates;
    n_i rebuilds its set of super-peer candidates.
end if
if State(n_i)∈ is rebuilt **then**
    for each neighbor n_{neig} of n_i **do**
      n_{neig} deletes SP(n_i) from its set of super-peer candidates.
      if n_{neig} is a client node, SP(n_{neig})≠null and is down **then**
        n_{neig} changes its state to be rebuilt and removes its super-peer from the set
        of super-peer candidates; n_{neig} rebuilds its set of super-peer candidates.
    end if
    end for
end if
if n_i has different super-peer candidates with its neighbors **then**
    n_i gets the super-peer candidates of each neighbor and compares their capabilities
    to get a new set of super-peer candidates with higher capacity *CanSP* ;
    n_i updates its super-peer candidates to be *CanSP*;
        for each neighbor n_{neig} of n_i **do**
          n_{neig} updates its set of super-peer candidates to be *CanSP*;
          if n_{neig} is client and n_{neig}∈ *CanSP* **then**
          then n_{neig} changes its role as a super-peer;
          if n_{neig} is SP and n_{neig}∉ *CanSP* **then**
          n_{neig} changes its role as a client node;
          if $S_c(n_{neig})$ ≠ null **then**
          n_{neig} transfers its clients to the super-peers in *CanSP*.
        end if
      end for
    if n_i∈ *CanSP* **then** n_i changes its role as a super-peer.
else if n_i has the same super-peer candidates with its neighbors **then**
    n_i searches its neighbors to get one under-loaded super-peer;
    if n_i finds one super peer SP$_j$ **then** n_i joins the peer group managed by SP$_j$.
    else
      n_i searches the super-peers of its neighbors that are under-loaded;
      if n_i finds one super-peer SP$_{j,}$ **then**
        n_i joins the peer group managed by SP$_j$.
      else if all the super-peers are full-loaded **then**
        n_i declares itself as a super-peer.
    end else
end else

Fig. 1. The action of a client node in the GSPS

Input: A super node n_i and n_i is under-loaded
Operation:
if State(n_i) is rebuilt **then**
    for each neighbor n_{neig} of n_i
        if n_{neig} is a client node, SP(n_{neig})≠null and is down **then**
            n_{neig} deletes SP(n_i) from list of super-peer candidates;
            n_{neig} changes its state to be rebuilt;
            n_{neig} rebuilds its set of super-peer candidates.
        end if
    end for
end if
if there is one node whose super-peer candidates are larger than n_i **then**
    n_i gets the set of super-peer candidates of each neighbor and compares their capacity to get a new set of super-peer candidates with higher capacity-*CanSP*;
    n_i updates its super-peer candidates to be *CanSP*.
    for each neighbor n_{neig} of n_i **do**
        n_{neig} updates its set of super-peer candidates to be *CanSP*;
        if n_{neig} is client and $n_{neig} \in$ *CanSP* **then**
            n_{neig} changes its role as a super node.
        if n_{neig} is SP and $n_{neig} \notin$ *CanSP* **then**
            n_{neig} changes its role of n_{neig} as a client node;
            n_{neig} transfers its clients to the super-peers in the set *CanSP*.
        end if
        end for
        if $n_i \notin$ CanSP **then**
            n_i transfers its clients to the super-peers in the set *CanSP*;
            n_i changes its role to be a client node.
        end if
else **for each** neighbor n_{neig} of n_i **do**
        if n_{neig} is client, SP(n_{neig})=null and n_i is under-loaded **then**
            n_i adds n_{neig} as its client.
        if n_i is under-loaded **then**
            n_i searches its neighbours to get a client node n_{neig} whose super-peer is null and then adds n_{neig} as its client.
    end for
end else

Fig. 2. The action of a super-peer in the GSPS

Fig. 2 shows the action of a super-peer in the GSPS algorithm. It also includes two scenarios: the joining process and rebuild process. In the rebuild process, each neighbor of a super-peer removes the failed super-peer from its set of the super-peer candidates. To make the algorithm converge fast, a two-hop search method is utilized. That is, the super-peer first searches its neighbors and then searches the neighbors of its neighbors. The reason why we use the two-hop search is to prevent the worst case from happening that would increase the convergence time. Here, the worst case is as follows: all the neighbors of a peer have joined one service group, and these peer groups are full-loaded and cannot accept any more client nodes. In the worst case, the peer cannot join any of the peer groups of its one-hop neighbors. Therefore, the two-hop search method is employed to help the peer to find a peer group of its neighbors for joining.

3 Evaluation of the GSPS Algorithm

We have conducted experiments with PeerSim [24], which is a round driven P2P simulator, to validate the operation of the GSPS protocol. Here, a simulation round means all the nodes have finished performing the protocols deployed on the nodes one time. We focus on three main questions: (i) the impact of the GSPS's parameters on the performance of the GSPS protocol; (ii) the robustness of the protocol in the case of the super-peer failure; and (iii) the performance comparison with other related protocols. For the simulation, the size of the overlay is 10^5 if not separately specified. The initial simulation topology is a random graph and all the nodes take the role of a client node in the beginning. The frequency of information sharing among peers using the gossip protocol is set to take place every 10s (seconds).

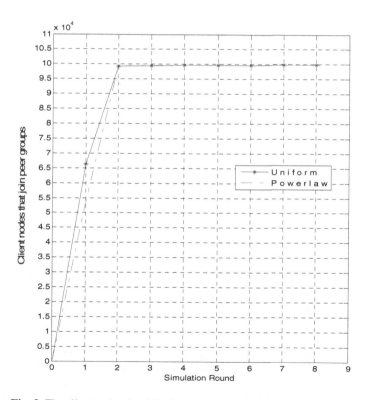

Fig. 3. The client nodes that join the super-peers during simulation rounds

Fig. 3 shows the efficiency of convergence of our GSPS algorithm over simulation time. We can find out using the uniform distribution that on average it takes about eight rounds for all client nodes to join one of the selected super-peers. However, for the power-law distribution, it takes approximately four rounds. During the initialization of the simulation, we selected a random topology where all the peers take the role of a client-peer. The reason is twofold. On one side, every node joins the network and declares itself as a client node, after that, these nodes can execute the GSPS algorithm to select a super-peer. On the other side, the initial topology is the farthest from the target overlay and provides a better chance to verify the efficiency of our GSPS algorithm. The curves in Fig. 3 represent the number of client nodes that have joined the overlay after a number of simulation rounds. In the first round, the entire set of client nodes exchange information with their neighbors and select the required number of super-peers. After that, the client nodes join the peer groups managed by the selected super-peers. For the capacity of the nodes, two types of distributions are evaluated, the uniform distribution and the power-law distribution. Based on the above results, we can say that the GSPS algorithm performs fast when measured with the convergence time to the target overlay.

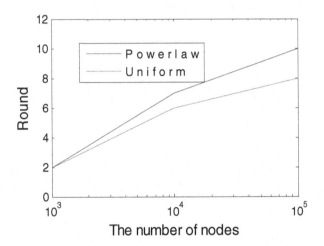

Fig. 4. The scalability in terms of different distribution of nodes' capacity

Fig. 4 demonstrates the scalability of the GSPS. Specifically, as the number of the peers in the network increases, what is the variation of the simulation rounds that are needed to make the overlay converge to the target overlay. In this experiment, two types of distribution of the peers' capacity are utilized: the power-law distribution and the uniform distribution. One can find out from the figure that the number of simulation rounds needed to achieve the target configuration grows a little bit with respect to the size of the network. The reason is that: even there is huge increase in the number of the nodes in the overlay, most of the super-peers can be selected in the first simulation round by all the nodes in the overlay; and only a few super-peers are not selected but they can be selected in the following second or third round. Based on these selected super-peers, the client nodes can join these super-peers based on their set of super-peers candidates very quickly to make the overlay converge to its target. Therefore, the increase in the number of the nodes in the overlay only has a little impact on the convergence to the target overlay. This result proves that the GSPS supports scalability very well.

Fig. 5 shows the comparison between the RASP, and the SG-1, which is implemented in [13], in terms of the influence of the super-peers' maximum capacity on the convergence to the target overlay. In this experiment, only the number of simulation rounds needed to achieve the target topology is depicted. From this figure, we can see that, as the super-peers' maximum capacity increases, our GSPS takes a few more simulation rounds to converge the target overlay, peaking at 8.5 rounds on average when the capacity is equal to 600. However, the SG-1 takes a little longer simulation time to achieve the target overlay with the increase of the super-peers' maximum capacity, peaking at 14 rounds when the capacity is equal to 600 on average. This reason for this result is due to fact that different methods are utilized in the SG-1 and our GSPS. More specifically, when the super-peers' maximum capacity increases (that is, a super-peer can manage more client nodes), the number of required super-peers is reduced. However, in our GSPS, most of the super-peers can be selected in the first simulation round, no matter the number of the super-peer is reduces or not. Based on the selected super-peers, the client nodes can join one of the peer groups managed by one of the super-peers. Therefore, the increases of the super-peers' maximum capacity has a little impact on the GSPS algorithm. For the SG-1, when the maximum capacity of the super-peers increases, the number of the required super-peers that manage the client nodes in the overlay becomes less. That is to say, more information exchanges between the super-peers are required to change these super-peers to the client nodes, because all the peers in the overlay take the role of a super-peer in the beginning of the simulation. Thus, it takes longer time to build the target overlay with fewer super-peers. As conclusion, the increases of the super-peers' maximum capacity has a little influence on our GSPS algorithm in comparison to the SG-1.

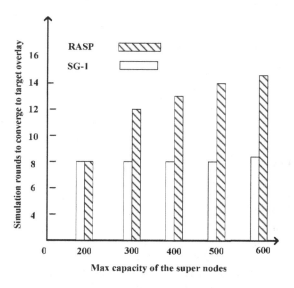

Fig. 5. The influence of the super- nodes' max capacity on the convergence to the target overlay

Fig. 6 demonstrates the robustness of the GSPS. We examined three catastrophic scenarios : 10% of the super-peers are removed at simulation round six; 20% of the super-peers are removed at round six and 30% of the super-peers are removed at round six. One can find out that even when the number of the failed super-peers increases, it almost takes the same number of simulation rounds for the GSPS algorithm to reach the steady overlay state again. The rationale behind this result is as follows. When the crash of the super-peers happens, these failed super-peers are removed from the overlay; meanwhile, all the client peers, whose super-peers have crashed, remove their super-peer from the set of super-peer candidates and rebuild their set of super-peers as shown in Fig. 1. After that, these client nodes execute the GSPS algorithm to select new super-peers as usual and join the peer groups managed by these super-peers. Based on the simulation result, we can say that the GSPS is not only robust to the failure of super-peers but also efficient in re-organizing the overlay into a new topology.

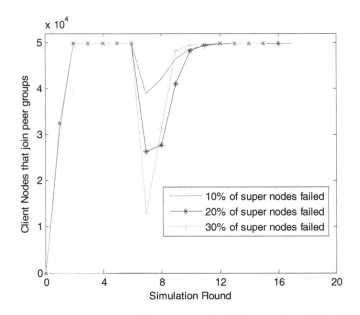

Fig. 6. The failure scenario: 50% of the super nodes are removed at the round 6

4   Related Work

In this section, we review the related work on the building and maintaining the P2P overlay for different aims. Meanwhile, we also compare our GSPS algorithm with other research studies.

Some overlay management work focus on the diameter or degree of the overlay. For example, Angluin et al. [3] describe an asynchronous distributed algorithm to quickly convert the nodes in a weakly-connected pointer graph into the leaves of a Patricia tree by the length of node identifiers. Pandurangan et al. [4] present a protocol to build P2P networks with constant degree and logarithmic diameter in a distributed fashion. In [5], an algorithm is proposed that can construct low-diameter resilient topologies, where the degree of the nodes distribution follows a power-law. In [6], Swap Links approach utilizing random walks as a component is proposed to construct required graphs for the overlay, where the degree of each node is the only parameter that needs setting. In [7], Mushtaq et al. present a quality adaptive mechanism for the multimedia streaming and video on demand services over hybrid P2P overlay networks. Their overlay is built by organization the sender peers in the networks based on the category of their offered video quality and the end-to-end probing among the sender and receiver peers. Different from these work, our work focus on building a super-peer overlay, where the role of a super-peer is identified.

Some researchers work on the construction of the unstructured overlay with random walk. For example, in [8], to build an unstructured overlay, a random walk is used to select neighbors for the new incoming peers in the joining process, in terms of capacity and connectivity to achieve load balancing. Li et al. [25] focus on the layer management in a super-peer architecture, specifically, employing workload model to maintain the optimal size ratio between the leaf-layer and the super-layer. Ganesh et al. [26] focus providing partial views for each node in the overlay without the knowledge of the system size. Thus, the memory cost and the synchronization overhead between nodes are reduced when build the overlay. Different from the above work, our work focuses on building the connection between the nodes, taking account of the nodes' heterogeneity.

Many works have discussed the performance trade-offs and the advantages of structuring peers into two layers: a super-layer, where the super-peers (i.e., the nodes with relatively long lifetime and large capacities) behave like proxies for the peers in the "normal" layer. Montresor [13] proposes a robust protocol SG-1 to construct and maintain overlay topology based on super-peers. In SG-1, a node exchanges information with randomly selected neighbor nodes to identify a super-peer and rearrange the topology according to the application requirements. Jesi et al. [27] propose a novel proximity-aware protocol SG-2 to manage super-peer topologies. The SG-2 employs a gossip-based protocol to spread messages to nearby nodes and a biology-inspired task allocation mechanism to promote the "best" nodes into a super-peer status. The comparisons between the SG-1, the SG-2 and our work are as follows. In the SG-1, the super-peers are selected through comparing the capacity between each two neighboring nodes recursively, where the node with the high capacity takes the role of a super-peer. The SG-2 utilizes a complex biology-inspired method to select the super-peer, considering the locality factor. In our GSPS, we first build a set of the super-peer candidates, and then a super-peer is selected in the way that if a client node belongs to the set of super-peer candidates, which is simple but does not take account of the locality.

5 Conclusion and Future Work

In this paper, we have presented a gossip based super-peer selection algorithm (GSPS) that is robust in managing the super-peer overlay, e.g. selecting the super-peers and maintaining the relationship between the super-peers and the client peers. In the GSPS, the peers with higher capacity are selected to be the better super-peers candidates through exchanging information with the neighboring nodes. If a node belongs to the set of super-peer candidates, the node takes a role a super-peer and recruits client nodes. Otherwise, a node chooses to join a super-peer. Moreover, the simulation results show that the GSPS is 1) efficient in building the target topology, 2) robust to the churn of nodes joining and leaving as well as to the failure of the super-peers.

In our future work, we will evaluate the communication overhead to build the target overlay. Specifically, we take account of two kinds of communication overheads. One is the total number of exchanged message sent to query the load of the neighboring super-peers on average and their sets of super-peer candidates. The other is the total number of communication overhead during the construction of the overlay on average. Another future work is to introduce the locality factor for the location-based optimization, which can improve the communication performance.

Acknowledgements

The authors would like to thank the anonymous reviewers for their valuable advice. This work was supported by the ITEA2 Expeshare project, funded by the Finnish Funding Agency for Technology and Innovation (Tekes), and the project of SOPSCC (Pervasive Service Computing: A Solution Based on Web Services), funded in the Ubiquitous Computing and Diversity of Communication (MOTIVE) program by the Academy of Finland.

References

1. Oram, A.: Peer-to-Peer: Harnessing the Benefits of a Disruptive Technology, ch. 8, March 2001. O'Reilly & Associates, Sebastopol (2001)
2. Milojicic, D.S., et al.: Peer-to-Peer Computing. Technical Report HPL-2002-57, HP Labs, Palo Alto (2002)
3. Angluin, D., Aspnes, J., Chen, J., Wu, Y., Yin, Y.: Fast Construction of Overlay Networks. In: Proceedings of the seventeenth annual ACM symposium on Parallelism in algorithms and architectures (2005)
4. Pandurangan, G., Raghavan, P., Upfal, E.: Building low-diameter peer-to-peer networks. IEEE Journal on Selected Areas in Communications (2003)
5. Wouhaybi, R.H., Campbell, A.T.: Phenix: Supporting Resilient Low-Diameter Peer-to-Peer Topologies. In: Proc. INFOCOM 2004 (2004)
6. Vishnumurthy, V., Francis, P.: On heterogeneous overlay construction and random node selection in unstructured P2P networks. In: Proc. IEEE INFOCOM 2006 (2006)
7. Mushtaq, M., Ahmed, T.: Hybrid Overlay Networks Management for Real-Time Multimedia Streaming over P2P Networks. In: Krishnaswamy, D., Pfeifer, T., Raz, D. (eds.) MMNS 2007. LNCS, vol. 4787, pp. 1–13. Springer, Heidelberg (2007)
8. Kwong, K.W., Tsang, D.H.K.: Building heterogeneous peer-to-peer networks: protocol and analysis. IEEE/ACM Transactions on Networking (2008)
9. Lime Wire LLC, Rfc-Gnutella 0.6,
   http://rfcgnutella.sourceforce.net/development
10. Kazaa,
   http://www.kazaa.com/us/help/glossary/p2p.htm
   (accessed 17-07-2009)

11. Saroiu, S., Gummadi, P.K., Gribble, S.D.: A measurement study of peer-to-peer file sharing systems. In: Proc. of Multimedia Computing and Networking (MMCN), San Jose, CA, USA (January 2002)
12. Yang, B., Garcia-Molina, H.: Designing a Super-peer Network. In: Proc. of the 19th Int. Conf. on Data Engineering (ICDE), Bangalore, India (March 2003)
13. Montresor, A.: A robust protocol for building super-peer overlay topologies. In: Proceedings of the 4th International Conference on Peer-to-Peer Computing, pp. 202–209 (2004)
14. Wang, F., Liu, J., Xiong, Y.: Stable peers: Existence, importance, and application in peer-to-peer live video streaming. In: IEEE INFOCOM 2008 (2008)
15. Zhou, J., Ou, Z., Rautiainen, M., Ylianttila, M.: P2P SCCM: Service-oriented Community Coordinated Multimedia over P2P. In: Proc. IEEE Congress on Services Part II (2008)
16. Jelasity, M., Montresor, A.: Epidemic-Style Proactive Aggregationin Large Overlay Networks. In: Proc. of the 24th International Conf. Distributed Computing Systems (2004)
17. Jelasity, M., Kowalczyk, W., van Steen, M.: "Newscast computing.Technical Report IR-CS-006", Vrije Universiteit Amsterdam, Dept. of Computer Science (November 2003)
18. Chen, Y., Pandurangan, G., Xu, D.: Robust Computation of Aggregates in Wireless Sensor Networks: Distributed Randomized Algorithms and Analysis. IEEE Transactions on Parallel and Distributed Systems (2006)
19. Lua, E.K., Crowcroft, J., Pias, M., Sharma, R., Lim, S.: A Survey and Comparison of Peer-to-Peer Overlay Network Schemes. IEEE Comm. Surveys and Tutorials 7(2), 72–93 (2005)
20. Stutzbach, D., Rejaie, R.: Characterizing the two-tier Gnutella topology. In: Proc. ACM SIGMETRICS (2005)
21. Voulgaris, S., Gavidia, D., Van Steen, M.: YCLON: Inexpensive Membership Management for Unstructured P2P Overlays. Journal of Network and Systems Management (2005)
22. Yuan, Q., Wu, J.: DRIP: A Dynamic VoRonoi RegIons-Based Publish/Subscribe Protocol in Mobile Networks. In: Proc. IEEE INFOCOM 2008 (2008)
23. Basagni, S.: Distributed clustering for ad hoc networks. Journal of Parallel Architectures, Algorithms, and Networks (1999)
24. PeerSim P2P Simulator, http://peersim.sourceforge.net/
25. Li, X., Zhuang, Z., Liu, Y.: Dynamic Layer Management in Superpeer Architectures. IEEE Transactions on Parallel and Distributed Systems 16 (2005)
26. Ganesh, A.J., Kermarrec, A.M., Massoulie, L.: Peer-to-peer membership management for gossip-based protocols. IEEE transactions on computers (2003)
27. Jesi, G.P., Montresor, A., Babaoglu, O.: Proximity-aware superpeer overlay topologies. IEEE Transactions on Network and Service Management (2007)

An Evaluation Criterion for Adaptive Neighbor Selection in Heterogeneous Peer-to-Peer Networks

Marco Picone, Michele Amoretti, and Francesco Zanichelli

Department of Information Engineering, Univ. of Parma, Italy
picone@ce.unipr.it
http://dsg.ce.unipr.it

Abstract. The peer-to-peer paradigm potentially enables low-cost and highly scalable distributed systems where user nodes have at the same time the roles of consumer and provider of resources. Nowadays, the computational power and storage capacity of mobile devices has notably increased, for which their inclusion in the physical network that supports P2P overlays can be realistically considered. For those applications where the quality of service is a fundamental constraint, such as live streaming, it is important to have overlay network level strategies to dynamically reconfigure the active connections among peers. In this paper we propose a simple but effective strategy for the evaluation of neighbors, taking into account their capabilities, to support the dynamic selection of resource providers. We apply the formal framework to P2P Internet Live Streaming, simulating three realistic scenarios and discussing the results.

1 Introduction

Peer-to-Peer (P2P) applications have recently emerged as an effective solution for large-scale content distribution over the Internet, from the early Napster (1999) to today's widespread fully decentralized delivery of multimedia streams, without relying on the traditional client-server paradigm.

In general, P2P approaches potentially enable low-cost and highly scalable distributed systems where user nodes have at the same time the consumer and provider roles. Sharing their own resources, peers contribute to the achievement of a global task which needs only a limited (if any) infrastructure since it exploits the large pool of user resources. *P2P Internet Streaming* is becoming one of most popular services on the global network and by means of application-level multicasting techniques achieves large-scale distribution of massive amounts of data with strong temporal constraints without compromising the provided quality of service [5,7,8]. These applications are mostly targeted to a set of wired nodes which are considered heterogeneous only with respect to the connection type and speed.

Recent years have also seen the relentless market success of a plethora of mobile devices (PDAs, smartphones, MIDs, PMPs, netbooks, ...), whose ever

T. Pfeifer and P. Bellavista (Eds.): MMNS 2009, LNCS 5842, pp. 144–156, 2009.

increasing capabilities make them attractive to a growing number of network applications in *business* and *infotainment* domains to be fully experienced in mobility. Although the computing, storage and communication resources available on many modern mobile devices are often not far from those available on common PCs, the specific issues of reduced connection stability (because of being wireless and moving across different access networks) and limited autonomy (because of being battery-powered) should be addressed in any distributed application which includes support for mobile nodes.

This work presents an adaptive peer selection strategy for heterogeneous peer-to-peer networks, with particular reference to Internet live streaming applications. The prioritization strategy supports extremely heterogeneous P2P networks where nodes exhibit very diverse nature and performance. Given that neighbor selection, *i.e.* one the critical functions of any P2P system, is generally based only upon the availability of required resources and the evaluation of the bandwidth capabilities of prospective partners, a more general selection criterion is required to cope with node heterogeneity. The adaptive selection strategy in our approach compares nodes by taking into account a certain number of their features (as required by the application domain) to the purpose of increasing the experienced quality of service by performing uniform evaluation of highly heterogenous peers.

The paper is organized as follows. Section 2 outlines a brief review of the main challenges to be faced when designing P2P applications supporting mobile devices. In section 3 some related work is discussed. Section 4 provides a formal characterization of the evaluation criterion for peer selection and introduces a set of node features appropriate for P2P live streaming applications.

In section 5 the proposed selection strategy is preliminarly evaluated by means of simulation on a number of heterogenous P2P live streaming scenarios.

2   Design Challenges

So far, P2P applications have been mostly designed and implemented considering personal computers as hosts and resource providers, rather than mobile devices. Nowadays, the computational power and storage capacity of mobile devices has notably increased, for which their inclusion in a physical network that supports a P2P overlay can be realistically considered. In this section we recall some general considerations to better define the issues that arise when mobile devices participate in a distributed system [6].

Different interfaces for data connectivity. In particular, mobile phones may have different kinds of data connections (*e.g.* CDMA/GPRS/3G) or in addition, as in the case of most modern devices, they can access WiFi networks. Applications like P2P media streaming are very sensitive to delays and loss of segments. For all these reasons, the different nature of connections and the possibility of sudden switches from an access network to another, are factors to take into account in order to dynamically adapt the overlay network to the characteristics of individual nodes.

Intrinsic mobility of devices. Physical mobility may involve changes in access speed to the network, but can also cause prolonged or momentary disconnections of peers, more frequently with respect to peer hosted by personal computers. Redundancy of resources and quick discovery of new providers is the general solution to this problem, but a purely reactive approach is not sufficient for applications like P2P multimedia streaming, for which proactive strategies should pursued instead (*e.g.* each peer should have a list of suitable neighbors, in the sense that if a new segment provider is selected when the current one disconnects from the network or offers poor performance, packet losses are minimized).

Limited resources. As mentioned above, with respect to personal computers, mobile devices are characterized by limited battery autonomy low memory and reduced computational power. This aspect is very important and requires several optimizations for the software to be run on the device, in order to guarantee a good quality service. Compared to the previous issue, this one is fortunately becoming less and less relevant, since an increasing number of mobile devices with very high autonomy and generous computational and storage capacities is entering the market. These new mobile devices will allow the developers to create richer applications, improving the experience for the user.

3   Related Work

Dynamic neighbor evaluation and selection is used in several P2P systems described in the literature.

In KaZaA [3] and Gnutella2 [2], the most powerful nodes (*e.g.* those with higher bandwidth) are set as super-nodes to form the backbone of the P2P overlay network, which manages most of the messaging load for resource discovery. In BitTorrent[1] systems, central servers store information about trackers, *i.e.* agents that are responsible for helping peers find each other. The BitTorrent protocol focuses on high data transfer speed rather than on search capabilities. When joining the torrent, the peer asks to the tracker a list of IP address of peers to build its initial peer set, *i.e.* the list of other peers it knows about. A peer can only send data to a subset of its peer set, called active peer set. The "choke algorithm" determines the peers being part of the active peer set. Each downloader reports to all its peers what pieces it has, thus each peer knows the distribution of the pieces for each peer in its peer set. The piece selection strategy used in BitTorrent is based on rarest first strategy.

Kwong et al. [9] propose a simple but interesting protocol for building heterogeneous unstructured P2P networks. The basic idea is to take into account node capacity during the joining and rebuilding process. In a first step, incoming new peers select as neighbors those peers that are more suitable in terms of capacity and connectivity, with the purpose of achieving good load-balancing. The rebuilding process describes how the nodes act to re-establish an efficient topology when some of their links are broken. To the same purpose, *i.e.* dynamically re-shaping the overlay network topology, interesting strategies based on genetic algorithms have ben proposed [10,11].

In applications like P2P Internet live streaming, where the quality of service (QoS) plays a very important role, neighbor selection must be carefully performed. The basic solution is random neighbor selection from the list received by the bootstrap node of the system or by a decentralized mechanism. A better solution is adopted by other protocols like CoolStreaming[5], where nodes periodically exchange information about their status, e.g. about the stream segments that they own and they can share, and about their actual bandwidth. These information are used by the provider selection strategy during the start-up process of each single node, and for managing changes of provider during the life of the peer.

To create a P2P streaming protocol that can be applied to a network of heterogeneous hosts, including mobile devices, it is important to introduce a peer selection criterion that dynamically evaluates the QoS of the neighbors, in order to personalize the behavior of each peer. A work of Nemati et al. [7] tries to analyze and model a network with mobile and heterogeneous devices in terms of mobility and QoS. The protocol defines two kinds of mobile peers: indirectly mobile peers whose hosts are mobile, and directly mobile peers that are realized as mobile agents. A mobile peer can manipulate a multimedia content in a host. QoS supported by the peer depends on the host. Movements of mobile peers are modeled in terms of changes of QoS, which is described and characterized by bandwidth, delay and packet-loss-ratio under overlay level and at the overlay by frame-rate, resolution, number of colors, quality of sound, etc. With this model the peers of the network can analyze the parameters of other nodes to select the best provider, trying to maximize the obtained QoS in a dynamic way.

4   Formal Statement of the Evaluation Criterion

We consider a network with N peers as a graph $\mathcal{G} = (\mathcal{V}, \mathcal{E})$, where $\mathcal{V}$ is the set of vertices and $\mathcal{E}$ is the set of edges. Each peer has a number of resources, whose domain is defined as $\mathcal{R}$. Moreover, each peer can distinguish principal resources, in a set $\mathcal{R}_p$, from secondary resources, in a set $\mathcal{R}_s$, such that $\mathcal{R} = \mathcal{R}_p \cup \mathcal{R}_s$.

The status of both main and secondary resources should be taken into account for a peer that has to be evaluated by another peer. But in a heterogeneous network some kinds of peer could be lacking one or more kinds of resources, with respect to other richer peers. For this reason we introduce a unique parameter to characterize any kind of peer, i.e. the *fitness*. In other words, we state that for each peer in V $\exists f_i > 0$ defined as:

$$f_i = f(g_i, h_i) = \frac{g_i(\mathbf{r}_s)}{K_0 + h_i(\mathbf{r}_m)} \quad K_0 > 0 \quad \mathbf{r}_s \in \mathcal{R}_s^{m_i} \quad \mathbf{r}_m \in \mathcal{R}_p^{n_i} \tag{1}$$

where

$$g : \mathcal{R}_s^m \to \mathbb{R} \quad m \in \mathbb{N} \tag{2}$$

and

$$h : \mathcal{R}_m^n \to \mathbb{R} \quad n \in \mathbb{N} \tag{3}$$

As illustrated in figure 1, the fitness is a family of curves that depend on the value of functions h and g. For a given peer i, with n_i principal resources and m_i secondary resources, the fitness value and h_i are inversely proportional, while the fitness value and g_i are directly proportional. The curve progress of functions g, h, as well as the value of K_0 must be defined based on the application, always avoiding the following situation:

$$f_1(h_1, g_1) > f_2(h_2, g_2) \quad h_1 > h_2 \tag{4}$$

in which the node with lowest h has the highest fitness value.

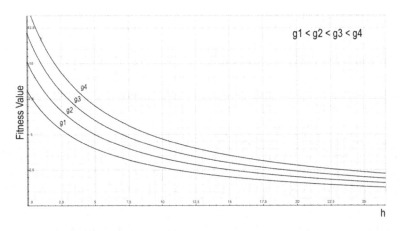

Fig. 1. Fitness curve progress with respect to h and g

This evaluation criterion can be used in a wide range of P2P applications. For example we consider a P2P Internet Live Streaming application based on the data-driven approach, where the stream is distributed depending on the availability or need of data chunks, unlike traditional Internet streaming systems (*e.g.* those based on the source-driven paradigm) that perform explicit search of the optimal streaming paths from the source(s) to the sinks. The fitness-based approach introduces adaptiveness in the data-driven system, to maintain a high degree of efficiency even in presence of heterogeneous nodes with different availability profiles (*e.g.* mobile nodes versus stable nodes). Each node is periodically evaluated according to the status of its resources, *i.e.* its dynamic features (residual battery, type of network connection, available bandwidth, on-line permanence time), with a fitness value being computed. By comparing the fitness of its neighbors (*i.e.* known peers), each peer can select the locally optimal multimedia stream providers. This allow to reduce the impact on the system of least performing nodes (*e.g.* nodes with reduced bandwidth and computational capacity), and to improve the overall quality of service.

The fitness value of a single node is computed considering the following parameters (which represent resources characterizing every node):

- actual upload bandwidth (U): the nominal transmission rate of a node, over the number of neighbors being served by that node
- battery percentage (B): in case of PC node, its value is always 100; for a mobile node, the value decreases depending on node usage
- on-line permanence time (T_o): its value defines how long the peer has been connected to the network

Among these resources, we considered U as principal, while B and T_o are secondary. Since all nodes are characterized by the same number of resources (*i.e.* $m_i = m$ and $n_i = n$ for each $i = 1, .., N$), the h and g functions are the same for every node. Supposing a node i evaluates another node j, the h function applied to the latter is defined as

$$h(U_j) = \left(\frac{min\{D_i, \frac{U_j}{k_j+1}\}}{S} \right)^{-1} \tag{5}$$

where D_i is the download rate of node i, S is the stream rate of the multimedia source assumed to be constant, and

$$k_j = \sum_{l=1}^{N} e_{lj} \tag{6}$$

where $e_{lj} \in \{0, 1\}$ has non-zero value if node l is being serviced by node j. In (5), the numerator represents the transmission rate that will be devoted to node i from node j, if selected. U_j is evaluated with respect to already active outgoing connections (which in general are less than the number of known nodes by each peer), plus the envisioned connection (for which neighbors are being evaluated by node i).

The g function applied to node j is defined as

$$g(B_j, T_{oj}) = K_1 \frac{B_j}{B_{Max}} + K_2 \frac{T_{oj}}{T_{oMax}} \quad K_1 > 0 \quad K_2 > 0 \tag{7}$$

Thus the fitness function applied to node j is

$$f_j = f(g_j, h_j) = \frac{g(B_j, T_{oj})}{K_0 + h_j(U_j)} \tag{8}$$

Fitness-based evaluation can be applied to the following phases of a generic data-driven protocol (see also figure 2):

1. *Neighbor list update*: to limit the negative effects of random disconnections and to monitor the quality of service of the system, each peer periodically updates its neighbor list; this is done by sending messages to all known nodes, which in turn respond with their updated resource values; if a contacted node does not respond before a given deadline, it is removed from the neighbor list, and replaced with another node.

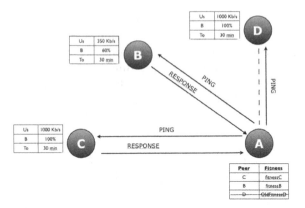

Fig. 2. Example of neighbor list update, performed by node A

2. *Provider selection*: once the peer has updated its neighbor list, it selects the neighbor with the higher fitness value to be the provider of the multimedia stream.

5   Simulation Results

The adaptive peer selection strategy applied to live streaming has been implemented and preliminary evaluated using the Discrete Event Universal Simulator (DEUS) [4], which is an open source tool that provides a simple Java API for the implementation of nodes, events and processes, and a straightforward but powerful XML schema to configure the experiments. DEUS aims to be one of the reference tools in the field of complex system simulation, thanks to its high flexibility and performance.

Three node types have been modelled with the parameters illustrated in Table 1: PC with high performance in terms of computational capacity and bandwidth, Mobile-WiFi nodes with limited resources but accessing the network with a Wireless Lan connection, and 3G Mobile nodes using a connection with lower bandwidth and subject to the variability of cellular networks.

For the behavioral modeling of mobile devices two types of specific events have been considered:

Table 1. Parameters of the simulated nodes

Node type	Uplink	DownLink	Battery
Mobile3G-Node	50 Kbit/sec	400 Kbit/sec	[20,100]
MobileWiFi-Node	100 Kbit/sec	2 Mbit/sec	[20,100]
PC-Node	300 Kbit/sec	4 Mbit/sec	100%

- The transition from a 3G to a 2G connection, *i.e.* a connection with low performance that has a reduced uplink bandwidth of only 25Kbit/sec and a downlink bandwidth of 100 Kbit/sec.
- Battery consumption; each peer enters the network with a random fraction of battery capacity; this value (Q_B) is periodically decreased according to elapsed time and to the number of outgoing active connections:

$$Q'_B = f(Q_B, k_{out}) \tag{9}$$

In general, we assumed that with a charge of 100%, a mobile peer can stay active for 1 hour and 30 minutes of playback. When the remaining battery falls below a certain threshold, the node leaves the system with a consequent reconfiguration of the peers which were directly connected to it.

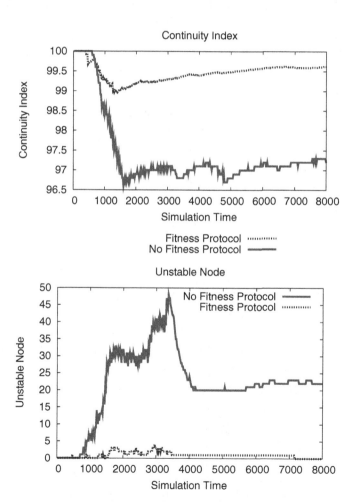

Fig. 3. Comparison of Continuity Index and Unstable Nodes in the first scenario

Initially we considered a simple data-driven protocol [8] in which each node has a single segment provider. We compared the peer selection strategy based on the evaluation of the fitness value associated to each node with a simple random selection of the supplier for the media stream.

The first analyzed scenario has a higher percentage of PC nodes and Mobile-WiFi and consequently a large amount of available resources. Applying the fitness strategy allows to select the most efficient suppliers, reduces the load on the source node and prevents the undesirable effect of having Mobile Wi-Fi and 3G nodes that become suppliers for subgroups of nodes. Obtained simulation results (figure 3) show a small percentage of links to nodes with poor performance, thus increasing the Continuity Index (CI), which is the percentage of video segments received before the playback deadline, and reducing the number of unstable nodes in the system (*i.e.* nodes with a CI under 90%).

The second scenario shows a higher number of Mobile3G compared to other types of nodes and implies a reduced availability of resources. In this situation, when no evaluation of the nodes is performed, a remarkable reduction of the CI can be noticed along with a significant increase of unstable nodes in the system as in figure 4. The reason is that selected nodes are inefficient suppliers

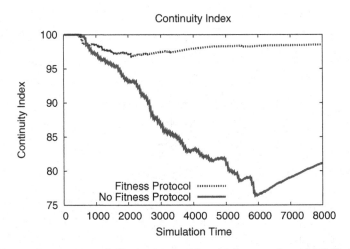

Fig. 4. Comparison of CI obtained with a higher number of 3G Nodes

Table 2. CoolStreaming simulations parameters

Name	Value
Total Nodes	712
Num. Of PC-Node	396
Num. Of MobileWiFi-Node	141
Num. Of Mobile3G-Node	179
Simulation MaxTime	110000 VT
Real MaxTime	1:30 h

for their subgroups of peers in the system. This choice involves a reduction of performance and a progressive deterioration of the system. Instead, the use of the fitness-based strategy reduces these negative effects, trying to exploit as much as possible the ability of the most efficient peers.

The increase of the CI without fitness criterion after 6000VT is a consequence of the disconnection of mobile nodes that in this scenario have to manage a lot of connections, which cause a fast decrease of the battery level. At the end of the simulation there are less mobile nodes compared with the beginning of the simulaton, for which PC nodes can manage the distribution of the media stream with better performance, in terms of continuity index.

Obviously the impact of mobile nodes is very important in a system with only one segment provider per peer, where the disconnection or the presence of low-performing intermediate providers readily affects the system's performance. More

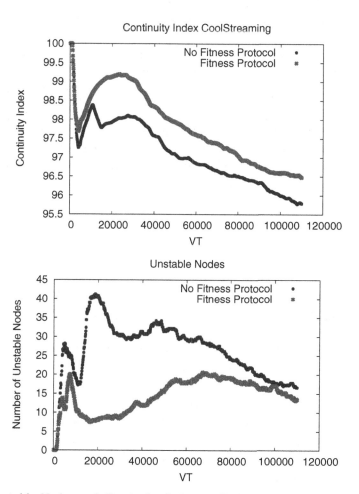

Fig. 5. Unstable Nodes and Continuity Index in CoolStreaming, with and without fitness

complex protocols, involving multiple suppliers per peer, are more robust against temporary loss of suppliers, because the responsibility of the flow is distributed among multiple nodes. For this reason, the second phase of analysis of the fitness criterion has been focused to its application to the popular multi-supplier protocol for P2P live streaming, *i.e.* CoolStreaming [5]. This protocol assigns a set of segment providers to each peer, with an evaluation strategy that analyzes the available bandwidth and resources of nodes with which the other peers come into contact. This value is used for the selection of the appropriate provider for the media-stream. For the reasons explained previously in a network that shows heterogeneity in terms of devices, a more detailed and specific strategy is necessary, for which we added the fitness-based strategy to the CoolStreaming protocol. Simulations have been carried out using DEUS, using the same types of nodes and events that have been used for the analysis of the simple data-driven protocol. The evaluation is based on the characteristics listed in Table 2.

In this second analysis the fitness strategy replaces only the bandwidth strategy of CoolStreaming, not the stream segments evaluation that is to much tied together with the protocol and can not be changed. The results show that also in case of a real system like CoolStreaming with a high heterogeneous network in term of kinds of devices, connections and behaviours can experience an increase of performance using the fitness selection strategy. Figure 5 shows that during the simulated time there is an increase of CI and a decrease in the number of unstable nodes. Near the end of the simulation, where the number of devices and the global battery level are reduced, there is still a small group of high performance nodes. For this reason there is a reduced range of good potential providers

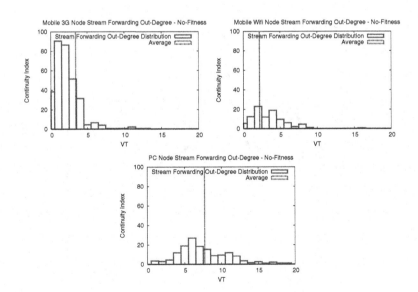

Fig. 6. Distribution of the number of outgoing active connections (k_out) for each peer, for the standard CoolStreaming protocol

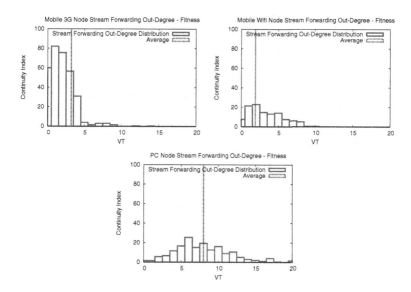

Fig. 7. Distribution of the number of outgoing active connections (k_out) for each peer, for CoolStreaming protocol enhanced with fitness-based strategy

and the difference of performance between the two approaches is less evident. In figures 7 and 6 we compare the stream forwarding out-degree distribution (at simulation's virtual time 50000) without and with fitness-based strategy for each kind of node. They show that with the adaptive strategy there is a little advantage and that nodes with higher capacities are used more than nodes with lower capacities.

6   Conclusions

In this work we have proposed an evaluation criterion for neighbor selection in distributed systems based on the peer-to-peer paradigm, where peer processes are hosted by heterogeneous devices, including mobile devices. Our approach is based on the concept of fitness, which allows to compare resource providers with different characteristics. We have shown that the general approach can be specialized to a particularly challenging problem, i.e. P2P Internet Live Streaming. Simulation results are encouraging, showing that the fitness-based strategy can be applied to existing protocols, with effective performance improvements.

As future work, we will use our strategy in conjunction with techniques and protocols that have been specifically defined for constrained devices. For example, in the field of P2P Internet Live Streaming we will consider layered video coding, and multiple description coding. Those techniques allow to adapt multimedia content to differently featured devices. Moreover, we will investigate the application of the fitness-based strategy to other P2P applications, such as data-intensive computing and multi-player online gaming.

References

1. BitTorrent official site, http://www.bittorrent.org
2. Gnutella official site, http://www.gnutella.com
3. KaZaA official site, http://www.kazaa.com
4. Amoretti, M., Agosti, M., Zanichelli, F.: DEUS: a Discrete Event Universal Simulator. In: Proc. of the 2nd ICST/ACM International Conference on Simulation Tools and Techniques (SIMUTools 2009), Roma, Italy (March 2009)
5. Keung, G.Y., Xie, X.Z.S., Li, B.: CoolStreaming: Design, Theory, and Pratice, pages. IEEE Transactions on Multimedia 9(8), 1661–1671 (2007)
6. Ahmed, T., Mushtaq, M.: P2P-based Mobile IPTV: Challenges and Opportunities. In: Proc. Computer Systems and Applications, AICCSA 2008. IEEE/ACS International Conference, pp. 975–980 (2008)
7. Takizawa, M., Nemati, A.G., Enokido, T.: A Multi-Source Streaming Model for Mobile Peer-to-Peer (P2P) Overlay Networks. In: Proc. The 28th International Conference on Distributed Computing Systems Workshops, pp. 18–23 (2008)
8. Fourmaux, O., Silverston, T.: Source vs Data-driven Approach for Live P2P Streaming. In: Proc. International Conference on Networking, Internation Conference on Systems and Intenation Conference on Mobile Communications and Learning Technologies, pp. 99–104 (2006)
9. Kwong, K.W., Tsang, D.H.K.: Building heterogeneous peer-to-peer networks: Protocol and analysis. IEEE-ACM Transactions on Networking 12(2) (April 2008)
10. Koo, S.G.M., Kannan, K., George Lee, C.S.: On neighbor-selection strategy in hybrid peer-to-peer networks. Future Generation Computer Systems 22, 732–741 (2006)
11. Abraham, A., Yue, B., Xian, C., Liu, H., Pant, M.: Multi-objective Peer-to-Peer Neighbor-Selection Strategy Using Genetic Algorithm. In: Aluru, S., Parashar, M., Badrinath, R., Prasanna, V.K. (eds.) HiPC 2007. LNCS, vol. 4873, pp. 443–451. Springer, Heidelberg (2007)

Improving Performance of ALM Systems with Bayesian Estimation of Peers Dynamics

Ihsan Ullah, Grégory Bonnet, Guillaume Doyen, and Dominique Gaïti

ERA/Institut Charles Delaunay – FRE CNRS 2848
Université de Technologie de Troyes
12 rue Marie Curie, 10000 TROYES, France
{ihsan.ullah,bonnet,doyen,gaiti}@utt.fr

Abstract. P2P-based Application Layer Multicast (ALM) systems have shown a great success for several group communication applications. But some performance problems still await a major breakthrough from these systems for critical services such as live video streaming. For these applications, one of the problems is the dynamics of users' presence since the unannounced departure of a peer causes an interruption in service for all dependent ones. In this paper, we address this issue and propose a probabilistic approach based on Bayesian inference to anticipate users' departures and let peers react proactively. Through simulations and experimental evaluation, we prove that our approach improves significantly the performance of ALM systems with a low overhead.

1 Introduction

Services such as Video-on-Demand (VoD) and live video streaming are becoming very popular due to the availability of broadband access. These services are highly bandwidth consuming and, for the unicast-oriented architecture of the Internet, it is not feasible to deploy them. Therefore to support these services, dedicated group communication mechanisms are required. IP multicast [1] is the natural solution for it but it can not be deployed at the Internet scale due to several reasons given in [2]. On the other hand, Content Delivery Networks (CDNs) [3] distribute the content diffusion load of an origin server to several other servers deployed at strategic geographic locations. Nevertheless they are very expensive and the number of servers must grow with the number of users.

P2P-based Application Layer Multicast (ALM) has emerged as a promising approach to enable group communication applications. ALM systems form an overlay network over the physical one by establishing direct links among end-hosts in a P2P manner. Multicast groups are created and maintained at the application level and content is disseminated without requiring any support from the physical network infrastructure. Hence these systems are easy to deploy and require low cost. Since ALM systems are overlay networks composed of nodes, which are owned and controlled by the end-users, they face problems due to both the overlay itself and end-users. Most of the overlay related issues are addressed in previous works but the problem of peer dynamics, which is user related,

T. Pfeifer and P. Bellavista (Eds.): MMNS 2009, LNCS 5842, pp. 157–169, 2009.

requires some more attention. It is not only a hurdle in the success of tree-based systems, but also impacts the performance of other P2P-based systems. In currently deployed systems, the impact of peer dynamics is attempted to be reduced indirectly through the use of buffers of a very large size. The buffer provides the continuity of service but induces a time range delay. In our work, we address this issue and propose a probabilistic approach based on a Bayesian inference which enables ALM nodes to analyze their past presence in the system, and estimate the current session duration. Each node cooperates with other nodes to provide this information to them on request. A node, knowing the estimated session duration of the node it is currently depending upon, can react proactively in such a way to minimize the impact of peer dynamics. Moreover, it improves the performance of ALM systems through reducing the required buffer size and thus delay. Our work does not consider the start-up delay because peer dynamics causes a disruption in service after once it is started.

The rest of the paper is organized as follows. Section 2 outlines the work related to the same issue. In section 3, we present our approach, its validation and a comparison with a previous one. Section 4 deals with the dynamics management algorithms for ALM systems. In section 5, we present the experimental validation we perfomed to evaluate our propopsal in real conditions. Finally, section 6 draws some conclusions and gives directions of the future work.

2   Related Work

Since ALM systems are overlays formed by end-hosts, they face performance problems due to both the overlay topology and the end-users. Topology related problems include heterogenous resources and overlay mismatching with the physical network. These issues are already addressed in the research community and solutions have been given in [4,5,6]. On the other side, user related problems cover two aspects, which are resource sharing and dynamics of user's presence. Although the former has been addressed in [7,8,9], the latter requires some more attention especially for content delivery services such as live video streaming and VoD. The related work to this problem mostly consists in studies over different P2P-based video streaming systems, Video-on-Demand systems and telco-managed IPTV systems. These studies provide useful insights towards understanding the user behavior and modeling it in the proper context. We discuss now three of them.

In Yu et al [10], a statistical study of user behavior in a Video-on-Demand system is presented. They show that the number of users watching videos decreases during working hours of the day and increases in the breaks and in the evening times. Similarly, the number of users increases at the weekends, which shows that users watch more videos in their free times. The user arrival rate in this particular VoD matches a modified form of the Poisson distribution. The study of session lengths reveals that about 37% of users go offline within 5 minutes after arrival. On the other hand about 25% of users watch a video for more than 25 minutes. The later group of users is relatively stable and can be utilized to improve the performance. A second analysis study of an IPTV system

[11] shows similar patterns as above, namely that users watch more TV during breaks and in the dining hours. But, interestingly, Friday and Saturday got less online users as compared to other days of the week. The study of the IPTV system finds that the number of online users increases gradually but it decreases sharply due to batch departures. Moreover, the arrival and departure processes follow exponential distribution at short timescales. According to a third study of a Peer-to-peer IPTV system [12], user participation shows diurnal patterns with two peaks, one at the mid day and other at the evening time. The number of users does not vary too much on the weekends and on the working days. The study of users' session durations shows the same phenomenon as identified in the work presented above, namely that most of the users stay for a short time.

These user behavior analysis show that a large portion of users stay in the system for a very short time. Hence, on the departure of these users, other depending ones will face a service disruption. On the other hand, another category of users stay for sufficiently long time. Adapting ALM nodes to rely more on the stable part of the peers can reduce the service disruption.

Apart from the analysis studies, a work very close to our's is given in [13,14]. Authors first present an analysis which statistically reveals that a peer's remaining online duration is positively correlated with its elapsed online duration. Based on this finding they propose a mechanism which chooses a content provider node as the one which elapsed the longest time in the system. To support this function, a centralized authority is used to keep sessions' information of all peers in the system. As a conclusion, considering the elapsed time as a stability indication assumes all recently joining peers unlikely to stay longer. Moreover, a centralized authority is not a scalable and robust solution.

3   Peer's Dynamics Estimation

In this section, we first give a brief overview of a previous estimator we proposed in [15], based on Exponential Moving Average (EMA). Then we present a new estimator, which relies on a Bayesian estimation technique. Before comparing both techniques, we describe the associated decision making mechanism. In the sequel, we term the content providing node as a *provider* and the content receiving node as a *consumer*.

3.1   EMA-Based Estimation

In our previous work [15], we used an EMA-based estimation. EMA is a statistical technique which estimates an average from a set of values by giving exponentially decreasing weights to older values. As given in (1a), ES_t is the current session duration, S_{t-1} is the actual duration of last session, ES_{t-1} is the length of the last estimated session and α is a weighting factor in $[0, 1]$. The chosen optimal value of α is 0.7 suggesting to give more weights to the recent session durations. A node having no session history sets ES_0 at its elapsed time as the estimated current session duration. We define two enhancements for the estimator. Firstly, we decrease the estimated session duration by 20%. Such approach is called EMA_{20}. Secondly, we add the trend of the session length in the estimation as given in (1b) and (1c). β is a weighting factor in $[0, 1]$ and we choose 0.6 which gives overall good results. Such an approach is called EMA_T and is combined with EMA_{20} in EMA_{T20}.

$$ES_t = \alpha \times S_{t-1} + (1 - \alpha) \times ES_{t-1} \tag{1a}$$

$$T_t = (1 - \beta) \times T_{t-1} + \beta \times (ES_t - E_{t-1}) \tag{1b}$$

$$ES_t = \alpha \times S_{t-1} + (1 - \alpha) \times ES_{t-1} + T_t \tag{1c}$$

3.2 Bayesian Estimation

We propose another estimation technique: a probabilistic approach based on Bayesian inference, which enables an ALM peer to estimate its current session duration in the presence or absence of past sessions' history. In classical statistics, computing a probability distribution requires a set of observations to be infered. In our problem, a peer joining the system for the first time has no previous observations of the user behavior: this very limited number of observations is not appropriate to use classical statistics. Bayesian inference considers a prior probability distribution in the absence of any observation. Moreover, when a new observation arrives, this distribution is updated into posterior probability distribution accordingly. We assume that the prior probability distribution is a uniform one. Hence, we do not make any strong assumption on the user's behavior. Thus the Bayesian model we use is as follows.

Let $T \in \mathbb{R}$ be the maximum possible session duration of a node A. Let us partition T in k time steps $\{t_1, t_2 \ldots t_k\}$ such that $t_1 < t_2 \ldots t_{k-1} < t_k$. For each time interval $[t_i, t_{i+1}[$ we define a binomial variable α_i. The prior probability of the event ϕ_j, meaning that the next session duration S_i will be at least equal to t_j, can be modeled by the Dirichlet density function as given in (2a) where α_j is the number of observations when $S_i \geq t_j$. The estimated prior probability of $(S_i \geq t_j)$ is given by (2b) where $|O|$ is the set of already observed session durations. Let us notice that the variables α are not independent. So we define a mechanism to update the $\langle \alpha \rangle$ vector. After observing a set O' of some new session durations, the posterior probability of a session duration S_i to be at least equal to t_j is computed through (2c) where $o_j \subseteq O$ and $|o_j|$ is the number of observations where $S_i \geq t_j$.

$$f(\phi_1 \cdots \phi_{k-1} \mid \alpha_1 \cdots \alpha_k) = \frac{\Gamma(\alpha_1 + \alpha_2 + \cdots + \alpha_k)}{\Gamma(\alpha_1)\Gamma(\alpha_2) \cdots \Gamma(\alpha_k)} (\phi^{\alpha_1 - 1} \phi^{\alpha_2 - 1} \cdots \phi^{\alpha_k - 1}) \tag{2a}$$

$$f(\phi_j) = \frac{\alpha_j + 1}{|O| + 2} \tag{2b}$$

$$f(\phi_j | \beta, O) = \frac{\alpha_j + |o_j| + 1}{|O| + |O'| + 2} \tag{2c}$$

Using this estimator each peer updates its posterior probability after each session and keeps a list of probabilities corresponding to each t_j.

3.3   Decision Making Mechanism

The *consumer* node requests the session estimation from the *provider*. If we use the EMA-based estimation, each node estimates the length of its current session and provides it to other nodes on request. If we use the Bayesian estimation, the *consumer* specifies a given probability threshold P_{Th} and the *provider* estimates the length t_i of the current session with (3).

$$t^* = \max_{t_j}(f(\phi_j) \geq P_{th}) \tag{3}$$

In both cases, the *provider* also sends its *join time* in order to compute its elapsed and remaining time durations. When the elapsed time duration of the *provider* is reaching to its estimated one, the *consumer* sends a request to all neighbor nodes for their estimated dynamics. The neighbor nodes respond with their estimated time durations, *join times* and capacity status. Capacity status shows the possibility of serving a new consumer. This parameter is important to control the load on stable nodes. On receiving responses from neighbor nodes, the *consumer* selects the node with a capacity to provide content to a new node and having the highest estimated remaining time duration as a new *provider* and leaves the previous one.

3.4   Estimator Evaluation

In order to compare both techniques, we first introduce the session generation model. Then we present a comparison between both approaches.

Sessions Generation. The analysis studies of ALM systems do not show the individual user behavior, instead they give insights of collectively all users in the systems. We choose one of these studies [10] and model the session durations as a lognormal distribution with parameters ($\mu = 2.2, \sigma = 1.5$). Since it shows a collective behavior (and not an individual one), we define two kinds of users: users whose behavior changes from session to session and have uncorrelated session durations and users having a persistent behavior whose sessions are auto-correlated. Firstly, we generate randomly uncorrelated sessions in lognormal form which show the first behavior. Then we apply (4) to make them correlated.

$$S_t = f \times L_t + (1 - f) \times S_{t-1} \tag{4}$$

Here, S_t is the adapted session duration, L_t is the session in lognormal form and S_{t-1} is the last session duration. f is called the auto-correlation factor having a value between 0 and 1. We have chosen the value 0.2 to generate correlated sessions and 1 to generate uncorrelated sessions.

Comparison. To compare the estimators, we generate one thousand session durations and estimate each next session starting from the first one. By going forward the previous sessions are taken as a history. Firstly, we measure *success* which stands for the number of times our estimated session duration is less than or equal to the actual session duration. *Success* is important to react before the departure of the *provider* node. Secondly, we measure the *early reaction time.* Early reaction time is the difference between the actual session duration and estimated duration when the later is less than the former one. This measurement shows how optimal the reactions are. The lower the early reaction time, the lower is the overhead because *consumer* nodes stay over *provider nodes* as long as they can and they minimize the number of reactions. Thirdly, we measure the *error* that is the difference between the actual session duration and estimated session duration whatever the success. We made α, β varying on $]0,1[$ for EMA and EMA_T and the threshold varying on $]0,1[$ for Bayesian estimation. We kept the most interesting results. For Bayesian estimation, we kept three thresholds: 0.7, 0.8 and 0.9. We show our results in Table 3.4. In case of uncorrelated sessions, Bayesian estimation performs better on all criteria than all other estimators. By contrast, in case of correlated sessions, the EMA_{20} and EMA_{T20}-based estimations perform better than Bayesian estimation. Thus the most interesting approach depends on the correlation factor that models the users.

In order to refine our comparison, we analyze the *ratio* of the *early reaction time* to the actual session duration of the *provider* node as well as the *evolution* of the *error.* Figure 1 depicts the frequency distribution of these ratios and the evolution of the error for EMA_{20}, EMA_{T20} and Bayesian estimator. For Bayesian estimation, we set the threshold at 0.7 which is representative of the results. In case of uncorrelated sessions, the ratio distributions have the same structure for the three estimators. Thus, Bayesian estimation performs better than the others estimators due to its higher success. Concerning the evolution of the error, we can notice that Bayesian estimation does not overestimate the session compared to others estimators. Now in case of correlated sessions, ratio distributions have not the same structure. EMA_{20} and EMA_{T20} are better than Bayesian estimator. EMA_{20} does not over-estimate sessions compare to the others estimators. EMA_{T20} slightly overestimate due to the trend that might be

Table 1. Comparison between EMA-, EMA_T-based and Bayesian estimation

Estimator	Uncorrelated sessions			Correlated sessions		
	Success	Early Reaction Time	Error	Success	Early Reaction Time	Error
EMA	41.7%	32.3576	26.9371	32.3%	7.6659	4.9135
EMA_{20}	45.4%	31.8811	24.4678	**81.7%**	**5.5993**	**4.6996**
EMA_{T20}	58.4%	28.4502	28.79	**87.3%**	**5.3565**	**4.9191**
BAYES_0.7	69.1%	**27.0214**	**19.3771**	66.7%	14.2141	10.6827
BAYES_0.8	76.3%	25.6273	19.9028	76.7%	14.3295	11.6206
BAYES_0.9	**83.7%**	24.3352	**20.5066**	87.7%	14.9109	13.3018

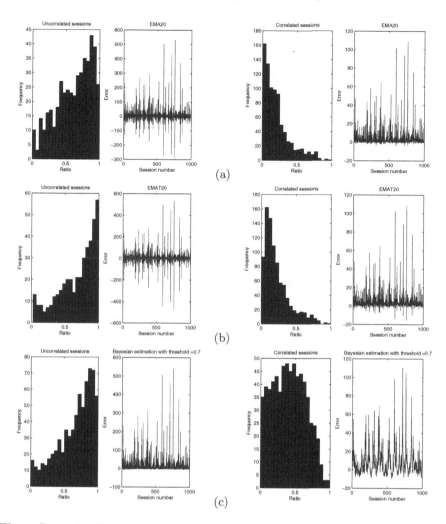

Fig. 1. Ratio distributions and evolution of the error for (a) EMA_{20}-based estimator; (b) EMA_{T20}-based estimator; (c) Bayesian estimator

incorrect. Bayesian estimation is very sensitive to sudden variations in the session durations and it has difficulty to converge. As previously, Bayesian estimator is better in uncorrelated cases whereas EMA_{20} and EMA_{T20}-based estimator are better in correlated cases.

To summarize, in case of uncorrelated session durations Bayesian approach does less underestimations and have less ratios than EMA-based approaches. Moreover they achieve more success than EMA-based approaches, therefore Bayesian approach is better than EMA-based approaches for uncorrelated session durations. On the other hand, for strongly correlated session durations, EMA-based approaches are better in terms of success, underestimation and ratio. Thus EMA-based approaches are better for strongly correlated session durations.

4   Dynamics Management Algorithm

In this section, we discuss our mechanism for making application layer multicast systems dynamics-aware. We explain this process through three algorithms. All these algorithms are run by the *consumer* node. Algorithm 1 describes investigation of the current *provider* and scheduling a move. Algorithm 2 allows a *consumer* node to find *potential providers* and request them for their dynamics. To choose a new *provider* node, the consumer runs Algorithm 3.

Algorithm 1. Investigating the provider node and scheduling a move

---
1: send DynamicReq(provider)
2: $providerElapsedTime \leftarrow currentTime - providerResponse.joinTime$
3: $providerRemTime \leftarrow providerResponse.estSession - providerElapsedTime$
4: scheduleMove(providerRemTime)

As a node joins the ALM system, it starts Algorithm 1. In the first step, the *consumer* sends a message to its *provider* inquiring for his estimated current session duration and *joinTime* as shown in line 1. The *provider* responds with the two values. After receiving the response, the *consumer* estimates the remaining online time of the *provider* as given in lines 2 and 3. Then it schedules a *move* after the remaining online time of the *provider* as given in line 4. The execution of move is shown in Algorithm 2.

Algorithm 2. Execution of scheduled move

1: potentialProviders=getPotentialProviders(groupId, k)
2: **for** each potentialProvider **do**
3:     send(DynamicsRequest, potentialProvider)
4: **end for**
5: **for** each DynamicsResponse dr **do**
6:     **if** $((dr.capacity\_status = true)$ **then**
7:         List.add(dr.source,dr)
8:     **end if**
9: **end for**

As time scheduled in Algorithm 1 is up, Algorithm 2 starts. In the first step the *consumer* node queries the list of the neighbor nodes and chooses k nodes from it as shown in line 1. We term them the *potential providers*. After getting the *potential provider* nodes, it sends a request to each of them asking their current estimated session duration and *joinTime* as shown in lines 2 and 3. On receiving responses from the *potential providers* each response is analyzed in line 6. If the capacity status of a *potential provider* is true: the number of *consumer* nodes it is currently serving is not reached to the maximum limit, then the *consumer* stores the response in a list as given in line 7. Algorithm 3 uses this list for choosing a new *provider*.

After receiving responses from all the *potential providers*, the *consumer* starts choosing the most stable node. We show this process in Algorithm 3. It chooses a node with maximum remaining online time from the list by analyzing their responses as shown in lines 2 to 5. Then it sends a join request to the node with the longest remaining online time. If the request is accepted, it leaves the current *provider*, otherwise it restarts the process with the next node. All these steps are shown in lines 8 to 14.

Algorithm 3. Choosing a new provider

1: $longestRemTime \leftarrow 0$
2: **for** each List.dr **do**
3:    **if** $dr.estSession > longestRemTime$ **then**
4:       $logestRemTime \leftarrow dr.estSession$
5:       $provider \leftarrow dr.source$
6:    **end if**
7: **end for**
8: send(JoinRequest, newprovider)
9: wait()
10: **if** JoinAckMessage is received **then**
11:    send(LeaveMessage, previousProvider)
12: **else**
13:    List.remove(newProvider.dr)
14:    goto line 1
15: **end if**

The overall process in these three algorithms requires ALM nodes to exchange $2(k + 2)$ messages for each *move*, where k is the number of potential provider nodes. The two other exchanges are for leaving the current provider node and joining the new one. This algorithm runs only when the estimated session duration of the current provider node is expired. Therefore, the overall overhead of the approach is low.

5   Experimental Evaluation

Apart from simulations we carry out experiments on an ALM system to validate our approach and notice the performance improvement. We choose Scribe [16] for our experiment, which is a tree-based ALM system that forms a tree for each multicast group enabling the content to be disseminated from the root towards leaf nodes. It is built upon Pastry [17], which is a structured P2P overlay. Scribe does not implement a buffering mechanism. Hence, the departure of a peer interrupts the availability of content to its descendent nodes until the next execution of maintenance process and the finding of a new parent node. Next we discuss the experimental setup and the results we have collected.

5.1   Experimental Setup

We carry out all experiments on a LAN environment consisting of 12 computers connected through a switch. We use the Scribe implementation built upon FreePastry[1]: an open source Java-based implementation of Pastry. In order to coordinate the 12 computers during the experiment, we use DELTA[2] [18], a generic environment for testing and measuring Java-based distributed applications. We launch several nodes on each machine all subscribing to the same Scribe group. The root node stays online throughout the experiment and also works as a source node. All other nodes stay in the system for specified session durations. To avoid the case of many nodes connecting with the stable peers we limit the out-degree of each node to 5 child nodes.

To simulate a user behavior, we base our experiment on the analysis study given in [10], where the session durations of collectively all users follow a lognormal distribution with parameters ($\mu = 2.2, \sigma = 1.5$). Therefore, we generate random session durations in lognormal form with parameters ($\mu = 2.2, \sigma = 1.5$), and assign each node a history of 10 sessions for the estimation of the next session. Similarly, to simulate nodes arrivals into the system, we create them according to the modified Poisson distribution [10] until the maximum limit of nodes on a machine is reached. Concerning the video flow, we use a video trace file of *Jurassic Park* encoded with *H*.263 format with a target bit rate of 256 *kbps* [19]. The trace file has the statistics for one-hour video, therefore each experiment lasts for one hour time. The source generates dummy frames with the sizes specified in the trace file and makes it available to the root node after time intervals synthesized in the trace file.

5.2   Results

Although our simulations consider two kinds of users' behavior (i.e. users with correlated session durations and uncorrelated session durations), for the validation experiments we choose the uncorrelated case which is more difficult to anticipate. We configure DELTA to collect measurement results from each node on each machine after each 5 seconds time. These results contain lost frames, number of attempted moves and number of nodes in the network. Lost frames are those lost by a node between the first frame it receives after its arrival and the last frame it receives before the departure. It shows the impact of peer dynamics on Scribe and the improvement of our proposed approach. An attempted move is counted when a *consumer* tries to find another *provider* node. Since the overhead of our approach is caused by a move attempt which involves exchange of messages among the nodes, therefore we show them in our results. Number of nodes gives an idea of the network size. We perform three experiments: (1) Scribe without any dynamics anticipation mechanism; (2) with EMA_{20}; (3) with our statistical Bayesian approach. In Figure 2 (a), we show the number of active nodes in the system. We can notice that the number of nodes vary in a

---

[1] http://freepastry.org
[2] Distributed Environment for Large-scale Tests of Applications.

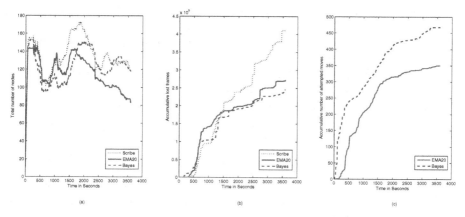

Fig. 2. Experimental results for uncorrelated sessions. (a) Number of nodes; (b) Frames loss; (c) Number of attempted moves.

similar way and the three experiments follow a similar shape which indicates a similar experimentation behavior. We depict the accumulated frames loss in Figure 2 (b). Here we can see that without any estimation Scribe looses the highest number of frames with a value equal to $411,581$. On the other hand, EMA_{20} performs better since it reduces the frame loss by 33%. Finally, the Bayesian approach reduces the Scribe frames loss by 40%. It clearly shows a significant performance improvement of the Bayesian estimation in Scribe. Now, concerning the overhead, we show the number of attempted moves for both EMA_{20} and Bayesian-based approach. We consider moves attempts instead of the successful moves because all the attempted moves are not successful in Scribe due to three reasons: (1) there is no *potential provider* which fulfils the Pastry's prefix routing constraint (2) the capacity of all the available *potential providers* is reached to the maximum limit; (3) the estimated remaining session durations of available potential providers are reached to zero. As shown in Figure 2 (c), EMA_{20} attempts 5.8 moves, while Bayesian-based approach attempts 7.8 moves every minute in the overall community. The average moves per node in one hour are 3.74 for Bayesian approach. although it is more than the EMA_{20}-based approach but still it is a low overhead.

6   Conclusion and Future Work

In this paper we address the problem of peer dynamics in P2P-based ALM systems. We propose a statistical approach based on a Bayesian inference to anticipate the departure of a peer by considering its online presence in the past. We also compare it with previously proposed EMA-based approaches. Moreover we proposed a generic algorithm to make ALM systems dynamics-aware. We validated our proposal with both simulations and experimentation. Simulations validate the accuracy of the estimator. Experimentations demonstrate the performance improvement of an ALM system in a context very close to what happens in a concrete P2P broadcasting system. Especially, our experimental results show that the performance of ALM systems can be improved by reducing significantly the number of frames lost by peers during a movie broadcast. Thus, benefits of our approach are twofold: (1) it minimizes the impact of peer dynamics on the performance of ALM systems; (2) it reduces the size of the required buffer in P2P-base video streaming systems, which will decrease the delay. Our approach is not limited to ALM systems. It can also be applied to other P2P systems where dynamics has an impact on the performance of the system.

Concerning short time future work, we will perform the same experiment for the users with correlated session durations and will test our approach on other types of ALM systems (e.g. mesh-based). We will also work on integration of other impacting parameters like type of application and time of the day with a Bayesian network. After that, we will consider other performance issues like heterogeneity of resources and overlay mismatching together with the peer dynamics. Some of performance parameters related to these issues are conflicting in nature and addressing them altogether will be interesting.

References

1. Deering, S., Cheriton, D.: Multicast routing in datagram internetworks and extended lans. In: ACM Transactions on Computer Systems, pp. 85–110 (1990)
2. Chu, Y., Seshan, S., Zhang, H.: A case for end system multicast. IEEE Journal on Selected Areas in Communication (JSAC) 20(8) (2002)
3. Dilley, J., Maggs, B., Parikh, J., Prokop, H., Sitaraman, R., Weihl, B.: Globally distributed content delivery. In: Internet Computing, pp. 50–58. IEEE, Los Alamitos (2002)
4. Kostic, D., Rodriguez, A., Albrecht, J., Vahdat, A.: Bullet: high bandwidth data dissemination using an overlay mesh. In: Proceedings of the Nineteenth ACM Symposium on Operating Systems Principles, pp. 282–297. ACM Press, New York (2003)
5. Xiao, L., Liu, Y., Ni, L.M.: Improving unstructured peer-to-peer systems by adaptive connection establishment. IEEE Trans. Comput. 54(9), 1091–1103 (2005)
6. Zhao, J., Lu, J.: Solving overlay mismatching of unstructured p2p networks using physical locality information. In: Proceedings of the 6th International Conference on P2P Computing. IEEE, Los Alamitos (2006)
7. Castro, M., Druschel, P., Rowstron, A., Kermarrec, A., Singh, A., Nandi, A.: Splitstream: high-bandwidth multicast in cooperative environments. In: 19th ACM Symposium on Operating Systems Principles (2003)
8. Ngan, T., Wallach, D., Druschel, P.: Incentives-compatible peer-to-peer multicast. In: Proceedings of the Second Workshop on the Economics of Peer-to-Peer Systems (2004)
9. Liuy, Z., Shen, Y., Panwar, S.S., Ross, K.W., Wang, Y.: Using layered video to provide incentives in p2p live streaming. In: Proceedings of the 2007 workshop on Peer-to-peer streaming and IP-TV, pp. 311–316. ACM, New York (2007)
10. Yu, H., Zheng, D., Zhao, B.Y., Zheng, W.: Understanding user behavior in large-scale video-on-demand systems. SIGOPS Oper. Syst. Rev. 40(4), 333–344 (2006)

11. Cha, M., Rodriguez, P., Crowcroft, J., Moon, S., Amatriain, X.: Watching television over an ip network. In: Proceedings of the 8th ACM SIGCOMM Conference on Internet Measurement, pp. 71–84. ACM Press, New York (2008)
12. Hei, X., Liang, C., Liang, J., Liu, Y., Ross, K.W.: A measurement study of a large-scale P2P IPTV system. IEEE Transactions on Multimedia (2007)
13. Tang, Y., Sun, L., Luo, J.-G., Zhong, Y.: Characterizing user behavior to improve quality of streaming service over P2P networks. In: Advances in Multimedia Information Processing, pp. 175–184 (2006)
14. Tang, Y., Sun, L., Luo, J.G., Yang, S., Zhong, Y.: Improving quality of live streaming service over P2P networks with user behavior model. In: Cham, T.-J., Cai, J., Dorai, C., Rajan, D., Chua, T.-S., Chia, L.-T. (eds.) MMM 2007. LNCS, vol. 4352, pp. 333–342. Springer, Heidelberg (2006)
15. Ullah, I., Doyen, G., Khatoun, R., Gaïti, D.: A decentralized approach to make application layer multicast systems dynamics-aware. In: 10émes journées doctorales en informatique et réseaux, UTBM, pp. 43–48 (2009)
16. Castro, M., Rowstron, A., Kermarrec, A.M., Druschel, P.: Scribe: a large-scale and decentralised application-level multicast infrastructure. Journal on Selected Areas in Communication 20(8) (2002)
17. Rowstron, A., Druschel, P.: Pastry: Scalable, decentralized object location, and routing for large-scale peer-to-peer systems. In: Guerraoui, R. (ed.) Middleware 2001. LNCS, vol. 2218, pp. 329–350. Springer, Heidelberg (2001)
18. Doyen, G., Ploix, A., Lemercier, M., Khatoun, R.: Towards a generic environment for the large-scale evaluation of peer-to-peer protocols. In: Networking and Electronic Commerce Research Conference 2008 (2008)
19. Fitzek, F.H.P., Reisslein, M.: MPEG-4 and H.263 video traces for network performance evaluation. IEEE Network 15(6), 40–54 (2001)

Quality of Service for Multicasting in Content Addressable Networks

Marc Brogle, Luca Bettosini, and Torsten Braun

Institute of Computer Science and Applied Mathematics
Universität Bern, Neubrückstrasse 10, 3012 Bern, Switzerland
`brogle@iam.unibe.ch, bettosin@iam.unibe.ch, braun@iam.unibe.ch`

Abstract. Multicasting is an efficient mechanism for one to many data dissemination. Unfortunately, IP Multicasting is not widely available to end-users today, but Application Layer Multicast (ALM), such as Content Addressable Network, helps to overcome this limitation. Our OM-QoS framework offers Quality of Service support for ALMs. We evaluated OM-QoS applied to CAN and show that we can guarantee that all multicast paths support certain QoS requirements.

1 Introduction

The OM-QoS framework [1,2] aims to enable different Application Layer Multicast (ALM) protocols to support Quality of Service (QoS). In [1], we focused on how to make Scribe ALM, which runs on-top of Pastry Peer-to-Peer (P2P), QoS aware. To support more P2P/ALM protocols, we also analyzed in [2] how to enable QoS for NICE, Content Addressable Networks (CAN) [3], and how to create a general solution using a layered approach, in order to support different P2P/ALM networks.

As described in [1,2], the multicast tree has to be built in such way that the QoS requirements or capabilities are monotonically decreasing from the root to the leafs. To manage different QoS parameters, we introduced the concept of QoS classes, which need to have a natural order. Such a QoS class could be a combination of bandwidth, jitter and CPU requirements. An example of a QoS aware tree is depicted in Fig. 1.

In this paper, we evaluate OM-QoS for CAN, which is the reference implementation for the OM-QoS framework's general solution (layered approach). For each QoS class, we use a dedicated CAN. Those CAN layers are then ordered and interconnected with each other using gateway links, to build a QoS aware aware multicast tree. For an overview of CAN, see [3]. A more detailed description of OM-QOS is available in [2].

2 Evaluation of QoS Enabled Content Addressable Network

We evaluated the application of OM-QoS to CAN using the OMNet++[1] simulator. Therefore, we implemented the CAN protocol and made some enhancements to fully support join and leave functionality. Due to the possibility of nodes leaving at any time during the simulation, we also needed to support temporary key-space assignment as

---

[1] Official OMNet++ simulator website: http://www.omnetpp.org

T. Pfeifer and P. Bellavista (Eds.): MMNS 2009, LNCS 5842, pp. 170–175, 2009.

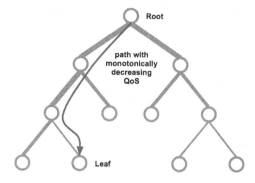

Fig. 1. QoS Supporting Multicast Tree

well as zone handover and merge mechanisms. If the multicast sender leaves its CAN, its responsibility to transmit continuously multicast messages has also to be passed to another CAN node. The CAN protocol was implemented in a fully decentralized manner, the network was built and maintained using only message transmission among the nodes. This original "native" CAN implementation has no QoS awareness/support. Therefore, it would be quite simple to modify our solution to also work in real networks.

We analyzed the CAN implementation and our OM-QoS extensions to CAN using various scenarios. We present the results for a scenario consisting of a CAN network without QoS support, where the nodes have one of 64 possible QoS classes assigned, in order to verify the QoS properties of the multicast paths for "native" CAN. Further, we present the results for a scenarios consisting of an OM-QoS enabled CAN with one of 64 QoS classes assigned to a node. All nodes get their QoS class (out of 64 possible QoS classes, depending on the scenario) assigned on startup. We then compare how many of the multicast message paths fulfill the previously described QoS property in native CAN (without any QoS mechanisms for multicast tree construction) and in OM-QoS enabled CAN with a QoS aware multicast tree construction mechanism. The latencies between all the nodes are determined using distance matrices, defining the latencies for each possible node pair connection. The distance matrices were built using topologies generated by Brite[2]. The minimum, maximum and median delay values of those matrices are depicted in Table 1. For each of the scenarios, we looked at various networks ranging with a node count from 100 to 2000 in steps of 100. Each node step was evaluated using 13 different distance matrices, which we evaluated each with 20 different random seeds influencing arrival, departure and other random based decisions. Therefore, each scenario consists of 5200 simulations. We removed 1% of the outliers (0.5% of the min. and max. values each) for the figures and results in this paper. Figure 2 shows the simulation results for a native CAN scenario without any QoS support but where each node gets one of 64 QoS classes assigned at startup. All nodes reside in one single CAN consisting of up to 2000 nodes. In Fig. 3, we show the simulation results for an OM-QoS enabled CAN scenario with 64 QoS classes. For the OM-QoS enabled CAN scenario with 64 QoS classes, we have 64 distinct CAN layers consisting

---

[2] Website for Brite topology generator: http://www.cs.bu.edu/brite/

Table 1. Delay Properties of Distance Matrices in ms

Matrix	min RTT (ms)	mean RTT (ms)	max RTT (ms)
Matrix 0	0.08	22.47	48.44
Matrix 1	0.09	30.35	90.48
Matrix 2	0.05	30.56	94.58
Matrix 3	0.05	29.76	90.23
Matrix 4	0.07	23.26	57.52
Matrix 5	0.09	22.78	51.82
Matrix 6	0.04	22.77	49.24
Matrix 7	0.08	23.27	52.30
Matrix 8	0.05	22.91	53.92
Matrix 9	0.05	23.27	50.83
Matrix 10	0.08	22.47	48.44
Matrix 11	0.05	22.91	54.00
Matrix 12	0.01	23.13	54.17

of an estimated average of 1.56 to 31.25 nodes for the scenarios with 100 to 2000 nodes in total. We compare the average, minimum and maximum values for the OM-QoS enabled CAN scenario with the results for the native CAN scenario without QoS support. Figures 2(a) and 3(a) present the duplicates received per multicast message. The average for the native CAN scenario is between 0.3 to 0.5 duplicates per message, which is due to the nature of CAN. As the minimum shows, duplicates can be often avoided. For some nodes the worst case is between 2 to 2.5 duplicates per multicast message. Comparing the average with the OM-QoS enabled CAN scenario, we see that the values behave now more or less constant due to the fact that we have smaller CAN networks. On the other hand, the average for less nodes has risen slightly, because of the duplicates that can be introduced by inter-layer forwarding. Our mechanisms between layers focuses more on reliability than on duplicate avoidance. This has the same effect on the maximum and minimum values.

Figures 2(b) and 3(b) show the multicast fan-out, the number of direct downstream children of a node. For the native CAN scenario, the average fan-out of 3 per node is very acceptable and remains more or less constant for the different amount of nodes. As expected, there are also leaf nodes that do not forward any messages (minimum of 0). For the worst case, the maximum is at 19, which seems to grow only very slowly for more nodes. Looking at the OM-QoS enabled CAN scenario, the average has been increased by 1 to 2 children. These additional children are introduced by the inter-layer forwarding mechanism. The maximum has been reduced because of having smaller CAN on the different layers, but the values grow more steadily with more nodes in a scenario. The minimum did not change, because there will always be pure leaf nodes.

In Figures 2(c) and 3(c), we present the hop-count of multicast messages. The hop-count on average grows slowly when there are more nodes in a CAN. Minimum and maximum values for the hop-count behave as expected, with the minimum being more or less constant while the maximum grows steadily when more nodes are in a CAN. The average hop-count in the OM-QoS enabled CAN scenario is generally increased due to inter-layer forwarding, but behaves now more or less constant due to smaller CAN sizes. This has a similar effect on the maximum. Figures 2(d) and 3(d) show the RTT of nodes to the root of the multicast tree. This value behaves the same as the hop-count with an average between 0.1 to 0.35 seconds and a maximum of 1 second for

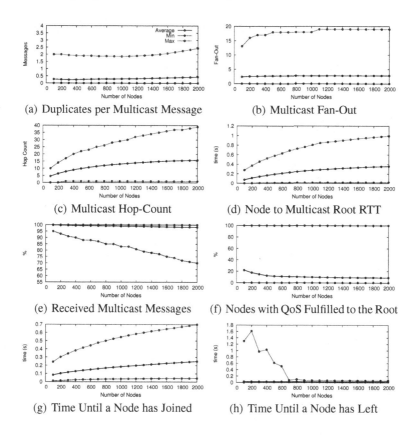

(a) Duplicates per Multicast Message

(b) Multicast Fan-Out

(c) Multicast Hop-Count

(d) Node to Multicast Root RTT

(e) Received Multicast Messages

(f) Nodes with QoS Fulfilled to the Root

(g) Time Until a Node has Joined

(h) Time Until a Node has Left

Fig. 2. Simulation Results for a Native CAN without QoS Support (with 64 virtual QoS classes)

the native CAN scenario. In the OM-QoS enabled scenario, the RTT values receive the same impact as for hop-count. They are on average a bit higher than in the native CAN scenario but behaving more or less constant with more nodes in the scenario.

In Figures 2(e) and 3(e), we depict the percentage of received multicast messages. More nodes in a CAN result in less multicast messages being successfully delivered to every node, as can been seen looking at the behavior of the minimum values for the native CAN scenario. The range for the average is between 98 to 100 percent, with a maximum of 100 percent as expected. The amount of the received multicast messages in the OM-QoS enabled CAN scenario is improved, because there are only small number of nodes in a CAN and due to the reliability optimized inter-layer forwarding mechanism. The minimum value behaves less predictably, because there are now multiple CAN in parallel behaving completely different than when just having one big CAN for all nodes. In Figures 2(f) and 3(f), we present the percentage of nodes that hold the previously described property on their full path to the root of the multicast tree. Although the paths in the multicast tree are not constructed in a QoS aware manner in the native CAN scenario, on average 10 to 20 percent of the paths may hold the previously mentioned QoS property. As expected, all the paths fulfill the QoS property in the OM-QoS

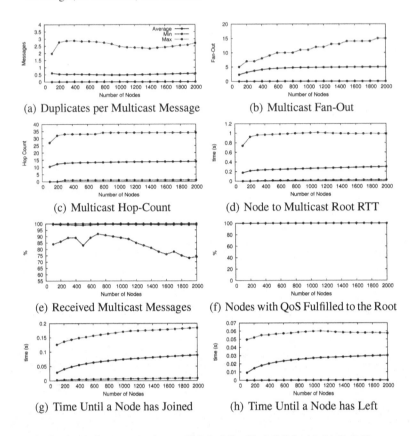

(a) Duplicates per Multicast Message

(b) Multicast Fan-Out

(c) Multicast Hop-Count

(d) Node to Multicast Root RTT

(e) Received Multicast Messages

(f) Nodes with QoS Fulfilled to the Root

(g) Time Until a Node has Joined

(h) Time Until a Node has Left

Fig. 3. Simulation Results for an OM-QoS Enabled CAN with 64 QoS Classes

enable CAN scenario. Figures 2(g) and 3(g) show the time a node required to fully join a CAN. The values in the native CAN scenario grow steadily with the amount of nodes, having an average ranging between 0.1 and 0.25 seconds, while the maximum is still in an acceptable range from 0.25 to 0.7 seconds. The minimum remains more or less constantly low close to 0.05 seconds, which reflects the early moments of a CAN, where there are only a few nodes in the network and join related messages have only to be passed among few nodes. The OM-QoS enabled CAN scenario has smaller CAN in the different layer. Therefore, joining time on average is reduced significantly. The maximum and minimum values behave accordingly.

In Figures 2(h) and 3(h), we present the time a node required to successfully leave. On average, nodes can quickly leave a CAN, but sometimes the handover of zones to other nodes may take more time if multiple nodes want to leave at the same time. With less nodes in the native CAN scenario having only one single CAN, the effect of multiple nodes wanting to leave at the same time is stronger and can result in leaving times up to 1.6 seconds. In the OM-QoS enabled CAN scenario, nodes can leave faster due to having a lower probability of nodes simultaneously leaving from the same CAN layer. Therefore, the average and maximum values grow slowly and turn to behave almost constant with more nodes being distributed evenly over the multiple layers. Since there are also CAN layers that only consist of one node when having multiple layers, no handover of zones has to be done and leaving is performed instantly (0s minimum). We also ran the simulations for an OM-QoS enabled CAN with 256 QoS classes (4 times more layers). The duplicates increased for small number of nodes. The average fan-out for small amount of nodes in a scenario is reduced, because only one or very few nodes are in each CAN. Therefore, multicast messages mainly have to be forwarded to other layers and rarely inside the same CAN. With more nodes in the system, the average and maximum match the behavior of the scenario with 64 QoS classes in relation to the amount of nodes per CAN in a layer. The average hop-count is increased by more than the factor 2, while the maximum is more than 3 times higher, the average RTT to root values are tripled, while the maximum is almost 4 times larger. The average of lost multicast messages is smaller because of our inter-layer forwarding improvements.

3 Conclusions

In this paper we have presented OM-QoS (Quality of Service for Overlay Multicast) applied to CAN (Content Addressable Networks), which enables CAN to support Quality of Service (QoS) enabled multicasting. The concept of QoS classes allows an abstract view of QoS requirements. For each QoS class, a dedicated CAN is established. These layers of CAN are interconnect using gateway nodes. Multicast messages are passed from a higher QoS class layer to a lower QoS layer, therefore building multicast trees that support QoS requirements. We have evaluated our approach using OMNET++. Simulations of networks with 100 to 2000 nodes have been performed and analyzed. OM-QoS is a self-managing middleware, which supports efficient and reliable usage of content distribution networks and other multimedia applications such as (real-time) A/V streaming based on Application Layer Multicast (ALM).

Enabling QoS for CAN using OM-QoS slightly increases the average fan-out of nodes and duplicates received per multicast message, but in consequence, this improves the percentage of multicast messages received. Other properties of CAN are not changed significantly when using OM-QoS.

References

1. Brogle, M., Milic, D., Braun, T.: QoS enabled multicast for structured P2P networks. In: P2PM 2007 at IEEE Consumer Communications and Networking Conference, January 2007. IEEE, Los Alamitos (2007)
2. Brogle, M., Milic, D., Braun, T.: Quality of service for peer-to-peer based networked virtual environments. In: P2P-NVE 2008 Workshop at the 14th IEEE International Conference on Parallel and Distributed Systems, Melbourne, Victoria, Australia, December 2008. IEEE, Los Alamitos (2008)
3. Ratnasamy, S., Francis, P., Handley, M., Karp, R., Schenker, S.: A scalable content-addressable network. In: Proceedings of the 2001 conference on Applications, technologies, architectures, and protocols for computer communications, vol. 31. ACM, New York (2001)

An Architecture for IMS Services Using Open Source Infrastructure

Robert Mullins, Shane Dempsey, and Tom Pfeifer

Telecommunications Software & Systems Group [TSSG]
Waterford Institute of Technology [WIT]
Cork Road, Waterford, Ireland
rmullins@tssg.org, sdempsey@tssg.org, t.pfeifer@computer.org

Abstract. IMS ARCS is an Industrial and Academic cooperative program conducting research in the area of IMS technology with a view to creating a body of intellectual property for the use of project partners, and serving as a case study on how to develop IMS end user and enabling services. The project employs the OpenIMS testbed from Fraunhofer Fokus, as the basis for the development and execution of services, and has built upon the facilities available in the OpenIMS testbed, while adding value to these through the development of enabling services. This paper describes the general architecture for both enabling and end user services developed during the project and shows how these have been used to create a useful location aware service which can help a user maximise use of public transport facilities in a city.

Keywords: IMS, OpenIMS, services, enablers, architecture.

1 Introduction

The IMS ARCS research project [1] was conceived as a means of bringing together a group of academic institutions to work with a number of companies in the telecommunications field. The companies bring their commercial experience and market knowledge; the academic group bring their research and development skills and knowledge of leading edge technology and trends. Together, through discussions and the application of their respective expertise, they create innovative new product concepts, prototypes and processes for developing future applications. The output from the project, such as prototype code and documents, is freely available to all members of the project to develop and commercialise, and after a period of time will become open source and freely available to the general public.

The initial objective of the project focused on end-user and enabling services for IMS, by developing a number of end-user service concepts and analysing these under a number of headings, including value proposition, service functionality and implementation requirements. This was followed by the development of a number of working service prototypes which had been deployed on the OpenIMS [2] testbed. As the project evolved it became apparent that a further objective would be to create a general architecture for both enabling and end-user services.

T. Pfeifer and P. Bellavista (Eds.): MMNS 2009, LNCS 5842, pp. 176–182, 2009.

2   Prior Work and State of the Art

The participants in the project had previously lead the Pervasive Services Management aspect of the IST Daidalos project in FP6 [3] [4]. This project had concentrated on developing a platform to support a set of context aware and personalised end-user services across a range of connectivity technologies. The IMS ARCS project aimed to build upon the experiences in this area, but focused on IMS as the platform of choice on which to create the services. The project also chose to aim for service development which was commercialisable in the near to medium term, so reliance on sophisticated network capabilities or demonstrating concepts that could not be reliably implemented was avoided. Instead, the emphasis is on value proposition, and practical use of technologies provided by IMS such as location awareness, presence, call control and rich internet.

As a key objective of the project was to develop a light weight service oriented architectural model for services and to achieve this using open source and freely available tools, attention was paid to the existing work of Fraunhofer Fokus in the area of Service Oriented Architecture and IMS, and to their portfolio of products in this area [5] [6]. However the IMS ARCS project aims to be of more general availability and for this reason has avoided the use of proprietary software. Instead it was focussing on SOA tools.

3   Technology Description

The IMS ARCS team analysed the features of a number of services, how the user would interact with them and how the services would interact with the underlying IMS network. The issue of what development tools and infrastructure could be used was also considered, based on considerable experience in the area of Web2.0 development. These included mobility, location awareness, user profile and authentication, authorisation and accounting (AAA). The services needed to provide a general "context awareness", where the service could react to changes in location, presence and profile.

As such the general approach adopted for the services was to follow a Web pattern where core functionality (backend) resides on an application server and the service is accessed via a web browser on the client. A rich interface for the service is enabled through the use of a Mashup AJAX framework. The application server backend interfaces with the IMS network and the various service enablers to deliver the functionality characterised by IMS.

A further focus of the project was to use open source and freely available software throughout development. This helps the output of the project to be easily distributed and reusable without users needing to incur commercial license costs. Additionally, the output of the project will itself eventually become open source in which case dependencies on commercial licenses would not be feasible.

Figure 1 provides a overview of the general architecture, as discussed in the following sections.

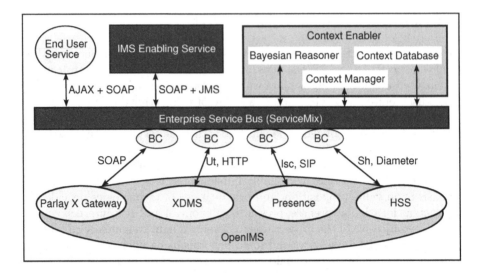

Fig. 1. Components of the general architecture

3.1 Enabling Services

An analysis of the functionality of the end-user service prototypes showed that many of the features and functionality were common across the various services. These included:

- User's location and presence,
- Other users' locations and presence,
- Rich presence (including device capabilities information),
- Service personalisation to a user's preferences,
- One to One SIP Call setup and Messaging,
- User Identity features and Anonymisation,
- Service login.

For the purpose of reuse, modularity and consistency, it made sense to isolate common functionality as *Enabling Services* which could then be used as the building blocks for the end-user services. The enabling services would also function as an abstraction of the underlying IMS network so that from an application developer perspective, they could interact with enablers without needing explicit knowledge of the IMS specific protocols such as SIP [7] or DIAMETER [8]. To provide such an abstraction, the enablers would need to support interfaces that would be familiar to a typical web developer, so it was decided that a web service interface based on the use of WSDL/SOAP would be supported by enabling services.

To have a cohesive and consistent architecture, both the end-user services and the enablers would all follow a similar architectural pattern, would communicate with each other in a similar manner, and – as far as possible – would use similar concepts and identifiers to interoperate. As such one of the first steps was to decide on a communications framework. As noted above the end-user service would communicate with the enablers via a web services framework. However the enablers would also need to communicate with each other and various communication patterns such as Query/Response and Publish/Subscribe needed to be allowed. In keeping with the use of enablers as service building blocks, a further requirement was to support a means of service composition and orchestration, using a language such as BPEL. To facilitate this, an Enterprise Service Bus was adopted as the middleware for the architecture.

The appropriate language for enabler development was judged to be Java, because of its ubiquity among developers, its rich development environment with a huge choice of tools, runtime libraries and infrastructure which would be suitable for the type of development and functionality. As such the ESB chosen was one that was based around the Java Business Integration (JBI) standard [9]. One of the most popular implementations of this standard is Apache ServiceMix [10]. This had the advantage of being widely used and supported across a number of different application servers including a number of open source ones. It also had the advantage of having a commercially supported variant, called FUSE ESB [11], which was an important consideration if an enabling or end-user service was to be commercialised. It is also closely integrated with other related tools such as Apache ActiveMQ and an Orchestration engine which plugs into ServiceMix, called Apache ODE (Orchestration Director Engine) and uses BPEL.

The project needed to select an application server to host the enabler components and also the end-user services. Because many of the enablers and components would use the SIP protocol for call setup, the application server needed to be SIP enabled. Glassfish/Sailfin [12] was chosen because of our preference for an open source and freely available option, without restrictions. An enabler can comprise of a number of sub-components that link together via the service bus. Some of these are written as service assemblies which run in the context of ServiceMix. Typically the binding components (BC) which implement the protocol translation follow this pattern. They are specific to the OpenIMS component that they interface with. Other sub-components within the enabler which encapsulate business logic may run within an application server and communicate via either SOAP or JMS with the other sub-components. However, where an enabler communicates with either the end-user services or with another enabling service, this communication takes place via the service bus using SOAP.

To allow the end-user services to avail of web technologies such as AJAX, HTTP requests can also be routed through the service bus to enabling services. The ESB also incorporates reusable Enterprise Integration Patterns (EIPs) which facilitate scalable message routing, for example Publish/Subscribe.

Information can typically be retrieved from the underlying IMS network using two different methods and a combination of these is typically implemented by the binding component. The first is where the components within the IMS network can be queried directly for information. The second approach is where asynchronous notifications are received when new information is created or changes in existing information occurs. If the underlying component is capable of delivering asynchronous notifications then the binding component subscribes to these, however if such is not possible or unavailable then this can be achieved by polling the underlying components regularly, however this is less efficient.

3.2   Context Management Enabler

Much of the information being gathered from the IMS network refers to what is generally classed as "Context" information. This refers to current and historical information about users in the network, where they are, what they are doing, what types of devices they are using and their capabilities, in addition to any information that can be inferred from this [13]. As such it acts as an abstraction of the underlying IMS network as a source of information, while not changing the state of the network through proactive functionality such as management or call setup.

The enabler architecture described above has been used to implement a Context Enabler as part of the IMS ARCS project. The Context Enabler interfaces with the end-user service via a publish/subscribe interface. The end-user service subscribes for context information relating to a specific user or set of users. The criteria used are a user identifier(s), a filter expression and an identifier that will allow the Context Enabler send notifications to the service. The user identifier identifies the user whose context information (presence, location etc.) the service wishes to be informed of. The filter criterion is an XQuery statement, with an additional reference to the URI of an XML Schema file that describes the schema of the data on which the condition acts. This can be used to exclude data and events that the service is not interested in, or to place thresholds for changes. An example of this may be that the end-user service only wishes to know about changes in a user's location of more than 100 metres (rather than presence changes etc.). The notification that the Context Enabler sends to the end-user service will contain a URI reference to an XML document whose contents will contain the context information that the service subscribed for.

As shown in the above, the context enabler avails of the data collected from the OpenIMS and this is delivered via the service bus. The Context Manager subcomponent specifically manages the subscriptions from end-user services through monitoring which services have registered for information on users and the associated filter criteria. This component is then responsible for publishing the appropriate events to be delivered on the service bus. Where security considerations exist, these will also be managed by this component.

The context database manages the storage of the context events in their XML representation. The context database leverages prior work from the Daidalos project on the development of a spatially aware database [14]. It provides both the URIs for such events, acts as an event cache to store the stream of events coming from the network and allows queries to be created so that sets of events relating a user can be retrieved. This allows value added functionality, such as inferences, to be made.

The Bayesian Reasoner observes the user information in the database, and where an end-user service has registered an interest in a user's context, the reasoner can make inferences based on the context information. These inferences are stored as a reusable XML document in the database and an event is generated and published to the subscribed services. Because of the nature of Bayesian reasoning, all inferences will have an associated probability which qualifies the reliability of the inference. The services are free to use these inferences or discard them. An example of the type of inference that may be created may be based around the changes in a user location. If a user's location is changing frequently and such changes correspond with the coordinates of a road, then it is reasonable to infer that the user is travelling along that road in a particular direction. If the rate the user is travelling is greater than 40km/hour then it is reasonable to infer the person is travelling in a motorised vehicle. Depending on time and presence information, various other inferences may be made such as whether the person is driving or caught in traffic.

3.3   End-User Services

To demonstrate both enabling and end-user services, a number of end-user services have been developed and these services are integrated with the described context enabler and can be used to demonstrate the functionality that is offered by it. Some of these services have been demonstrated at public events such the Mobile World Congress 2008 in Barcelona. The end-user services have been designed in consultation with a project partner whose specialisation is Software Usability and Human Computer interactivity.

The Public Transport Advisor service is a typical example of a service offering a value proposition, using context information on the user and delivering a Web 2.0 type experience over an IMS network. The objective of the public transport advisor is to help a user to maximise their use of public transport infrastructure in a metropolitan area, particularly one which may be unfamiliar to them, where they are not aware of what services exist or what routes are available.

When a user invokes the service, the service backend subscribes to the context enabler for information on the users location. The user can select the destination. The service can then calculate optimal routes, plot a map, monitor the changing user location and notify the user about points to change transport or approaching the destination. This can be done via a number of methods, such as instant message or a voice call with instructions.

4   Conclusions

The project has been of significant benefit to a number of small and medium enterprises engaged in the telecommunications software industry in Europe and specifically in Ireland, in addition to a number of operators who are interested in rolling out sophisticated services over their next generation networks. The general architecture, toolset and exemplar services provide an ideal proof of concept and starting point for companies interested in developing and deploying such services.

To support this, the project team has developed a "Jumpbox" DVD, which contains a VMWare image of a Linux machine with the OpenIMS, ServiceMix, Glassfish/Sailfin, Java, Maven and Subversion installation, together with the codebase of the various services and enablers that are used in the project.

Acknowledgement

The work described in this paper has been funded by Enterprise Ireland as an Industry Lead Research project, IMS ARCS, consisting of an academic consortium lead by TSSG and a number of companies.

References

1. IMS ARCS project (2008), http://www.ims-arcs.com/
2. Fraunhofer FOKUS OpenIMS Testbed (2008), http://www.open-ims.org
3. Daidalos (2008), http://www.ist-daidalos.org/
4. Mullins, R., Mahon, F., Kuhmuench, C., Crotty, M., Mitic, J., Pfeifer, T.: Daidalos: A platform for facilitating pervasive services. In: Pfeifer, T., et al. (eds.) Pervasive 2006: 4th International Conference on Pervasive Computing, Advances in Pervasive Computing 2006. Adjunct Proceedings (Dublin, Ireland), May 2006, pp. 167–172. Austrian Computer Society, Vienna (2006)
5. Blum, N., Magedanz, T., Schreiner, F.: Definition of a service delivery platform for service exposure and service orchestration in next generation networks. UbiCC Journal 3(3)
6. Blum, N., Magedanz, T.P.W.: In: The Integration of IMS into Service Delivery Platforms based on ServiceOriented Architectures, November 2008. Taylor & Francis, New York (2008)
7. SIP: Session Initiation Protocol, RFC 3261 (2002), http://www.ietf.org/rfc/rfc3261.txt
8. Diameter Base Protocol, RFC 3588 (2003), http://www.ietf.org/rfc/rfc3588.txt
9. JSR 208 Java Business Integration (2008), http://jcp.org/aboutJava/communityprocess/final/jsr208/index.html
10. Apache ServiceMix (2008), http://servicemix.apache.org
11. FUSE ESB (2008), http://fusesource.com/products/enterprise-servicemix
12. SailFin Application Server (2008), https://sailfin.dev.java.net
13. Abowd, G.D., Dey, A.K., Brown, P.J., Davies, N., Smith, M., Steggles, P.: Towards a better understanding of context and context-awareness. In: Gellersen, H.-W. (ed.) HUC 1999. LNCS, vol. 1707, pp. 304–307. Springer, Heidelberg (1999)
14. Pils, C., Roussaki, I., Strimpakou, M.: Distributed spatial database management for context aware computing systems. In: 16th ICT Mobile & Wireless Communications Summit, ICT, Budapest, Hungary, July 2-4 (2007)

Data Aggregation Scheme for a Multi-Application WSN

Ahmad Sardouk, Rana Rahim-Amoud, Leïla Merghem-Boulahia,
and Dominique Gaïti

ICD/ERA, FRE CNRS 2848, Université de Technologies de Troyes,
12 rue Marie Curie, 10010 Troyes Cedex, France
{ahmad.sardouk,rana.amoud,leila.boulahia,dominique.gaiti}@utt.fr

Abstract. Wireless Sensor Networks (WSNs) are still designed and deployed for one specific application, while it is vital to deploy several applications over the same WSN in order to reduce the deployment and the
administrative costs. One of the remaining problems, in this domain, resides in the data aggregation solutions, which are proposed generally for
one application and may drain the WSN power in a multi-application
context. Therefore, we propose a data aggregation scheme based on a
multi-agent system to aggregate the WSN information in an energy-
efficient manner even if we are deploying several applications over this
network. This proposal has proved its performance in the context of one
and several applications through successive simulations in different network scales.

1 Introduction

The basic role of a Wireless Sensor Network is to collect information from the
environment by many sensor nodes (SNs). Even due to hardware limits the
WSNs have been predominantly tasked with a single application in the past [1].
The recent advances, in the hardware part of an SN, have lead to the creation
of more powerful SNs. For instance, the SNs produced by Sun (Sun SPOT) [2]
are a good example of these advances, where each SN has a 180Mhz, 512KB of
RAM and 4MB of flash memory. These advances have allowed/pushed a growing
interest in deploying several applications over the same WSN.

The solutions proposed to deploy several applications could be divided into
two categories. The first one [3] [4] proposes to change the code of the running
application if needed. The second category [1] [5] manages the access of the
different applications to the SN resources (CPU and Memory).

The SNs have a finite battery life and nodes failures can lead to a loss of data
or network partition. Therefore, in addition to these kinds of solutions, we need
to optimize the power consumption of the SNs, which is mainly related to the
information communication.

In this paper, we propose an energy-efficient data gathering scheme, which
optimizes the power consumption of WSNs deployed for one or several applications. This solution is based on a multi-agent system (MAS) to reduce the

T. Pfeifer and P. Bellavista (Eds.): MMNS 2009, LNCS 5842, pp. 183–188, 2009.

amount of the gathered information by treating and filtering the information locally at the SNs. Moreover, The deployed MAS will be empowered by a strategy allowing the agent to make more appropriate decisions and to prioritize a running application in favor of another one.

The remaining of this paper is organized as follows. In section 2, we present our proposal and how the agent makes its cooperation decisions. Next, section 3 explains our simulations results. Finally, the conclusion is given in section 4.

2   Multi-Application WSN Data Aggregation (MADA)

2.1   System Design

In our proposal we implement an agent in each SN. Each agent will be able to control the power and radio entities of its SN. The proposed architecture is a two layers architecture and it is illustrated in Fig. 1. The low layer is constituted by the physical SNs and the high layer is formed by the agents.

Each agent manages several types of applications. For example, if we want to deploy two applications (monitoring and tracking), each agent will create two executive agents (EA): monitoring agent (MA) and tracking agent (TA). Once the work of an EA is acheived, it will be killed by the main agent, which created it. Hence, the role of the main agent will be to create EAs, attach them to applications, and then to kill them at the end of their tasks.

2.2   Agent States

Fig. 2 presents the state diagram of a typical EA in our proposal. The events are the transitions that allow an EA to pass from one state to another one.

To illustrate our proposal, we will use Fig. 1 as a reference and we will suppose that we have two simultaneously running applications (1) Monitoring application which corresponds to a fire detected by the node A (2) Tracking application related to a desired object detected by node X. We mention also that A, B and X are neighbor nodes. In the "listening" state (partially managed by the main agent), the agent waits for an interruption that could come from one of two main sources. The first one is when the sensing entity perceives new information from the environment (e.g., sensors of node A detect a fire or sensors of node X detect an object). This information will be sent to the corresponding agent, which will create an MA if it is not previously created. This MA passes to a "processing" state to treat the received information and to judge its importance degree. The second type of interruption is a cooperation request message sent by a neighbor agent (or EA). For example, receiving a cooperation request, from a TA_x, asking if this node has detected a defined object. Thus, the corresponding agent creates a TA for this tracking application. Then, the created TA passes to a "joining a cooperation" state to decide to participate in this cooperation or not.

In the "processing" state, the EA treats the perceived information and following its importance degree, a cooperation could be initiated. For example, for the

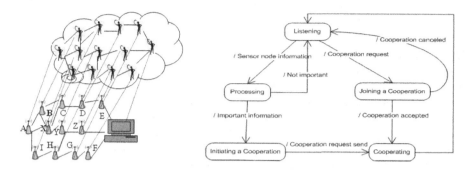

Fig. 1. Two Layers Architecture   **Fig. 2.** EA state diagram

monitoring application, the MA of A compares the detected temperature value with the previous one and finds a big difference. The MA considers that there is an weird event (like a fire). Based on the processing result, the EA can judge the information importance degree, which will be identified later.

The "processing" triggers "initiating a cooperation" state if it estimates the perceived information as important. Thus, the EA cooperates with other EAs in order to execute the task related to this information. For example, the TA of X sends the detected information to its one-hop neighbors to inform them about the existance of the desired object in its area and at which distance and when it was detected. The goal of sharing its information is to localize the object, which needs at least three EAs. This state appears as an intermediate state, it allows an EA to start cooperation and then it passes to a "cooperating state" to manage this cooperation.

"Joining a cooperation" state starts when an EA receives a cooperation request from another EA. For example, the MAs of agents B and X, which are neighbors of agent A, have received a cooperation request from the MA of A asking about their perceived temperatures. If the MAs of B and X have detected an important temperature variation, they send their information to A. Simultaneously, the TA of A has received a cooperation request from the TA of X concerning the object detection. If the TA of A has received similar signal, it sends the information obtained from the signal (estimated distance and detection time) to the TA of X. The "cooperating" state allows the EAs to communicate together. It is trigged from the "initiating a cooperation" state if an EA needs to cooperate with other EAs to achieve its goal. In addition, it could be trigged from the "joining a cooperation" state if a neighbor EA decides to cooperate or to answer positively a cooperation request. For example, when the TA of X waits for the cooperation of at least two other TAs.

An example of the data carrying method within the network and the cooperation message that summarizes the information of several SNs has been given in some of our previous works [6] [7].

2.3   Agent Strategy

Previously, we explained the importance of cooperating, but indeed, in some cases, not to join a cooperation could be better than joining it. For example, if the agent B does not have a lot of energy, B will prefer to cooperate for the fire detection instead of cooperating with X to localize the object. Hence, agent B gives more prioritory to its MA than its TA. Therefore, each EA should computes the relevance (R) of each cooperation. Thus, we defined four parameters: the energy E, the network density D, the position of an SN within the network P, and the information importance degree I, to compute the cooperation of each relevance. To simplify the computation of this relevance, we propose the equation (1).

$$R = E \times \alpha + \frac{1}{D} \times \beta + P \times \theta + I \times \omega \tag{1}$$

Where α, β, θ, and ω are the influence factors for the energy, the density, the position, and the information importance degree respectively. This strategy has been detailed in one of our previous work [8].

3   Results Discussion

To the best of our knowledge, we do not see any work treating the data aggregation for a multi-application WSN. Therefore, to evaluate the relevance of our proposal (MADA), we suggest to evaluate its performance compared to a well known data aggregation approach, which is the data fusion [9]. This approach could be described as follows. When a node sends its information to the sink, intermediate nodes merge their information with the first node information. As the information of multiple sensor nodes are merged into one message (one overhead instead of many ones), this solution reduces the information communications' power consumption.

We have implemented these approaches on Glomosim [10], which is a scalable simulation environment for wireless and wired network systems. The simulations parameters, which are related to the capacity of the SNs, have been defined according to the recommendation of sun SPOT [2] and [11]. The main simulations parameters are summarized in Table 1.

3.1   Power Consumption

Fig.3 presents the average power consumption per node in the case of 1 and 3 applications in data fusion and MADA. The results point out that MADA decreases significantly the average power consumption of an SN in both scenarios (1 and 3 applications). In addition, we can observe that to deal with 3 applications instead of only one application in MADA, an SN consumes approximately an additional power equal to 2 mJ. However, in data fusion, the aditional power is approximately equal to 27mJ.

These results prove also that for larger WSN, MADA maintains the SNs' consumption to low values, while the difference with data fusion becomes greater.

Table 1. Simulation parameters

Simulation Parameter	Values
Network size	5000mx5000m
Node distribution	Random
Radio range	87m
Throughput	1Mbps
Size of sensed data	24 byte per node
Sensed Data Interval	10 seconds
Simulation time	1000 seconds
α,θ,ω	0.25
β	0.1

Hence, these results prove the suitability of MADA for small and large scale WSNs.

3.2   End-to-End Delay

This parameter represents the average delay needed to carry a message from a source node till the sink, including the time of communication and processing. The performance of MADA and data fusion corresponding to this criterion is presented in Fig. 4. The obtained results show that MADA requires more latency than data fusion. This extra latency is due to the required cooperation time in MADA. However, we could mention that the difference between MADA and data fusion is never more than 150ms. This difference means that only the application which requires more than 0.15 seconds will be influenced. We can point out also that the number of running applications does not influence the delay (delay for 1 or 3 applications is the same). Otherwise, in term of scalability, the strobe of the curves show that both approaches are scalable.

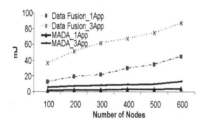

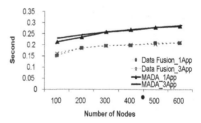

Fig. 3. Average power consumption per node   **Fig. 4.** Average end-to-end delay

4   Conclusion

In this paper, we have proposed a data aggregation scheme to optimize the power consumption of the sensor nodes, in the context of one and several applications deployed over the same WSN. This solution (MADA) is based on a multi-agent system to reduce the amount of communicated information by processing and filtering the information locally. MADA defines also a method based on several important parameters to decide the relevance of a cooperation. In addition, this method takes into consideration the priority of some applications compared to others ones (e.g. fire detection could be more important than object tracking if they are happening at the same time). MADA presents, through the results of the several simulations, a very good performance in term of power consumption.

Our future work will be based firstly on reducing the end-to-end latency. Then, we will optimize our agent strategy by integrating a more sophisticated mathematical model, which evaluates better the importance of each parameter.

References

1. Sangeeta, B., Chenyang, L., Gruia-Catalin, R.: Utility-based multi-application deployment in shared wireless sensor networks. Technical report, Washington University in St. Louis (2008)
2. Sun: Sun^{TM} Small Programmable Object Technology (Sun SPOT) Theory of Operation. Technical report, Sun Microsystem, Sun Labs (2008)
3. Levis, P., Gay, D., Culler, D.: Active sensor networks. In: NSDI, pp. 343–356. USENIX Association, Berkeley (2005)
4. Levis, P., Culler, D.: Maté: a tiny virtual machine for sensor networks. In: ASPLOS-X, pp. 85–95. ACM, New York (2002)
5. Yu, Y., Rittle, L.J., Bhandari, V., LeBrun, J.B.: Supporting concurrent applications in wireless sensor networks. In: SenSys., pp. 139–152. ACM, New York (2006)
6. Sardouk, A., Merghem-Boulahia, L., Gaiti, D.: Agent-Cooperation Based Communication Architecture for Wireless Sensor Network. In: IFIP Wireless Days/Ad-hoc and Wireless Sensor Networks, UAE, IFIP (2008)
7. Sardouk, A., Rahim-Amoud, R., Merghem-Boulahia, L., Gaiti, D.: Information-Importance Based Communication for Large-Scale WSN Data Processing. In: WMNC, Gdansk,Poland, IFIP (2009)
8. Sardouk, A., Rahim-Amoud, R., Merghem-Boulahia, L., Gaiti, D.: A Strategy for Multi-Agent Based Wireless Sensor Network Optimization. In: Sadre, R., Pras, A. (eds.) AIMS 2009. IFIP International Federation for Information Processing 2009. LNCS, vol. 5637, pp. 122–133. Springer, Heidelberg (2009)
9. Das, S.R., Nasipuri, A., Patil, S.: Serial Data Fusion Using Space-filling Curves in Wireless Sensor Networks. In: IEEE, ed.: First Annual IEEE Communications Society Conference on Sensor and Ad Hoc Communications and Networks, pp. 182–190 (2004)
10. Laboratory, U., Laboratory, W.: Glomosim: A scalable simulation environment for wireless and wired network systems. In: The 3rd International Working Conference on Performance Modeling and Evaluation of Heterogeneous Networks (2005)
11. Sohraby, K., Minoli, D., Znati, T.: Wireless Sensor Networks, Technology, Protocols, and Applications. Willey, Chichester (2007)

Context-Aware IPTV

Songbo Song[1], Hassnaa Moustafa[1], and Hossam Afifi[2]

[1] France Telecom R&D (Orange Labs), Issy les Moulineaux, France
{songbo.song,hassnaa.moustafa}@orange-ftgroup.com
[2] Telecom & Management South Paris (Institute Telecom), Evry, France
{hossam.afifi}@int-edu.eu

Abstract. The advances in IPTV technology enable a new user-centric and interactive TV model, in which context-awareness concept is promising in making users' interaction with the TV dynamic and transparent. In this paper we present several existing contributions that employ context-awareness concept to allow interactive services. Some of these contributions directly focus on TV, while others are proposed for specific NGN services. We analyze these contributions based upon some requirements that we define for enabling advanced IPTV services personalization.

Keywords: NGN, IPTV, Personalized Services, User-Centric IPTV.

1 Introduction

The new TV model will allow users not only to access new services and functionalities from their providers, but also to become active parts in the content creation and distribution process. With the consolidation of services, such as network Time Shifting (nTS) and network Personal Video Recorder (nPVR), users are allowed to record their own content and could also make them available to other users. The Next Generation Network (NGN) approach in coupling IPTV with IP Multimedia System (IMS) allows for services' convergence through using the IMS common architecture in providing a platform for interactive TV services. Although the rapid advancement in interactive TV technology (including IPTV and NGN technologies), IPTV service personalization is still in its infancy (for instance, content recommendation is not totally user-centric, choosing the desired channel in a manual mean could disturb the viewer). Context-awareness paradigm is promising in simplifying the viewer's life, through allowing content adaptation according to the user's needs and to the surrounding environment. We notice an increasing research trend for context-awareness IPTV systems, where promising applications and services' enhancements are expected. In this paper we focus on context-aware TV and NGN services.

The remainder of this paper is organized as follows. Section 2 defines a number of requirements that should be satisfied for TV services personalization. Section 3 presents the related contributions on context-aware interactive TV and context-aware NGN services based on IMS, analyzing them with respect to those defined requirements. We end the paper in Section 4 through giving a conclusion for the existing contributions, highlighting our future research work.

T. Pfeifer and P. Bellavista (Eds.): MMNS 2009, LNCS 5842, pp. 189–194, 2009.

2 Requirements for TV Services Personalization

In this section, we define a number of requirements for analyzing the existing contributions on context-aware TV and NGN services. These requirements help in evaluating the suitability and adaptability of each contribution to the interactive TV environment.

Context information domain (types): The architecture requirements for IPTV include four domains: consumers, network providers, service providers, and content providers. Based on these domains, we define our context information domains for TV environment as: user context, device context, network context, and service context. The user context and device context belong to the "consumer domain"; the network context belongs to the "network domain"; the service context presents the information from the "service and content domain".

Context information extension: Context information types and treatment methods can be designed either for general services or for special type of services. However, the extension/adaptation of the context information types and treatment methods to TV service is an important aspect which determines the possibility to integrate context-awareness into the NGN TV architecture.

Distributed versus centralized system: A distributed context-aware system is constituted by several entities that have the capacity to acquire, process, and store the context information. These entities can cooperate with each other to provide the context-aware services. In distributed systems, it is difficult to have a global view of the context information and the calculation capacity is limited to the distributed terminals capacities. A centralized context-aware system treats and stores the collected context information in a centralized server; however, the frequent communication between the devices and the server needs adequate network resources.

Support for mobility: Mobility is an important feature that should be supported in modern TV systems to allow the user to enjoy his personal TV content any time and any where. This requires context-aware TV systems to integrate appropriate mechanisms for continuous devices discovery and continuous location discovery for the user, in order to support the seamless TV service transfer and continuity.

Support for nomadism: With the new model of TV systems, users should be able to enjoy their personal TV content from anywhere. So, we define a new scope for nomadism to allow users to access their personal TV content and to pay through their own bill while passing by other's networks. To support such nomadic services, context-aware TV systems, beside acquiring the user identification should also be capable of acquiring other context information 'location, which connectivity, ...'.

Support for privacy protection: The privacy protection is the capability of a user or group of users to secure their personal information. Since any context-aware system is concerned to a great extent with personal information (user context), the privacy protection is necessary. Privacy protection in TV environment is mainly related to the following points: controlling the personal information sharing; not publishing the content information that the user is accessing (e.g., mastering the content sharing); user context storage and manipulation among authorized entities.

Performance and feasibility of implementation: Some context-aware functions may be not easy to implement due to the need of lot of processing power, calculation and storage capacity. Terminals capacity should then be considered in context-aware TV systems. Furthermore, the used protocols and the underlying architectures for context-aware TV systems should be compatible with the existing standards (especially those related to NGN).

Support for personalization: TV service personalization allows the content to meet the expectation/preference of the user. This refers to two points: identification of the user and finding out what content the user prefers. Furthermore, the support of mobility, nomadism and privacy protection present important requirements for achieving the provision of content in a personalized and user-centric manner.

Co-existence of multiple actors: Since modern TV services (especially IPTV) include multiple actors such as network operators, service providers, and content providers, the co-existence of these different actors should be assured by any context-aware TV system. Although IMS can provide some functional support to context-aware service, the dependence on IMS architecture has some implementation restrictions, especially when we look for compatibility among the various actors. Furthermore, the managing and sharing of context information among the various actors is not an easy task.

3   Contributions on Context-Aware Based Interactive Services

In this section, we present and discuss some existing contributions on Interactive TV (ITV), which employ context-awareness in order to enhance the user interaction with the TV environment. Other contributions are related to context-aware based NGN IMS services, which are not explicitly related to TV services, but we also discuss these contributions showing their suitability in TV environments based on our defined requirements.

A context-aware based advertisements (ads) insertion system is proposed in [1]. This work is based on the aggregation of past sequence of individual contexts (i.e. past viewing) and the association of the current user context to those past contexts in order to determine the most appropriate advertisement. The used context includes user's location and activity, user/device/content/event identity, and time and is organized as Current context (CCo) and Analyzed/Aggregated Context (ACo). The ACo is the analyzed and aggregated past context sequences presenting the past history of the CCo. This proposed ITV system is mainly targeting home networks and is realized through four entities: User Identification (UId), Context Derivation (CoD), Bulk Ad Retrieval (BAR) and Context-aware Ad Selection and Insertion (CaASI). This work presents a centralized system since the context information treatment is realized on the Set-Top-Box (STB). However the processing capacity of the STB limits its performance. No context discovery and service transfer mechanism are provided in this work, thus leading to a limited mobility support. Although a Channel Surfing Analysis algorithm is proposed to identify the users watching the TV, it is not very accurate since it is based on some hypothesis and also fails to detect visitors which restrict the nomadism. This work does not consider the privacy protection. The system in this work is in the application level and not dependent on the specific network architecture, so it can be implemented on any NGN platform.

An ITV system is proposed in [2] through applying context-awareness, considering the context information of users, terminals, network and content. Software Agents are implemented on top of physical devices for context acquisition, treatment and storage, composing a distributed ITV system. The agents' capacity in discovering other agents allows the devices to discover each other and the 'active network' used in this work which can decide the best way to route the TV content according to the context (traffic condition, user's location, etc.). However, the communication capacity between agents (for example the communication scope) is limited which impacts the mobility support. The lack of an identification mechanism and the distributed storage of context information stand as obstacles for nomadism. Furthermore, we notice that this work, does not apply any context inference mechanism or dynamic user experience analysis, so the service personalization is limited. Since this work is not dependent on a specific under-lying architecture, it can support co-existence of different actors.

In [3], a client/server based context-aware framework is proposed to enhance the TV services through including TV Set automatic control and personalized content recommendation. This framework is composed of two parts: Service Agent Managers (SAM) and the CAMUS Server. The SAM contains Service Agents (SA) and each SA detects the context information from the dedicated device (sensor or equipment) and forwards it to CAMUS server. The latter treats the context information through context manager which is responsible of the context representation, inference and storage as well as discovering the ongoing application through the service request. Then tasks are generated through a task manager included in CAMUS according to the stored rules, context information and ongoing applications. The SA then receives task commands from CAMUS and controls the device according to the commands. The context information mentioned in this work concerns the user, the devices and the content, and can be extended by adding new SAs. The centralized storage of context information and RFID based identification make the nomadism possible, but limited in the server implementation scope. Since this work does not consider the network context and does not allow the service transfer (no session control functionalities exist), the mobility support is limited. And since this work is not limited to a specific underlying architecture, it could allow for the co-existence of multiple actors; however the privacy protection is not considered.

In [4], the authors integrate the presence service into the IMS based emergency service aiming to provide context-awareness. The context information mentioned in this work is user's physiological information (as blood pressure) and environment information (as sound level) and is acquired by Wireless Sensor Networks (WSNs). It is then relayed to sensor gateways acting as interworking units between the WSN and the IMS core network. The gateway is considered as the presence external agent (PEA, an agent used to publish presence information in presence service), where it collects the information, processes it (e.g. through aggregation and filtering), and then forwards it to the presence server that plays the role of the Context Information Base (CIB) responsible for context information storage, management and dissemination. The two entities E(Emergency)-CSCF and location retrieval function (LRF) which are used to establish the emergency session in traditional emergency services are merged into the CIB. The Context retrieval function (CRF) at the service provider side retrieves different context information about the user. This presence service based system is centralized, where the presence agent allows the extension of context information, however no context information inference mechanism is provided which limits the service personalization. This work could benefit from the privacy protection in the classical presence service to assure users' privacy. The user's identification and authentication follow the IMS approach, attaching the user identification to that of devices which restricts the nomadism. Although the WSNs can discover devices, the lack of service's transfer among different devices limits the mobility support.

In [5], the IMS Push to Talk over Cellular (PoC) service is enhanced by adopting context-awareness through employing the presence service to master the storage, management and distribution of the context information. Compared to traditional PoC architecture, this proposed architecture adds a context-aware collector in the environment to collect the context information, and adds the presence service user agent in the PoC terminals to forward the context information to the presence server. Furthermore in the Group List Management Server (GLMS), besides the contact list of a certain user, stores the context-aware rules. Through the rules and the context information in the presence server the PoC server can infer which user will be added in the communication session. Although the context information considered in this work is limited to the user context, it can be extended through implementing the context-aware collector in different environments. The presence user agent located in each device helps the system to discover the devices, while the context collector can continuously acquire the user's location. The PoC server can also handle the session transmission allowing the system to support mobility. We notice that the user's identification follows, attaching the user identification to that of devices, which limits the nomadism. The privacy protection can be carried out through presence service.

In [6], a general context-aware service enabler based on the core IMS architecture is proposed. This contribution targets general IMS services and does not specify the context information domains. The enabler continuously communicates with the context sources which are located in the environment to acquire the context information and stores it in the Context Database. When the application server receives a request from the user, it firstly contacts the Context Query Engine which provides an abstract interface to the context-aware service enabler for applications to extract the desired contexts, where a Query Generator function creates the query according to the service description and forwards it to the Reasoning Engine through a query request. The Reasoning Engine includes a Reasoner function used to infer high-level context information from low level ones based on the rules stored in the Rule Manager and a Query Execution function treating the query sent by the Query Engine based on the context information in the context database and the reasoning results. At last, according to the query response, the Service instructor generates the service instruction used to configure the services. This centralized system treats the context information on a server which has enough capacity to provide adequate high-level user context information. Although no user's identification mechanism is provided, the context-aware enabler can identify the user based on the user context information, so the nomadism can be supported. Since the context sources can discover the devices and the session control is provided by the IMS, this work can support mobility. But this work does not mention the privacy protection. In order to support interactive TV service, the service functions (like content recommendation function) should be added.

4 Summary and Conclusion

In this paper, we focus on context-aware TV system (with a special interest on IPTV). Through our study and analysis to the different related contributions discussed in this paper, we notice that no existing contribution could satisfy service personalization in a complete and adequate manner. For ITV, most of the existing works treat the TV services personalization through only content recommendation and targeted advertisement insertion. However, the provision of content in a personalized and user-centric manner taking into consideration mobility and nomadic situations is not yet resolved. From the context-aware based IMS architecture, we can discover that the context-aware concept enhances the personalized information treatment in IMS. However, how to use the acquired context information to realize the personalized IMS based IPTV services is still a challenge. Furthermore, the privacy protection is another issue that is not resolved in the existing contributions, where user-context information should not be a way that threatens the user privacy.

Our next step is to benefit from this study and to integrate a context-awareness system into an IPTV/IMS platform that we have. Our future context-aware IPTV system will satisfy the different requirements that we defined in order to enhance the IPTV services and fulfill a number of use-cases that are promising for the network operator in opening new business opportunities.

References

1. Thawani, A., Gopalan, S., Sridhar, V.: Context Aware Personalized Ad Insertion in an Interactive TV Environment. In: 4th Workshop on Personalization in Future TV (2004)
2. Santos, J.B.D., Goularte, R., Faria, G.B., Moreira, E.D.S.: Modeling of user interaction in context-aware interactive television application on distributed environments. In: 1st Workshop on Personalization in Future TV, Sonthofen (2001)
3. Moon, A., Kim, H., Lee, K., Kim, H.: Designing CAMUS based Context-Awareness for Pervasive Home Environments. In: International Conference on Hybrid Information Technology, Cheju Island, pp. 666–672 (2006)
4. El Barachi, M., Kadiwal, A., Glitho, R., Khendek, F., Dssouli, R.: An Architecture for the Provision of Context-Aware Emergency Services in the IP Multimedia Subsystem. In: Vehicular Technology Conference, Singapore, pp. 2784–2788 (2008)
5. Hsu, J.M., Lain, W.B., Chan, C.C., Huang, Y.M.: Implementation of IMS-based PoC Service with Context-Aware Interaction. International Journal of Multimedia and Ubiquitous Engineering 3, 25–43 (2008)
6. Kim, J., Jeong, J., Nam, S.M., Song, O.: Intelligent Service Enabler based on Context-Aware in Next Generation Networks. In: International Symposium on Parallel and Distributed Processing with Applications, pp. 802–906 (2008)

COOCHING: Cooperative Prefetching Strategy for P2P Video-on-Demand System

Ubaid Abbasi and Toufik Ahmed

CNRS LaBRI Lab., University of Bordeaux 1
351 Cours de la Libération, Talence Cedex 33405, France
{abbasi,tad}@labri.fr

Abstract. Most P2P VoD schemes focused on service architectures and overlays optimization without considering segments rarity and the performance of prefetching strategies. As a result, they cannot better support VCR-oriented services. Despite the remarkable popularity in VoD systems, there exists no prior work that studies the performance gap between different prefetching strategies. In this paper we analyze and understand the performance of different prefetching strategies. Our analytical characterization brings us not only a better understanding of several fundamental tradeoffs in prefetching strategies, but also important insights on the design of P2P VoD system. On the basis of this analysis, we finally proposed a cooperative prefetching strategy namely "COOCHING". In this strategy, the segments requested in VCR interactivities are prefetched into session beforehand using the information collected through gossips.

1 Introduction

Over the past few years, multimedia communications have become essential part of people's daily life. Multimedia streaming is attracting extensive attention and becomes the most popular activity over the Internet. Video streaming supports a large number of simultaneous users and consumes more network bandwidth as compared to other internet applications [2]. It can be classified into two categories: Live streaming and Video on Demand (VoD). In live streaming systems, the source server broadcast the contents and all the clients play the contents at a same progress. On the other hand, VoD is an interactive multimedia service in which user enjoys the video with completely free choices due to the availability of VCR controls (i.e., forward, backward, resume). The important observation regarding P2P VoD systems is that, users don't watch the video from beginning to end [1]. VoD users performs the seek operations very frequently. This results in increase latency and causes excessive stress on streaming server.

Data Prefetching has been proposed as a technique for reducing the access latency. In this technique, peers prefetch and store various portions of the streaming media ahead of their playing position as shown in Fig. 1. Although it requires the additional bandwidth and storage for prefetching, considering the increasing bandwidth on network and storage capability on local peers, it actually offers a more desirable tradeoff between quality and cost. An effective prefetching strategy must prefetch the useful contents in a timely manner while introducing little overhead. Different prefetching

T. Pfeifer and P. Bellavista (Eds.): MMNS 2009, LNCS 5842, pp. 195–200, 2009.
© IFIP International Federation for Information Processing 2009

strategies are proposed up to date, but no one provides optimal performance. In this paper, we examine different prefetching strategies and discuss the design tradeoffs involved when implementing these strategies. To the best of our knowledge this is the first work, which provides a performance comparison between different prefetching strategies in P2P VoD systems. On the basis of this analysis we proposed a new prefetching strategy to overcome the discrepancies in existing prefetching strategies.

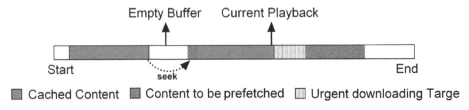

Fig. 1. Prefetching, caching and urgent downloading

The rest of the paper is organized in different sections. A brief related work and motivation is presented in section 2. In section 3, we provide a thorough analysis about the characteristics of user viewing behavior for different existing prefetching strategies. Section 4 discusses the proposed cooperative prefetching strategy. Section 5 illustrates the performance evaluation and section 6 presents a brief conclusion while highlighting some of the future perspectives.

2 Motivation and Related Works

In the past years, several researches have been proposed for multimedia caching and prefetching. The peer in a VoD system can prefetch the contents in many different ways. We first consider the simplest scheme, which is called no-prefetching [6]. Under this technique, each peer obtained the contents at streaming rate and don't prefetch contents for seek operations. The seek operation by a user results in increased latency due to runtime prefetching. This technique increases server stress because neighboring peers don't have the desired contents and most requests are satisfied by the server. The random prefetching [3] is used to prefetch the data in local cache before a seek operation is carried out. Rather than waiting for a cache miss to perform a prefetch, random prefetching anticipates such misses and issues a fetch to local cache in advance. The scheduler is responsible for randomly prefetching segments in periodic intervals. Although caching of data is considered in random prefetching but prefetching of data in unpredictable user behaviors has not been addressed. As a result more useless segments occupy the local cache.

The popularity aware prefetching technique [4] exploit user access patterns for prefetching the data segments. In this technique logs are maintained by a management server (also called tracker) regarding users access pattern. The statistics gathered on user requests are used to determine the optimal number and placement of replicates for each individual video file. These popular segments are distributed among the peers participating in VoD sessions. As a result popular data segments are obtained before playback. The popularity aware prefetching techniques improves hit ratio by considering user's access patterns, however large computation are required to be performed by management server for extracting the list of popular contents. The periodic exchange of seek operation's information with management server results in additional overhead. State maintenance and data mining [5] are used as another technique for prefetching more desirable segments of video. The playback history is exchanged among a set of peers (neighboring peers) which share the closest playhead positions. This playback history provides peers a data set for performing data mining operations. Unlike popularity aware prefetching, each peer performs data mining operations locally instead of central management server. Therefore, association rule mining is used to find maximum occurring segment with respect to current position.

3 Prefetching Technique Analysis

We defined two types of hit ratios regarding VCR operations. HR_r is the "relative hit ratio", defined as "the number of prefetching request satisfied locally". This means that the new segment pointed as a result of seek operation was already available. HR_g is the "global hit ratio", defined as the number of prefetching requests satisfied by requesting segments from neighboring peers. This means that the segment pointed as a result of seek operation was not available in local buffer, and therefore a prefetch request has been made to obtain the segment from other peers in same session.

Let us suppose, each peer has a memory to store s segments. Note that this is the maximum number of segments that can be prefetched before the occurrence of VCR operations. Let S be the maximum number of segments that can be prefetched by neighboring peers. We will denote L = {set of segments that can be requested using VCR control}. Obviously this set contains either those segments which are not played or those segments which are played but removed from memory later on. We denote L_i as the set of segment prefetched by peer i. Let P_i be the probability that the requested segment (as a result of VCR control) exists in L_i. In case of data-mining based prefetching mechanism for peer i, we have:

$$HR_r = \frac{P_i \times s}{L_i}, \quad HR_r + HR_g = \frac{P_i \times S}{L_i} \quad (1)$$

For no prefetching, there is no possibility that the requested segments exists in the set of available prefetched segments. Thus for no prefetching:

$$HR_r = 0, \ HR_r + HR_g = 0 \quad (2)$$

For popularity aware based prefetching we have:

$$HR_r = \frac{s}{L}, \quad HR_r + HR_g = \frac{S}{L} \quad (3)$$

Similarly for random prefetching:

$$HR_r = \frac{P_i \times s}{L}, \quad HR_r + HR_g = \frac{P_i \times S}{L} \quad (4)$$

The above equations show that both data-mining based prefetching and historical prefetching had better hit ratio comparatively. However, historical prefetching is based on a larger data set which didn't represent the user's behavior in a particular session. On the other hand, data mining based techniques prefetched the popular contents consumed by peers having closest playhead distance.

4   Cooperative Prefetching Technique

We observed a tradeoff between user behavior and overhead in different aforementioned prefetching techniques. Moreover either the management server (in case of popularity aware) or each peer (data mining based techniques) has to perform necessary computation which increase computational overhead. To overcome the above mentioned problem, we proposed "*cooperative prefetching technique*". We used a tree based overlay structure similar to P2Cast [7] in which peers are organized into different session according to their playhead position.

In cooperative prefetching technique, peers sharing the same session will exchange the *state information* with each other in periodic interval. This state information is the buffer map of available segments and the current play head position. For the management of buffer, each peer caches the latest 3 minutes of the video played. Apart from this each peer also holds the initial 3 minutes of video and never replaces this part during its existence in the network. This is due the "impatient" behavior of audience which scans through the beginning of videos to quickly determine their interest. The results indicates that caching the first few minutes of video is sufficient to serve 50% of all users session [1]. The format of the buffer map is *[PeerID, Playback segments, Current Playhead, Time stamp]*, where PeerID is the peer's IP address, Playback segments refers to the record of segments the peer plays after it generates the last state-messages. Instead of exchanging the complete record of available segment, each peer only sends *playback segments* in order to avoid extra overhead. *Time stamp* is the time when peer sends the state information. On receiving a state message, a peer performs relevant operations before it forwards the message to its neighbors. If peer 1 receives a state information message from peer 2, it compares the time stamp of current message with earlier time stamp. If the current time stamp is greater, then the state information record is updated. Once the state informations are collected from all peers (in same session) each peer creates a table of available segments in that particular session. Fig. 2 shows the state information table received by a particular peer *i*. Each peer performs the necessary computation to remove redundancy and creates a list of available non redundant segments in the session.

In case of Fig. 2 missing segments like 10, 18, and 19 would be requested from far neighbors (peers in other session) depending on current playhead position. This request is made to either far neighbors or server (if there is no response from other peers). As a result, those rare segments are obtained from other session that didn't exist in the current session. Later on, if a seek operation is carried out and the segment is available in the same session, it will take less time to acquire it from neighbor peers instead of server or far peers. It is important to note that each peer also prefetch the segments near to its playhead position as an *urgent downloading target*. In our case each peer prefetch the next 20 seconds of video segments as urgent downloading target. Apart from these segments, remaining segments are prefetched using cooperative prefetching strategy.

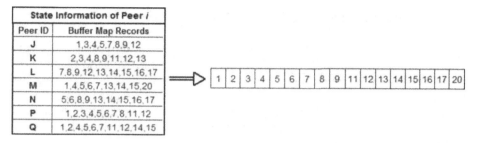

Fig. 2. Removing Segment Redundancy

5 Performance Evaluation

We organized the peers in an overlay structure proposed in P2Cast. In P2Cast, peers are distributed into sessions according to their playhead position. We used the BRITE universal topology generator in the top-down hierarchical mode to map the physical network. Each topology consists of 3 autonomous systems each of which has 10 routers. All AS are assumed to be in the Transit-Stub manner. The delay on the access links is randomly selected between 5 to 10 ms. The incoming and outgoing bandwidth of peers varies between 512 kbps to 5 Mbps and is uniformly distributed throughout the network. We deployed a single media source and the uplink bandwidth of media source is 5Mbps. When ever a peer receives the contents from a parent peer in the tree, it keeps tracks of the sequence number of the packets. The peer in same session exchanges the sequence number as part of state information.

5.1 Simulation Results

Fig. 3 and 4 shows the comparison of hit ratio and utilization ratio respectively. The obtained results suggest that cooperative prefetching increases the hit ratio and utilization ratio of the session. This is due to the reason that cooperative prefetching maximizes the availability of rare segments in the session. Both data mining and popularity aware prefetching techniques focused on certain number of segments according to user behavior, while ignoring segments rarity. That's why cooperative prefetching strategy has better performance.

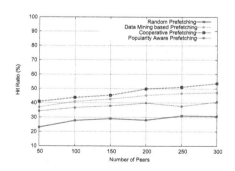

Fig. 3. Comparison of Hit Ratio

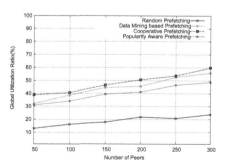

Fig. 4. Comparison of Utilization Ratio

6 Conclusion and Future Perspective

In this paper we analyzed different existing caching strategies for peer assisted VoD system. In order to provide a VCR-oriented VoD service for P2P networks, we proposed a cooperative prefetching strategy. Our strategy focuses on improving the availability of rarest contents in a session. Our proposed strategy improves the hit ratio and decrease the overhead significantly. For the future perspective, we aim to perform real test-bed evaluation for the more personalized VoD and IPTV services delivery over P2P network.

References

[1] Yu, H., Zheng, D., Zhao, B., Zheng, W.: Understanding User Behavior in Large-Scale Video-on-Demand Systems. In: Proc. of EuroSys 2006 (2006)
[2] Mushtaq, M., Ahmed, T., Meddour, D.: Adaptive packet video streaming over P2P networks. In: Proc. of the 1st International Conference on Scalable information systems
[3] Cheng, B., Jin, H., Liao, X.: Supporting VCR functions in P2P VoD services using ring-assisted overlays. In: Proc. of ICC 2007 (2007)
[4] Zheng, C., Shen, G., Li, S.: Distributed Prefetching Scheme for Random Seek Support in P2P Streaming Applications. In: Proc. of ACM P2P multimedia streaming 2005 (2005)
[5] He, Y., Liu, Y.: VOVO: VCR-Oriented Video-on-Demand in Large-Scale P2P Networks. Proc. of IEEE Trans. Parallel and Distributed Systems PP(99) (June 2008)
[6] Huang, C., Li, J., Ross, K.W.: Can Internet Video-on-Demand be Profitable. In: Proc. of ACM SigComm 2007 (2007)
[7] Guo, Y., Suh, K., Kurose, J., Towsley, D.: P2Cast: Peer-to-peer Patching Scheme for VoD Service. In: Proc. of International conference on World Wide Web 2003 (2003)

Author Index